HS

 Royal Horticultural Soc

Nature's Gardener

1620316 X

Royal Horticultural Society

Nature's Gardener
How to garden in the 21st century

Matthew Wilson

MITCHELL BEAZLEY

For Mum and Dad

'Man did not weave the web of life – he is merely a strand in it.
Whatever he does to the web, he does to himself.'
CHIEF SEATTLE, 1854

Matthew Wilson's *Nature's Gardener*
Previously published as *New Gardening* by Matthew Wilson

First published in Great Britain in 2007 by Mitchell Beazley,
a division of Octopus Publishing Group Limited,
Endeavour House, 189 Shaftesbury Avenue, London WC2H 8JY
www.octopusbooks.co.uk

in association with The Royal Horticultural Society.

First published in paperback in 2011

ISBN 9781845336523

A CIP catalogue record for this book is available from the British Library

Set in Interstate
Printed and bound in China

Royal Horticultural Society
PUBLISHER Rae Spencer-Jones
EDITOR Simon Maughan

Mitchell Beazley
PUBLISHER David Lamb and Lorraine Dickey
COMMISSIONING EDITOR Helen Griffin
ART DIRECTOR Tim Foster
ART EDITOR Victoria Burley
COVER DESIGN Juliette Norsworthy
PRODUCTION MANAGER Peter Hunt
PROJECT EDITOR FOR THIS EDITION Stephanie Milner

Created and produced for Mitchell Beazley
by The Bridgewater Book Company Ltd
CREATIVE DIRECTOR Peter Bridgewater
PROJECT EDITOR Susie Behar
ART DIRECTOR Michael Whitehead
EDITORS Hazel Songhurst, Judith Chamberlain-Webber
PROJECT DESIGNER Simon Goggin
PICTURE RESEARCH Liz Eddison
ILLUSTRATIONS Coral Mula

Contents

Foreword

by Inga Grimsey FORMER DIRECTOR GENERAL OF THE ROYAL HORTICULTURAL SOCIETY

As the UK's leading gardening organization, the Royal Horticultural Society (RHS) is concerned with ensuring that we provide the appropriate advice to our members and the wider public, so that they gain the greatest pleasure from their gardens while gardening in a manner that is as environmentally sound as possible. With concern over the impact of climate change and the depletion of natural resources very much on the agenda, it can be difficult for gardeners to know how best to tackle such significant issues and where to find clear, practical and well-informed guidance.

The RHS aims to help gardeners to continue to enjoy the life- enhancing benefits of gardens and gardening whilst coping with climate change and the issues around it: care of the environment, enhancing biodiversity and reducing carbon footprints. The knowledge gained from the four RHS gardens, supported by our scientific work and the knowledge of our plant committees and partner gardens, allows us access to an unparalleled range of information to draw on. This can be utilized to provide gardeners with the sort of practical, clear information that can be lacking during times of change. Matthew Wilson's book supports this initiative.

During his career with the RHS, Matthew has curated two of our gardens in parts of the country with distinctly different and challenging growing conditions; Hyde Hall in Essex with its low rainfall, heavy soil and exposed conditions, and Harlow Carr in North Yorkshire, where rainfall is greater but exposure to cold

Tulips (right) have been enjoyed in our gardens for centuries; they are also perfectly adapted to a hotter, drier climate.

winds and frost are major factors for consideration. At both gardens, Matthew has established a culture of gardening with the environment, protecting and enhancing biodiversity, and reducing or phasing out entirely the use of artificial irrigation, chemicals and inorganic fertilizers.

This book reflects and imparts the practical experience he has garnered, but goes beyond the perceived boundaries of gardening. Uniquely, it looks at the bigger picture – how our gardening activities can positively affect the environment and reduce our impact on natural resources. By looking 'over the garden fence', this book encompasses issues that typically fall outside more conventional gardening publications. It looks at where the materials and plants we purchase for our gardens come from and how they are produced, at how to tackle waste and recycle creatively, at the relationship between climate, soil and plant choice, and perhaps the biggest concern for gardeners today – at how to use water responsibly.

Gardeners have always had the knack of responding proactively to the changing seasons, and now that we are facing a greater challenge we should take some comfort from that inherent ability. But what we most need is practical, accessible information that can be employed in our own gardens, large or small. *Nature's Gardener* provides precisely that sort of information, and more besides, making it an important book for the RHS and, I believe, anyone with an interest in gardening and the environment.

Autumn berries (right) provide a visual treat and a vital food source for wildlife. Gardens can make a genuine contribution to the enhancement of biodiversity.

How to garden in the 21st century
'New Gardening' - A holistic approach

This book is the culmination of five years of dreaming, scheming, researching and, eventually, writing, but the practical experiences behind it date back to when I left horticultural college in 1993. Armed with a 'conventional' training, I struggled to see how a deep-seated childhood love of wildlife and the countryside could balance with what I had been taught - chemical control and intervention in the pursuit of 'perfection'. But in the intervening years I have been fortunate enough to meet inspiring people and to be exposed to new ideas, practices and possibilities that have shaped my thinking, and made me realise just how much can be achieved through enlightened, practical, 'new gardening'.

There is no doubt that gardening is a life-affirming and enriching activity; a means by which we can experience the joy that comes through the cultivation of plants. But I believe that an appreciation of gardens, and gardening, can be much more. Through them, we can gain an understanding of the environment and wildlife, witness the wonders and vagaries of nature, learn about science, art, design and colour. And I also believe that by gardening in a certain way we can positively affect the planet in a manner that is practical, enjoyable and easy to do.

A changing world
We live in rapidly changing and challenging times of great uncertainty, even fear. The human population on our beautiful planet is bigger than at any other time. It is consuming the Earth's finite natural resources at a phenomenal rate. And whatever your opinions on the causes of climate change, there can be no doubt that it is very real, and very much with us today. In the coming years the reality of climate change and its impact, and our need to lead a more sustainable existence, will affect us all in every aspect of our lives, including gardening. The implications can seem impossible to take in - how on earth can we act positively to reduce our impact on the planet?

I believe that gardening is one 'can do' activity that can help us to lead more sustainable lives, while enjoying all the life-enriching benefits that come with it. But I also believe that in order to do so we must change our gardening habits and embrace new ideas

and new practices. For the last seven years I have tried to garden, both professionally (at the Royal Horticultural Society's gardens Hyde Hall in Essex and Harlow Carr in North Yorkshire), and at home, with one basic precept in mind: that whatever I do should not be to the detriment of the wider environment. This doesn't mean any loss of enjoyment in the garden. I believe that I am more content and at ease in the garden that I run, and in my own garden, than I could ever have been without embracing 'new gardening' principles. And it doesn't mean a loss of quality or beauty either. All that follows has been tried and tested, professionally and at home - and it works.

Gardening fads and fashions
Humans have always attempted to control and command nature. The inherent fallacy of this, typified by the legend of the Anglo-Saxon King Cnut attempting to hold back the tide, is something that we have always battled against. The growth of industry brought an even greater sense of misplaced self-confidence - if you wanted to hold back a river, for example, building a dam was the simple solution. Gardening was no more immune from this attitude than any other facet of life.

In Britain the exponents of the eighteenth-century Landscape and Picturesque Movements sought to 'improve' nature. Vast lakes were dug out and mature trees were transported by specially constructed railways from one part of the country to another. It's impossible not to be impressed by these endeavours. They transformed large tracts of the British countryside to such an extent that we now consider the resulting landscapes to be entirely natural.

On a smaller scale there were other developments that changed the way in which we gardened. The invention of the lawnmower by Edwin Budding in 1830 meant that a clipped green sward was no longer the sole preserve of those wealthy enough to employ skilled scythemen. And in the pursuit of stronger plant growth, natural resources were plundered to provide

This mixed planting (right) of pollen- and nectar-rich, robust perennials requires little feeding, watering or aftercare. Such plantings are not only beautiful but they also provide inspiration for a more sustainable gardening future.

fertilizers. The first type was guano (bird droppings), from huge seabird colonies around the world. It was followed by bonemeal. In fact, bone meal became so popular as a fertilizer that demand for it was met by disinterring the corpses of fallen combatants from the mass graves of European battlefields.

The chemical age

The end of the 19th century marked the dawning of a new age of confidence in the power of science and industry. Gardeners embraced the advances borne out by the intensification and industrialization of agriculture, driven by the need for cheap food and then perpetuated by misplaced and ill-conceived government policy. Chemical controls for pests and diseases seemed to offer the chance to keep garden plants in pristine condition, and to cultivate new types that might otherwise be considered too sickly to bother growing. But the opportunity came at a huge price, as many of these 'broad spectrum' pesticides were entirely indiscriminate, killing everything in their path. By the 1960s, chemicals derived – incredibly – from nerve gases used in the trenches during World War I, had entered the food chain to such an extent that species of birds, insects and mammals were on the verge of extinction. In Britain birds of prey, such as the European sparrowhawk, teetered on the brink of disappearance, as pesticides reduced the numbers of smaller birds available as prey. This happened directly through poisoning but also by causing egg shells to become so thin that only a small number could be successfully incubated. Traces of herbicides were getting into water courses, poisoning aquatic life, but also infiltrating human water supplies too. It has taken

A well-balanced garden (below) such as this, with its combination of trees, shrubs, perennials, and its lushly planted pond, will support and encourage biodiversity.

decades for UK wildlife – and worldwide biodiversity – to recover from the inappropriate and over-zealous use of chemical pesticides. In some instances it has never recovered.

Gardening choices

At the heart of 'new gardening' is the questioning of practices that are detrimental to the environment. I've gardened successfully – both professionally and at home – with negligible to zero chemical use. I've done this by encouraging and embracing natural cycles in the garden, choosing appropriate, disease-resistant plants that will thrive in the prevalent conditions and by taking care of the basic elements that keep a garden healthy. Not only is this immensely rewarding, it's also incredibly easy to do – it just requires a little science and a good helping of common sense, along with a willingness to question years of received wisdom.

Without questioning the way in which we garden, it can be all too easy to adhere to the ideals and techniques that existed in horticulture 100 years ago. This is partly because received wisdom is very much a part of gardening knowledge, as it is with so many craft skills. There is much to be said for learning the true craft of gardening – the correct way of using tools, the observational skills, the importance of timing and so on. But prescriptive gardening – doing things by rote because it is how it's always been done – can cause far more harm than good.

Redefining beauty

Imagine a scene full of native wild flowers. It doesn't matter where it is – it could be a British hay meadow in mid-June, or perhaps the extraordinary flush of wild flowers that appears after the rains in sub-Saharan Africa, a wet meadow in Eastern Europe or swathes of terrestrial orchids in a North American wood. Whatever you have in your mind's eye, I'm sure it is inherently beautiful. In fact, I would guess it would be impossible to improve in any way. The fact that we can interpret such scenes as beyond improvement demonstrates an ability to define what is aesthetically pleasing in a multitude of ways. It's the equivalent of 'one man's meat is another man's murder'.

For sure, personal taste has a part to play, but it's conditioning that affects our judgement and inability to accept the non-pristine as beautiful, in much the same way as the media influence our thinking on what makes humans attractive. The fact demonstrably remains that we can break free of conditioning and

The rigorously neat borders (above) favoured by the Edwardians used large quantities of chemicals, water, fertilizer and manpower to maintain.

decide for ourselves what turns us on. In gardening terms, we have been subjected to years of conditioning from a variety of sources. We continue to be influenced by the media and by public gardens, and by the big businesses that supply many of the plants and sundries that we use in our gardens. This isn't to say that the influence is all bad, but we can and should question what we see and hear, and work out for ourselves what makes sense.

Embracing biodiversity

'New gardening' rejects the idea of sterility in gardens through excessive intervention and purging with chemicals. It's pointless to try to do so anyway, as no garden can be hermetically sealed from the outside world. Instead, by redefining what makes a garden beautiful, our level of enjoyment of it can only increase. And why deny oneself the opportunity to experience the pleasure of appreciating the natural cycles of nature? There is as much to admire in the decaying seedheads and stems of a perennial as there is when it is in full summer flower – it's just a case of retuning. By embracing biodiversity and gardening in as sustainable a manner as possible, all sorts of opportunities arise. The presence of wildlife in a garden is an inherently good thing, but we can't cherry pick the 'good' wildlife over the 'bad' wildlife because they rely on one another. Encouraging what I call 'a virtuous circle' in the garden leads to healthier soil, happier plants and an altogether more rewarding gardening experience.

What's in the book

This book begins by exploring how an appreciation and understanding of macro- and microclimate and soil conditions can guide our planting choices. It explains how to positively manipulate the prevalent conditions in our gardens to ensure that they begin to become inherently sustainable by default. From there, it moves on to ways in which we can actively contribute to the environment by recycling materials back into our gardens, and by making informed decisions about how and what we put into them. One example of active contribution would be to reduce the amount of water and fertilizer we use. The book also considers ways of embracing wildlife as an integral component of a healthy garden – including the odd 'pest' as a consequence.

I have been fortunate enough to garden in many different environments requiring different plant selections, so this book also covers the particular challenges posed by hot, sunny gardens, dry and damp shade, and how plants have adapted to these challenges and can, therefore, be creatively utilized to our advantage without the need for excessive intervention. The last half of the book covers planting techniques, how to preserve soil moisture, thereby reduce our use of a precious resource, and plants – lots of plants. Even if your garden consists of a small balcony there are tips and ideas for ways you can garden creatively without harming the environment. In chapter twelve, I give my personal plant selections for different conditions, such as shady, dry, or winter gardens. There is much more besides for you to discover, of course.

Learning from the past

Not everything in this book is new. Indeed the basic principles of gardening with the seasons, learning through observation and the application of good science have been practised by gardeners for centuries. They are as relevant now as they have always been, perhaps even more so in our changing climate. Gardening really can make a genuine contribution to enhancing our environment on so many different levels, from life enrichment to reducing our carbon footprint – writing this book has convinced me of that.

Backbreaking work?

It is generally assumed that gardening is backbreaking work – it is one of those 'gardening traditions' that goes unquestioned. It is true that the most commonly used garden tools – the digging spade and fork – can leave you with an aching back after just a few hours. Surprisingly, there is no good reason why our garden tools have such short handles. They have remained much the same size for centuries, even though the human race is on average much taller now than we were 200 years ago. Moreover, garden spades and forks are based on mining tools, designed to be used kneeling down rather than standing up. It is possible to purchase long-handled tools. Although these may be initially more expensive than 'conventional' tools, they are made to last a lifetime and will hep to take take the backbreaking aspect out of gardening.

Nature provides us (right) with some of the most imperfectly perfect spectacles, such as these wild flowers blossoming after rain in the South African Transvaal.

CHAPTER ONE

South by Southwest?
Climate in the garden

It is surprising how many of us ignore the realities of prevailing climate when choosing plants for our plot. Macroclimate, the bigger climatic picture, is arguably easier to understand and predict, but it is microclimate that can make or break a garden and cause much scratching of heads and disappointment. How can a neighbour have such success with a plant or group of plants that fail spectacularly just along the road, for example? Soil characteristics will play their part, but microclimate – the climatic characteristics unique to an area but also to a comparatively small space – is often the real reason behind success or failure. As a gardener, however, measures can be taken to positively change a microclimate. This chapter shows you how to garden with the macro- and microclimates in mind, as well as explaining various techniques for manipulating your microclimate to get the most from the plants that are best suited to your garden.

High hedges and warm walls (left) create a protective microclimate for exotic species of succulents growing in this coastal garden at East Ruston, in Norfolk, UK. The plants here would not normally thrive without protection from strong, salt-laden winds.

The big picture
Macroclimate

Wherever you live on this marvellous planet, your garden will be subject to a macroclimate – the prevailing climatic conditions. In countries with vast landmasses, such as North America, the macroclimate for a particular area may be fairly consistent – albeit with the possibility of extreme weather events such as the tornados that cause such destruction in the Midwest. But, freakish events aside, the large size of a country tends to lend a level of predictability to its weather. Smaller landmasses and islands can experience far more variable weather, particularly on the coastal fringes of the big oceans. Pan-global weather features can then further affect places such as the British Isles, in this case mainly beneficially by the warm waters of the Gulf Stream. This has created a climate considerably more benign than other landmasses at the same latitude.

Macroclimate enables people to describe the climate in their part of the planet in generalities: hot, cold, wet, dry and so on. None of these adequately describes what might actually be happening up in the clouds but they are fine when all you need to know is whether or not to take a raincoat with you.

The response of the plant world to these differing macroclimates has been – over millennia – to adapt in order to survive and take advantage of any niches that arise. One consequence of these clever adaptations is that there are very few places in the world where plants don't grow. For gardeners the richly variable world of plants offers endless opportunities and the answer to just about every climatic challenge on the planet. But caution must be exercised. There are examples of plants that in their own home range behave as a component part of the native flora, but one removed from this home range become a dominant, invasive pest, compromising other plants and ultimately threatening entire ecosystems.

Climate change

So, to garden successfully, macroclimate is something we all need to understand. At the most basic level it means that growing desert plants in Alaska is not a good plan, but there will be plenty of other plants available to enjoy. Of course there are no guarantees that our macroclimates will remain stable. Climate change through global warming is now a very real

This Cornish headland (right), despite sharing its latitude with the cold, exposed desert regions of northern Mongolia, is rich in plant diversity. The proximity and size of landmasses and the effect of sea conditions can have a dramatic effect on what can and cannot grow. In this case, the southern tip of Britain is bathed by the warm waters of the Atlantic Gulf Stream, enabling plants such as *Echium pininana* and *Erigeron glaucus* to be grown. These would not survive a moment in Mongolia; it is the garden's microclimate that makes all the difference.

threat to the balance of nature, not because of the change itself but rather because of the the cause and rapidity of the change.

Macro-microclimate

Confusingly, microclimate works at many different levels. On the one hand are the tiny variations that exist within a confined space such as a garden; on the other are the changes in climate that are a consequence of topography and orientation to the sun. We'll look at the really micro microclimates next, but first it's essential to understand the specific climatic conditions that exist in a somewhat larger area – the macro-microclimate for want of a better term. These can make life tricky for the gardener.

I live and work in the Yorkshire Dales, an area of the UK typified by its hills and valleys (dales). Some of the hills are just under mountain height and the dales are therefore often equally deep. My home is at the edge of Wensleydale, close to a river and 80m (269ft) above sea level. By North Yorkshire standards the climate is benign. Frosts are less frequent and penetrating than elsewhere in the county and snow more fleeting. The ground rises gently to the west of the village providing some shelter, but even in the depths of winter we get whatever sunlight is available. I work at the Royal Horticulture Society (RHS) Garden Harlow Carr, just 18 miles (29km) away in Harrogate, where the climatic conditions are very different. The garden is in a valley but at a higher altitude – 172m (580ft) – than home. Driving to work during winter and watching the in-car thermometer tumble by 5 or 6°C (41 or 43°F) can be a sobering experience. The boundary of Harlow Carr is mainly deciduous woodland on rising ground covering around 9 hectares (22 acres). During winter, when the sun's trajectory is low, the woodland casts a shadow over half the garden and only the upper parts of the colder slope ever get any sun. So in cold frosty weather the bottom of the valley remains icy for weeks on end while the top of the slope freezes and thaws repeatedly. Added to that are the frequent strong winds for which the Harrogate area is renowned.

Common differences

Of course, in many parts of the world such pronounced differences in climate in comparatively small areas are rare, but this highlights a problem the gardener may be unaware of. My home garden has very little in common climatically with the garden I work at, despite their proximity. If I wanted ideas for plants to grow at home it would be better to look at gardens at low altitude in open riverine settings than at a garden in a high-altitude valley setting. Bearing this in mind, it follows that the best way to work out the vagaries of your garden's microclimate is by observing it at different times of the year.

This scrub desert landscape (left) in Australia demonstrates the ability of plants to survive in challenging terrain. Even this comparatively sparse vegetation provides vital food sources and habitats, as well as helping to prevent soil erosion by anchoring the thin, dry earth. Desert scrub is typified by searing daytime temperatures that can tumble to below freezing at night. Exposure to wind can desiccate plants, and rainfall is modest and sporadic – sometimes absent for years or even decades. To survive in such conditions, plants have evolved an impressive range of adaptations, from water-storing organs to long dormancy periods.

The small picture
Microclimate

Life may be full of uncertainties but it is definitely true to say that no two gardens are the same. My own garden is located at the end of a block of nine terraced houses, some of which are side-by-side but others, including ours, are back-to-back. The garden's position means it should catch the sunlight all day, but the buildings and structural features around it cause numerous variations in the way sunlight falls. At sunrise the alley at the side of the house allows light to strike a 2m- (6½ft-) wide bed for a couple of hours. A little later, as the sun appears to move through the sky, a large sycamore tree to the east casts this 2m (6½ft) border into shade. For most of the rest of the morning a low fence (1.2m/4ft) casts shadow on the plants adjacent to it, while the back wall of the house is permanently bathed in sunlight and can get very hot indeed. At midday the entire garden is in full sun and remains so for a few hours, but for the three hours before sunset in summer, a boundary formed by a block of garages casts shade on half of the garden. This is especially annoying on warm evenings when I want to enjoy a cool drink in the garden after a long day at work. So within a very small garden there are variations of light and shade, each offering a different opportunity (see p.22).

Rainfall and wind

There is more to microclimate than just sunlight, however. That big sycamore sucks all the moisture and nutrients from the soil around it, creating a dry impoverished area of about 5m x 2m (16ft x 6½ft) that is quite unlike the rest of the garden. The house is built from porous sandstone that can absorb masses of heat during the day and reflect some back too. The effect is so marked that at the end of a hot day it can be uncomfortably warm sitting against the sunniest wall. The walls of the house, the garage and a boundary fence also prevent rain from falling on the soil in their lee. The soil within this 'rain shadow' can be as dusty and depleted as that beneath the big sycamore. And then there is the wind. As our garden is completely open to one side, whenever the prevailing wind is from that direction the garden is breezy to say the least. But it is the effect of the solid walls of the surrounding houses and barns that has a more noticeable impact

During midwinter (above) frost can often linger in enclosed, shaded areas **(1)** for the entire day without lifting. The weak rays of the winter sun **(2)** and its low trajectory mean that sunlight is often entirely absent from parts of the garden. Elsewhere, frost may well thaw during the course of the day **(3)**, meaning that plants are likely to freeze and thaw repeatedly during winter. This makes appropriate plant selection vital. The bare branches of the small cherry tree **(4)** cast no shade on the surrounding grass.

By midsummer (above) the scene is very different. The old apple tree fronted with trellis **(1)** casts irregular shade in part of the garden that has little sun at this time of year. The small cherry tree **(2)** is now in leaf and casting light shade over part of the lawn, shade that will move around the tree like that cast by the gnomen of a sundial as the day unfolds. As the trajectory of the sun **(3)** is now higher and its rays stronger, there is greater intensity of light and shade than in winter.

on our garden. Solid objects cause the wind to eddy and swirl. This phenomenon is well-known to aircraft pilots operating in mountainous regions who appreciate just how unpredictable flying can get in such conditions. In a garden it can mean that some plants get flattened or desiccated while others are completely unaffected. In my own garden there is a particularly bizarre wind-related mystery. I have a clump of *Crocosmia* – tall plants with sword-shaped leaves that sway attractively in a light breeze. But on still days when there is just a breath of wind, one solitary leaf twitches uncontrollably while all those around it are motionless. The mysterious breeze that causes the leaf to twitch is blowing from somewhere and being channelled by something, but I cannot for the life of me work out how.

Complex conditions

With such a mix of conditions, plus the variable light and shade in my garden, the growing environment becomes even more complex. But what of the neighbouring plots?

The distance between my garden and that of our neighbours is just a few centimetres in places, yet the conditions couldn't be more different. On one side, the block of garages that prevents me enjoying the evening sun does exactly the reverse for the family next door. It casts shade in the morning but creates a lovely sheltered and sunny spot in late afternoon. And the man who lives in the house which is back-to-back with mine, has a garden that catches almost no direct sunlight. Even on really hot days it's also noticeably colder than our garden, which faces in the opposite direction.

It's clear then that understanding the microclimate in your garden is vital to success. We shouldn't be at all surprised when a plant that thrives next door fails conspicuously at home. Macroclimate is something we can do nothing about – short of moving to another part of the country or indeed to a completely different country. A hot, dry climate is likely to remain so throughout your lifetime, as is a cold wet one. But the subtle variations of microclimates are there to exploit – you just need to know how to observe and interpret the different conditions.

Watching the world go by
Observing microclimates

We have already established my penchant for a post-work alfresco drink. What if I were to suggest that this is part of a serious research programme that I strongly recommend you embrace? Sitting in your garden with a notepad, watch and compass – drink optional – to record the sun's position and where shade is cast at different times and for how long is a great way to understand all the small variations of your garden's microclimate. Should accusations of time-wasting and general lackadaisical behaviour be levelled at you, then you can argue that a few days each season spent observing the garden will save time, effort and a considerable amount of money when it comes to the planning and planting stages.

In my own garden (see the illustration below) the house wall that radiates heat after a day in the sun would be hopeless for shade-loving plants or for those with big soft leaves. As most of the wall abuts a patio this area is used for container plantings. Tomatoes,

bell and chilli peppers all thrive in the sheltered warmth and ripen considerably earlier than they would elsewhere in the garden. The small bed is home to a climbing rose and three lavenders, all of which are romping away, and half-hardy climbers such as the gorgeous canary creeper, *Tropaeolum peregrinum*. During the winter the wall of the house also protects tender plants. This is not because of heat escaping from the house, as is often believed, but because the rain shadow here also acts as a frost shadow, keeping the worst of the freezing wintry conditions at bay.

This illustration (below) highlights the light and shade areas in my garden at different times during the day, and notes their unique characteristics. Making an annotated plan like this of your own garden each season will help you to focus on the individual microclimates that exist within it. This knowledge is invaluable when it comes to deciding what plants to grow.

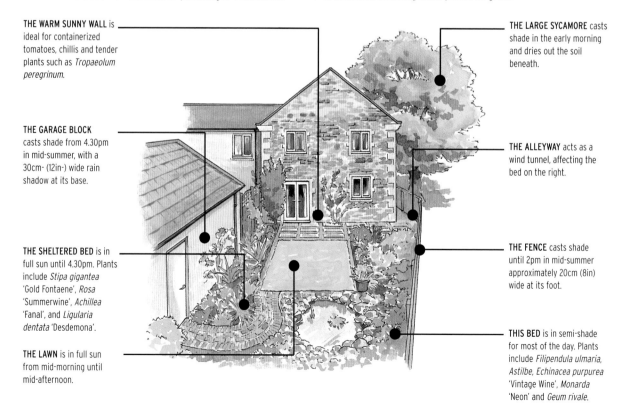

THE WARM SUNNY WALL is ideal for containerized tomatoes, chillis and tender plants such as *Tropaeolum peregrinum*.

THE GARAGE BLOCK casts shade from 4.30pm in mid-summer, with a 30cm- (12in-) wide rain shadow at its base.

THE SHELTERED BED is in full sun until 4.30pm. Plants include *Stipa gigantea* 'Gold Fontaene', *Rosa* 'Summerwine', *Achillea* 'Fanal', and *Ligularia dentata* 'Desdemona'.

THE LAWN is in full sun from mid-morning until mid-afternoon.

THE LARGE SYCAMORE casts shade in the early morning and dries out the soil beneath.

THE ALLEYWAY acts as a wind tunnel, affecting the bed on the right.

THE FENCE casts shade until 2pm in mid-summer approximately 20cm (8in) wide at its foot.

THIS BED is in semi-shade for most of the day. Plants include *Filipendula ulmaria*, *Astilbe*, *Echinacea purpurea* 'Vintage Wine', *Monarda* 'Neon' and *Geum rivale*.

Accepting the challenge

The plants in the border that gets the sun first thing, but is also most affected by channelled winds formed by the alleyway, tend to flower a little earlier than the same species elsewhere in the garden. However, the wind causes problems for large-leaved plants. This is illustrated by *Ligularia dentata* 'Desdemona' which grows in both the sheltered sunny border and the bed affected by the 'wind tunnel'. The former plant has grown perfectly well. Its big round leaves have good coverage and even growth to the ground. The latter's leaf coverage, however, is completely one-sided where the wind has 'pruned' the leafy growth (see p.26). Elsewhere in the garden the growing conditions are consistent: there is full sun from mid-morning to mid-afternoon and moderate wind exposure primarily from the southeast.

Each of the discrete microclimates existing within the garden offers opportunities and challenges. The 'old gardening' way of looking at the situation might be to shut out the world, change the soil, put up barriers to reduce the wind and so on. And there is always justification for manipulating microclimates in this way, up to a point. The 'new gardening' way of considering the many microclimates that can exist in a single area is to focus on the opportunities they present. The challenge is to use the conditions on offer to best effect, with some minor adjustments. Ultimately nature will have its own way, whatever devices we use in our attempts to control it.

Lush, subtropical plants (top) mixed with colourful hardy perennials thrive in a hot, sheltered environment.

The white walls (above) in this sunny courtyard enhance light levels throughout the day, making it possible to grow more exotic plants such as agave and bamboo.

Pineapples (left) given a sheltered, sunny spot and lots of care can thrive in the UK.

Let there be light!
Manipulating microclimates

All plants need sunlight in order to photosynthesize and thereby produce the food they need to grow. As we shall see later, plants have adapted to take advantage of a wide range of available light levels. This includes even deep shade where there appears to be almost no light at all. We humans also need light to feel happy and stay healthy and few of us relish the idea of a gloomy garden. So one element that is ripe for manipulation is the enhancement of light levels. There are a number of tricks that can be employed to make even the shadiest garden that little bit brighter.

Techniques to lift light levels

The simplest way to enhance light levels – or give the impression of brightness – in a dark garden is to use light-reflecting materials. This technique can be employed in all aspects of the garden from the hard landscaping materials to the containers. Painting surfaces with light-coloured paint or installing reflective features will further increase light levels. Colours such

as brown, black and dark green can be catastrophic in a shaded garden. In recent years, Moroccan blue has become a popular alternative for many European gardeners, a trend fuelled by frequent exposure on garden-makeover programmes on television. It's a colour that has its place, but only if you want to draw attention to something rather than hide it. Far better then to choose lighter, genuinely recessive colours for features that you would rather not emphasize. Better still, choose hardwood from a local sustainable source when using timber. It won't require treatment of any sort and will acquire a beautiful patina over time that is entirely natural and impossible to mimic with paint.

Hard landscaping materials such as paving and walling can be more difficult and costly to change in an established garden. If starting from scratch, light-reflecting materials are well worth considering. Most importantly, plants can be deployed to illuminate a garden. Those with gold- or silver-coloured foliage and others that have variegated leaves are invaluable when it comes to enhancing a garden with shady areas.

Max headroom

Plant pruning – or manipulation if you prefer – is a big part of the process of gardening. It is deployed to ensure good flowering, improve stem colour, prevent structural problems and so on. Pruning can also be used to manipulate microclimates by improving light levels around the base of the plant. When describing a plant, gardeners usually refer to its 'form'. Put simply, this is the shape of the plant in its natural state. Cultivated plants are selected because they display certain characteristics, including marked or different forms. For example, the flowering cherry tree *Prunus* 'Spire' may be selected for its fastigiate (pencil-shaped) form. A gardener may choose this particular tree because it is a tightly branched, upright tree.

Variegated or light-coloured foliage (top left) can help to raise light levels in a shaded garden. This variegated *Phormium* will tolerate sun and partial shade, and is ideal for containers.

Silver-leaved plants (left) often prefer full sun, so if you have just one sunny spot in a shaded garden try using a specimen such as *Artemisia* to create a dazzling contrast to the shade.

Clearly there would then be little point in hacking great chunks out of it to make it a different shape. Instead it would make far more sense to select a tree that displayed the desired form.

However, some plants benefit from, even require, intervention to bring out their best characteristics – and when it comes to light levels, some judicious pruning can make all the difference. 'Woody' plants – trees and shrubs – benefit from this treatment. In a dark and shady garden you can get more light in by lifting the skirts or maximizing the headroom of these, and create some interesting and even stylish results.

When to prune

The best time to carry out crown lifting is early in the plant's life. Careful pruning can be successfully carried out on more mature plants, too. However, a trunk could be seriously injured if too many lower branches are removed at any one time. Ideally half the foliage should originate from branches on the lower two-thirds of the tree and some major branches should be left on the lower half of the trunk. Apart from letting in more light, thinning-out densely packed branches has the added benefit of improving overall growing conditions for the plant and for any ground-covering plants beneath it.

Crown lifting to increase light

By careful pruning of the lower branches of a tree, you can increase light levels in a shady garden. This holly, *Ilex aquifolium,* is an ideal subject for crown lifting. Hollies can spread by layering their branches, forming roots at the point at which they touch the soil. Light levels at the base will be greatly improved and the removal of suckering shoots will enable surrounding foxgloves, snowdrops and wood sedge to migrate into the space around the base of the plant.

1. This holly has grown into an impenetrable thicket where nothing else will grow. You can barely see the trunk for the tangle of branches.

2. Start with the lowest branches and work upwards. Trace the route of each branch before you cut it to ensure you are removing the right one.

3. A good-quality pair of loppers is essential for this kind of work along with secateurs for thinner stems and, if needed, a sharp pruning saw.

4. As you remove the pruned material take time to stand back and observe the plant. The cut branches can be composted after shredding or chopping up.

5. On completion the holly now has a defined shape with the handsome bark colouration to the fore.

Sheltering plants
How to create a windbreak

One of the main threats to plant health is excessive transpiration (water loss through the leaves) caused by strong, desiccating winds that can cause wilting, leaf scorch and, ultimately, the demise of the plant. Strong, persistent winds can also lead to plants becoming 'wind pruned'. This means that growth is restricted and stunted as if the new tips have been continuously pinched out, and there is misshapen development of (usually) the leaves and branches on the leeward, more sheltered side of the plant. These phenomena will be known to anybody who is familiar with very open landscapes such as moorland or coastal cliff tops.

Reducing wind exposure

Appropriate plant selection is, of course, the key to establishing a garden in a windy site, and the majority of drought-tolerant plants have adaptations that reduce transpiration rates and the consequent ill-effects. But plants can also be used to establish a more benign microclimate by slowing down wind speed and creating shelter, even in the most exposed gardens. Solid objects such as walls and buildings may assist in reducing wind exposure, but they do so at the price of turbulence: as wind hits a solid object it swirls over or around it, accelerating as it travels and creating a vortex or eddy. The same principle enables an aircraft to fly – the profile of a plane wing is longer on top and shorter beneath, creating lift but also a vortex at the wing tip that leaves characteristic vapour trails.

Using permeable barriers

Permeable barriers reduce wind speed without creating turbulence by allowing the wind to pass through rather than accelerating around or over. Depending on the type of barrier, the beneficial effect can be felt over a distance of several metres. Woven fabric membranes fixed to fence posts are used commercially in farming and horticulture to reduce wind speed. Several types are available and, while they can't be described as being especially attractive, they

Making a windbreak with a laid hedge

A laid hedge forms a permeable barrier against the wind and a wildlife habitat. Native hedges comprising deciduous and evergreen species are the most suitable for this technique and should be at least five years older. You need to obtain hazel bindings and stakes from local conservation organizations, or milled timber stakes and cross pieces that can be bought from a timber merchant. You will also need the right tools: a billhook, mallet or club hammer, bow saw, secateurs and a pruning saw. The finished height of the windbreak is up to you; typically a 2.2m- (7ft-) high hedge will lay up to 1.2m (4ft). Before starting to lay, trim back the side shoots from the hedge.

1. Lean each stem over and use a billhook to cut it almost all the way through, leaving a flap of bark and wood behind to maintain the connection between the stem and the roots. For beginners, this may take several attempts.

2. Repeat along the length of the hedge, bending and cutting each stem until all the main stems are laid at an angle of about 45° to the ground. These stems are known as pleachings, and ideally at least 5–6m (16–20ft) of pleachings should be laid before binding takes place.

can be used domestically to aid the establishment of longer-term shelter plantings and, in particular, hedges.

Beneficial hedging

Historically, hedges were used as boundary markers rather than garden features. The planting of native-species hedges became widespread in Britain following the enclosure of common land in the seventeenth and eighteenth centuries. Their beneficial characteristics must have soon been appreciated, for as well as improving microclimates they also provided habitats for predators that helped to keep crops pest-free. Gardens tend to have ornamental hedges, typically evergreens such as yew, holly and box and deciduous or semi-evergreen hedges of privet, beech and hornbeam. All types provide nesting sites for birds and sheltered hiding places for insects, as well as food in the form of berries and nuts, but it is the correctly maintained native hedges that can most benefit biodiversity. In recent years there has been a resurgence in hedge laying, an ancient technique designed to make a hedge livestock-proof. Nowadays, it is used as a way of thickening up a hedge to create a strong, dense barrier that is better than a fence for deterring intruders and slows the wind gradually.

This hedge was laid two years ago (below), and though the hazel bindings are slowly deteriorating and unravelling, they have done their job and do not need replacing. Regeneration and regrowth are consistent along the length of the hedge, forming a permeable barrier that slows down the wind and acts as a deterrent to intruders.

?3. Stakes are driven in using a mallet or club hammer, vertically and adjacent to the pleachings. These can be cut from hazel coppice. Alternatively, milled tree stakes or square-cut softwood posts can be used. The stakes should be driven in at 50–80cm (20–32in) points and the tops then cut level using a bow saw.

4. Hazel bindings harvested from flexible material of around 1cm (½in) are wound together and between each stake like a rope, improving the rigidity of the hedge.

5. Within a year the cut stems have begun to regenerate from the base. In time these will form the next set of main stems and will themselves be laid within ten years.

CHAPTER TWO

Can You Dig It?
Soil improvement and maintenance

Let's be honest, soil isn't exactly the most glamorous stuff. It gets stuck on your boots when wet, making countryside winter walking a sticky and slippery business. Children and pets have an uncanny ability to get it all over them, and an equally well-honed knack of transferring it to sofas, carpets and adults. And in the summer months it turns to dust, coating cars and the washing on the line with a layer of grime – not to mention blowing into eyes, noses and mouths. So it should be no surprise that soil isn't the subject of polite conservation at dinner parties around the globe. But this is a shame, because soil is really rather wonderful stuff, and the better we understand it the more sustainable and rewarding our gardens become, with fewer costly mistakes and healthier, more beautiful plants. This chapter shows you how to get down, but hopefully not too dirty, with the soil in order to really get to know it; and how, when and what to use to improve it to create a healthy and balanced growing medium.

The knowledge accumulated (left) through a thorough understanding of the soil in your garden will help to inform how and when you improve it and the plants you choose to grow. Knowing your soil is a cornerstone of new gardening.

What lies beneath
Understanding your soil

Most well-cultivated soils contain 50-60 per cent mineral matter and around 5 per cent organic matter. The balance is made up of roughly equal parts of air and water. Organic matter comprises decomposed or decomposing organic material such as leaves. This is what gardeners seek to 'improve' by adding to in the form of manure, leaf mould, garden compost and so on. The air and water are crucial, not only to provide key growth elements but also because they make up the soil's pore space. If you've ever dug into airless soil – conditions known as anaerobic – you'll probably remember the awful smell forever, which is rather like that of damp, well-worn woollen socks left to stew in a laundry basket for a few days!

Soil layers
The surface layer is known as top soil, and is the part most associated with plant growth. Below is the subsoil. All gardeners should be intimately acquainted with the depth and composition of both, since they dictate what can and cannot be grown in a garden. Just to keep things interesting, soil type is amazingly variable and can change over a fairly small area, especially if you live in a part of the world that was once glacial.

At Beth Chatto's famous garden in Essex, UK, the soil varies from clay, to loam, to pure gravel in an area of under 2 hectares (6 acres). Some gardeners would be tempted to ship in tons of 'good' soil from elsewhere. Through research and observation, however, Beth has mastered these challenges by using appropriate management and improvement techniques – and by choosing the right plants.

It's rare to find a gardener who doesn't complain about the soil in their garden. But, in fact, all soil types have something to offer – it's a case of understanding what you have, and knowing how to get the best from it.

Rich soil and cooler conditions (right top) found in the pond area of Beth Chatto's garden allow this flowering bamboo (*Chusquea culeou*) to thrive.

In the woodland garden (right) at Beth Chatto's, dog's tooth violet (*Erythronium dens-canis*) thrives in the dappled to deep shade and the leaf-enriched soil.

Soil types
Along with an appreciation of the microclimate in your garden, understanding its soil is crucial if you are to garden successfully. One of the principle building blocks of gardening is knowing when to improve the soil and with what, and what will grow and what won't in a particular soil type. Different soils need different types of management and improvement.

Although soil is highly variable, often with subtle differences, soil types are grouped under four main headings according to their dominant characteristic (see p.35). These categories are clay, silt, chalk and sand. There is a fifth type, peat, but it is something of a specialist medium and uncommon in gardens. Somewhere in the middle of these types lies the holy grail of garden soils – loam – which is what all gardeners aim for through improvement and cultivation. Each soil type has its own properties, and as a consequence each requires different management to get the best from it. The starting point for any gardener is to discover what type their soil fits into.

Native plants as soil indicators

One of the easiest ways to assess the soil in your garden is to look for native plants growing in it, and in the countryside immediately around. Indigenous plants tend to be adapted to the characteristics of different soil types, so, armed with a native wildflower identification book that also tells you the soil types in which a plant thrives, a gardener can form a reasonable idea of the predominant characteristics of their garden soil. In my own garden the presence of a couple of native species (bugle and creeping buttercup) suggested that the soil was on the heavy side, held moisture pretty well and was fairly fertile.

Different soil conditions

There is much to learn about soil from understanding how plants grow in the wild. Along the edge of a stream, cowslips will favour the damp soil near the water, while sun-loving birds foot trefoil will thrive in the faster draining soil at the top of the bank. Such observations help us understand that soil conditions can vary over very short distances, to the benefit of different plants. Swathes of martagon lilies thrive in the silty soil along the river that runs through my local village. Every winter more silt is washed up on to the banks, but the lilies don't mind. Further out in the dale are limestone outcrops – typically fast-draining stone with a high pH – where native yew trees and stinking hellebore grow from the cliffs. They cling to the little organic matter that is washed down to their roots, and thrive in the ultra-sharp drainage. Yet gardeners are sometimes asked to plant yew hedges on pits filled with heavy manure, which has the opposite drainage features to limestone, and then wonder why they do not thrive.

In Beth Chatto's dry gravel garden (left top), the tall flower spikes of *Eremurus* can be see among the poppies. All thrive in this dry, well-drained medium.

In another area of the gravel garden (left) tulips (*Tulipa sprengeri*) bloom among *Nigella* seed heads in the summer.

Soil assessment
What you should know about your soil

An assessment of soil structure and texture can tell you much of what you need to know about your soil. The way in which soil bonds together is known as structure, and texture refers to the mineral component and its relative quantity. Well-cultivated soil will consist of mineral particles and pores of varying sizes. This happy medium can be achieved through cultivation and the incorporation of organic material.

Assessing your soil's structure

It's important to know how deep the top soil is, and what the underlying subsoil comprises. There is no better way to do this than to get digging and make a soil-profile test pit. In a small garden, a single test pit will do the job, but larger plots will benefit from two or more in different parts of the garden. A test pit will give you information on the depth of top soil which will vary according to soil type and the presence of

soil fauna. If invertebrates are absent, this is a sign of either low organic matter, compaction, water-logging, leaching or the presence of a foreign (introduced) predator such as New Zealand flatworm.

The soil-texture 'feel test'

A 'feel test' is a quick and easy way to assess the texture of your soil and thereby judge your soil type. Take enough soil from your garden to make a ball a little smaller than a golf ball. Remove any twigs, leaves and so on and wet it. Then try to roll the soil into a ball and rub a little of the wetted soil between your thumb and forefinger – you'll be able to feel the particles that are in it.
- *If the soil feels noticeably 'gritty' and won't roll into a ball, it's a sandy soil.*
- *If it feels a little gritty, rolls into a ball but some crumbles apart, it's a sandy loam.*

Digging a soil-profile test pit

This important technique ensures you get to know the soil in your garden. Before starting to dig, take a walk around your garden. If the soil feels noticeably wetter (softer) or drier (harder) in some areas you may need to dig a test pit in each area to understand better the varying characteristics. Soil can often lay wet in shaded areas, and bake hard in sunny spots. Once you have dug your pit, leave it for at least 24 hours in dry weather. If the base of the pit fills with water, this is an indication of a high water table, which will require improved drainage or the deployment of alternative planting techniques such as mound planting and raised beds.

1. Dig a pit about 1m (3ft) square and 60cm (24in) deep, removing the top soil (usually the darker layer) to one pile first and the subsoil to another. Visually check the depth of the dark top soil and look for structural problems such as a hard sub-surface pan layer which usually appears as a discoloured 'line' through the soil, and will be noticeably harder to dig through (see p.35).

2. Take a close look at the top soil and the subsoil. They usually vary greatly in colour, with top soil typically being browner or darker as a consequence of a greater amount of organic matter being present. Look for soil organisms and depth of root penetration. A lack of these suggest that the soil health and structure needs to be improved through the incorporation of organic matter.

The top layer of this soil profile, at around 20cm (8in) deep, is comprised of dark-brown top soil rich in organic matter. This is formed principally from leaf-litter accumulation.

Below the dark top soil is a layer of greyish-brown soil that is less fertile, with a lower organic content. However, you can still see plenty of evidence of root penetration from the surrounding vegetation.

The most obvious band is made up of orange clay, mixed with lumps of sandstone. The orange colouration is typical of soils where iron oxide is present.

Beneath the orange clay band the subsoil is distinctively bluish-grey, typical of heavy clay that has become anaerobic – where lack of soil fauna, organic matter and air cause the soil to become an impenetrable mass. Anaerobic soil is typified by its bad smell.

• *A loam soil rolls readily into a ball and has no noticeable grittiness.*
• *Clay loams are easy to roll into a ball, and when rubbed between thumb and forefinger, take on a noticeable shine.*
• *A clay soil will mould into a ball that will be hard to deform. It is sticky and, when rubbed, polishes easily.*

Some gardeners even test the texture of their soil by eating it. The human mouth can assess all manner of textures in food, and many gardeners and scientists swear by soil-eating as an accurate way of assessing soil types. I've never done it – and have no intention of ever doing it – just in case you were wondering.

Checklist: Understanding your soil

1. With the help of a wildflower identification book, use the native plants in and around your garden to help identify your soil type and provide an idea of what will grow without any soil improvement.
2. Use the soil texture 'feel test' to confirm the soil type.
3. Dig a soil-profile test pit to find out the depth of top soil and subsoil, and to check for any structural problems and waterlogging.
4. With the help of a tester kit, check the soil pH.

Soil pH and its effect on plants

The pH scale measures the acidity or alkalinity of soil. Neutral is expressed as 7 on the pH scale and values below that are acid and above it are alkaline. The ideal pH for most plants is slightly acid at 6.5 (confusingly referred to as 'neutral for plants') but there are plants that have adapted to most pH levels. Inexpensive tester kits are available from garden centres.

Understanding your soil's pH is the last element of soil knowledge you need before improvement and cultivation can begin. It is possible to change the soil's pH by applying chemical or mineral compounds or organic matter with specific pH qualities. Such techniques are often employed in vegetable production and arable farming, where particular crops usually require the application of lime to produce a good yield. Sometimes pH changes occur by accident and can have damaging effects. Where organic matter with a high pH has been used as mulch for many years, for example, gradually raising the pH of the soil to uncharacteristically high levels, it can adversely affect the growth and health of the plants grown in it.

Listen to nature

During the 1950s and 60s, before environmental considerations came to the fore, it was common for gardeners to instigate dramatic soil pH changes. At RHS Hyde Hall in Essex, UK, there is a small acid woodland, planted by the garden's founders in the 1960s. The soil here is heavy alkaline clay, so to make it suitable for plants that enjoy peaty, acidic soil, aluminium sulphate and Irish bog peat were applied. However, acid-loving plants need more than just the right soil, they also need the right climatic conditions, in particular regular rainfall and, crucially, moisture in the air – something that is distinctly lacking in the macroclimate of Essex, which is more akin to parts of the Middle East. Consequently, the woodland garden at Hyde Hall has never really thrived, whereas the plants that relished the prevalent pH and climatic conditions have romped away. Such a scale of soil manipulation is inherently unsustainable – as in all things, nature will always have the last word.

Rhododendrons (right top) are the quintessential plants for acidic soil conditions.

Plants (right bottom) such as *Eryngium* (sea holly) and *Papaver* (poppy) thrive in fast-draining sandy soil, where their adaptations to drought suit the conditions.

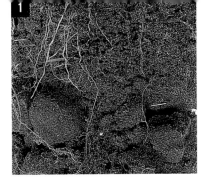

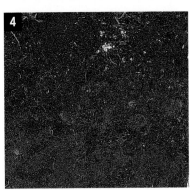

Types of soil and their properties

Once soil is cultivated, its characteristics will change – hopefully for the better. However, the underlying characteristics of the main soil types and the problems associated with them will remain largely the same, albeit with the extremes modified.

1. Sandy soils
Sandy soils are free-draining, quick to warm in spring and easy to cultivate, making them ideal for plants that come from hot and dry environments. They tend to be harder to 'improve' than soils with more body (since nutrients often wash through the top soil) and they don't hold water well. Consequently, they are less suited to plants requiring nutrient-rich soils and plenty of moisture. Erosion can be a problem and, to a lesser degree, capping (see p.37).

2. Clay soils
Clay soils are amongst the most challenging for gardeners. This is especially unfortunate since they are among the most common. They tend to be fertile, but their structure and composition make them unwilling to yield that fertility. Instability is a major problem, since clay soils can be as hard as concrete in the summer months but take on the consistency of cream cheese in winter. Clay soils tend to be hard to cultivate, poorly drained and prone to panning (see p.37) and compaction.

3. Chalk soils
Chalk soils share some of the characteristics of sandy soils, but vary depending on whether the chalk is mixed with loam or clay, and how close to the surface the chalk is. Cultivation techniques can vary accordingly. The most important aspect of chalk soils relates to its pH, which has a marked effect on the plants that can be grown.

4. Silt soils
Silt soils are often fertile but can be difficult to cultivate because they often behave like sandy soils. They are very prone to capping (see p.37) since the soil particles are so fine that they readily bind together. They can also be prone to compaction and erosion. Silt soils hold water well but can often dry out at the surface, which can cause problems when plants are being grown from seed.

5. Loam soils
Loam soils are the holy grail of soil types, with a consistent and stable structure because of their composition, which is achieved and maintained through the regular addition of organic matter and the presence of a sustainable population of soil fauna. All soil types have the potential to aspire to loam but how long it takes and how much effort is required will depend on the condition and type of soil at the start of the process.

Muck and magic
Good soil management

The improvement of soil has attracted more madcap ideas than just about any other aspect of horticulture. Generations of professional gardeners went to their graves guarding secret recipes for soil improvement. These often involved the most bizarre mixtures of ingredients such as ox blood, fish heads and cows' urine, resulting in the phrase 'muck and magic'. But given that all garden plants can either be found growing wild somewhere in the world or are the close relatives of native plants, surely plants can grow perfectly well without soil improvement?

Whatever the characteristics of your soil, cultivation will help to keep it healthy by improving the structure, nutrient levels and drainage. This will lead to better plant establishment and growth. Soil cultivation is the manipulation of the soil through the addition of other materials, to create a healthy, stable growing medium.

The American Midwest 'dustbowl' (below) during the 1920s and 30s was a tragedy caused by intensive farming and a lack of understanding of the effect of climate on soil.

A healthy growing medium will:
- *Have a range of particle and pore sizes that aid drainage, assist root penetration, retain moisture and nutrients, and allow air to penetrate*
- *Support the diversity of micro-organisms and soil fauna that keep the soil in balance, aid nutrient take-up and help break down organic matter*
- *Be easy to work and have good 'friable' crumb structure and dark colour – the only easy gauge of organic matter content.*

There's another factor at work here too. To talk of soil cultivation in general terms is to ignore the fact that different plants thrive in differing soil types and climatic conditions. At RHS Garden Hyde Hall the climate is perfect for drought-tolerant plants that thrive in low rainfall and in lean, fast-draining soils. But the soil is heavy clay. So rather than improving the nutrient levels with heavyweight organic matter in the soil, the primary focus for the gardeners is getting the drainage right, employing appropriate planting technique such as raised beds or mound planting and selecting plants that can thrive in those conditions.

Look after your soil
At Harlow Carr, the underlying subsoil in much of the garden is clay, typified by orange or blue colouration (see p.33) and mixed with lumps of sandstone and millstone grit – a conglomeration known as boulder clay. Above this jumble, the top soil is pretty good and fairly deep. The rainfall at Harlow Carr is twice that at Hyde Hall and the weather generally cooler. Because of this the range of plants we can grow is different from that at Hyde Hall, but the soil preparation is remarkably similar. Both involve improvement of drainage and the addition of lightweight organic matter that isn't too rich in nutrients and that won't impede drainage. Why? Because the soil at Harlow Carr is already fairly rich and moisture-retentive, and boosting the level of nutrients would only cause excessive, sappy plant growth that would then need constant watering to maintain.

Before embarking on soil cultivation of any type, it's important to have spent time getting to know the climatic conditions in your garden. That way you will

Although plants (above) can sometimes be the only thing preventing serious erosion; even an established tree can be affected by erosion, here leading to exposure of the root plate.

Widespread, repeated use of mechanical cultivators (above) to the same depth has resulted in sub soil pans becoming more common by causing the soil to form a hard layer underneath.

have an idea of what will grow there – sun-loving, drought-tolerant plants, lush-leaved moisture lovers or thrifty shade-tolerant specialists. This will in turn inform how you cultivate your soil and what to add.

We are all guilty of abusing soil at one time or another. We stomp around on it during wet weather when we should really keep well clear; we remove the plants that help to anchor the soil to the planet, causing environmental problems; and we don't bother to find out enough about our soil in the first place – a fundamental mistake.

The most common structural problems are listed below. Some occur naturally as part of the soil's characteristics, and some come about because of repeated cultivation or badly timed intervention.

- **Erosion** 'Thin' or 'light' soils (these terms refer to how the soil behaves when cultivated, rather than its physical weight) are prone to erosion by water and wind. If you have ever seen footage of the 'dustbowls' in the American Midwest during the 1920s and 30s you will appreciate the effect of erosion. In this case it was caused by removing indigenous plants in order to create vast field systems for farming.
- **Leaching** This is the term used to describe the loss of nutrients and minerals from the soil, and it occurs to some extent on all soils. Excessive leaching is a

particular problem on light, thin soils such as sand and chalk and can lead to nutrient deficiencies in plants, leading to increased reliance on the application of fertilizers to redress the balance.
- **Panning** Repeated cultivation to the same depth, with a rotary cultivator, for example, can lead to the formation of a hard layer within the soil that can act as a barrier to plant roots. This in turn can lead to the top growth becoming unstable, and cause problems with drainage. When you dig your test pit (see p.32), look out for this hard layer, which may well be a different colour from the soil above and below.
- **Capping** Soil with very fine particle size can become prone to capping, especially if it is repeatedly cultivated. Capping occurs when rainfall causes the surface soil to bind together, which prevents water from penetrating the surface and getting down to the plant roots. It can inhibit the germination of direct sown seeds that can't push through the surface.
- **Compaction** Heavier soils and those subject to a lot of wear – lawns are a classic example – can become compacted. This is when the pore space, made up of water and air, diminishes drastically through the top few centimetres of soil. The consequences are poor root penetration and nutrient take-up. This leads to weak, stunted growth, and a tendency for the soil to become waterlogged.

Soil improvers
How to enhance your soil

By cultivating the soil, you are altering – albeit modestly – its underlying characteristics in a bid to improve its health and, therefore, its potential as a growing medium. It's essential to get it right.

Timing

Some conditions are ideal for working the soil, and others are most definitely not, regardless of what soil type you have. In general you should never cultivate soil when it is waterlogged or frozen. This can exacerbate structural problems (see p.37). Nor should you dig over your soil in very dry weather, since this can cause it to lose what little moisture it has. In general, autumn and spring are the best seasons for soil cultivation, but only if the soil is right.

The overriding factor is the condition of the soil, rather than the time of year. Observation is everything when it comes to soil cultivation, so keep an eye on the weather and do a little test-digging to ascertain whether or not the soil is ready to work. If it falls away cleanly from a spade when it is dug over, then the soil is ready. If it sticks or lots of soil is left on the blade, then it's not.

Choosing a soil improver

There is huge variation within soil types – depending on its underlying traits, whether it has been cultivated before and with what, how high the water table is and so on. For this reason it can be somewhat challenging

Using a raised-bed system (below left) on light, fast-draining soil will allow you to grow a greater variety of plants.

If you have heavy soil (below), remember that you can always use containers to grow plants that like light soil, such as tulips.

to draw up a prescriptive list of soil improvers. The only sure way of knowing which soil improver to use in your garden is to do your homework on climate and microclimate, get to know your soil and experiment.

Locally produced organic matter, such as farmyard manure, green waste and garden compost, are the most sustainable materials to use – and by recycling a local waste product you are generating few carbon miles. Grit is not always widely available and it can be costly, but once it's in the soil it tends to stay there, needing only occasional additions. But with all soil improvers, check the pH for compatibility with your soil, and vary the material you use rather than sticking to one type which may, if used over a long period, adversely affect the soil's structure.

What to add to light, fast-draining soils

- *Farmyard manure* This should be allowed to rot for at least one year, if not two, in order to prevent damage to plants through the release of excess nitrogen. Let the manure stand in your own garden for a year before using it if you don't know how old it is.
- *Chopped up clothing*, wool waste and 'shoddy' (the waste from cotton and clothing manufacturing).
- *Water-retaining granules* These are crystalline granules that expand on contact with water, and then gradually release that water to the plants' root zone. Localized application may be helpful when establishing larger, woody plants.

What to add to heavy, slow-draining soils

- *Grit* The most important soil improver for heavy soils, it gives the soil structure, improves drainage and root penetration and holds on to moisture in dry times. Grit also helps to stabilise clay soils, enabling them to be 'worked' for longer periods of time.
- *Composted bark* This adds structure and improves drainage but does little to improve nutrient levels. It's essential to ensure it is well composted, as decaying bark uses nitrogen to rot, and so absorbs nitrogen, leaving little for the plants.
- *Spent mushroom compost* This is very well-rotted, inert farmyard muck to which lime has been added. Much lighter than manure, it doesn't bind heavy soil, but the lime can affect pH levels for short periods.
- *Mineralized straw* This is processed, chopped and partially composted straw waste from agriculture that has nutrients and minerals added to it. It's an excellent soil improver and very light in weight, so it uses less carbon to transport than heavier materials.

The perils of double digging

The RHS Garden Rosemoor (above), in North Devon, UK, provides us with a cautionary tale and one which has informed the soil cultivation techniques at Hyde Hall and Harlow Carr. Rosemoor is on heavy acidic clay combined with silt, a sticky and difficult-to-work soil. When development of the new part of the garden began in the late 1980s, great lengths were taken to improve the soil 'by the book' – which was to double dig and incorporate well-rotted manure.

Secret weapon

Double digging is one of the oldest techniques in gardening and there is no doubt it has its place. It is invaluable on thin, hungry soils where the addition of a deep layer of heavy organic matter can help to retain water and nutrients. It is useful in a vegetable garden where the crops being grown need a deep, rich root run. But on heavy, unadulterated soil, double digging can be a disaster. It's not surprising if you think about it: clay and muck have been the principal ingredients for building materials - in the form of mud bricks and daub - since Neolithic times. Double digging on clay binds the thick, sticky manure with the soil to form an impenetrable mass, while the top soil ends up buried at the bottom of the trench underneath stodgy subsoil.

Over the five years following the new garden development, the gardeners at Rosemoor watched as the soil returned to its native state. Test pits showed that much of the manure laid in the trenches had remained perfectly preserved, entombed in a clay coffin. Worse still, the plants they had lovingly tended began to die in droves. There was only one thing to do; dig up the plants and prepare the soil all over again, but this time with Rosemoor's secret weapon: grit. All their hard work paid off in the end - today it is a beautiful and inspirationally planted garden and their experience has provided others with the expertise needed to tame heavy soils.

Loam soils

Gardeners blessed with loam can use whatever they like in moderation. Be careful not to overfeed already nutrient-rich loam, especially in areas with dry climates, as this will cause unsustainably lush and sappy growth that will demand constant watering. Not only is excessive watering inherently unsustainable, it may well be illegal, depending on where you live.

General improvers for all soils

- *Leaf litter* This is the prince of soil improvers and nature's compost.
- *Garden compost* All gardens create waste, so you may as well recycle it.
- *Green waste compost* This is produced by local authorities or contractors from the waste we throw out. This waste is then 'hot composted', a process that takes advantage of the aerobic bacteria that cause decomposition. Environmentally sound, it's a good, lightweight soil improver, although the nutrient value can vary.
- *Green manure* If you are starting a garden from scratch on bare earth then green manures can be an option. Typically these are legumes such as vetches and clover, which use nodules on their roots to fix nitrogen in the soil so that it can then be taken up by plants. Similarly, cover crops such as mustard and grazing rye improve structure when they are dug in.

This isn't an exhaustive list, and there may well be other soil improvers locally available. There are some by-products from processing, such as spent hops from brewing, or wheat straw from agriculture, which are useful. In the case of the latter product, a processed form with added minerals is now available for use as a soil improver or mulch.

Incorporating soil improvers

For most ornamental garden plants, right up to big forest trees, the most important part of the soil and the bit that requires the greatest attention and care is the top 20–40cm (8–16in) layer. Even on really well-cultivated soils, most plant roots grow comparatively near the surface, and horizontally rather than vertically. Moreover, it is now widely recognized that once soil has been cultivated and sufficient organic matter and drainage material added, the best way to maintain its health is to dig as little as possible (see p.43). 'Low-dig' or 'no-dig' regimes help to preserve soil health by reducing disturbance, so preserving the fragile balance of soil fauna that keep the soil healthy.

Improving light, fast-draining soils

The major objective with light, fast-draining soils is to improve their ability to retain moisture and nutrients. But no matter how much organic matter you add, the characteristics of the soil will remain largely the same. As ever, the most satisfactory and sustainable solution is to make the soil suitable for plants that enjoy well-drained soil and are not nutrient hungry. Heavyweight soil improvers will soon break down and dissipate in fast-draining soils. If possible, store the manure under a tarpaulin to keep it dry, which will make it easier to handle and less prone to sticking.

Improving heavy, slow-draining soils

Although some especially adapted plants will cope even if their roots are in soggy soil, most will not, so the improvement of drainage in the top soil should be the main objective when working heavy soil. Sharp grit, with a particle size of around 6mm (¼in), is ideal for this purpose. A layer of around 10cm (4in), worked into the top 20cm (8in) of soil will improve drainage in the root zone, which can be further enhanced with the use of lightweight soil improvers.

Careful improvements (left) of the silty clay at Harlow Carr, North Yorkshire, UK have enabled grasses and perennials to be grown successfully with minimal watering.

The layer-cake method

If you are starting a new bed from scratch, begin by applying layers of organic matter (and grit on heavy soils) to the surface of the soil. If you can be patient and do this over the course of a few months you will find that weathering, and the activities of soil fauna, will break down the organic matter into the soil. The ideal time to start this process is in autumn, in readiness for final cultivation and planting in spring.

This technique can also be applied to existing plantings. By applying a surface layer of soil improver and either allowing it to break down into the soil or gently working it in around plants, improvements can be made to that crucial top 30cm (12in).

Fertilizers

As a general rule, fertilizers should be used only to supply specific nutrients or minerals that are missing from the soil. Most ornamental plants need little or no additional fertilizers, but they can help in certain situations, such as where digging in soil improvers may cause root damage to vegetables and fruit.

The manufacture and use of inorganic fertilizers is hugely damaging to the environment. In a garden, excessive levels of nutrients, especially nitrogen, leads to soft, sappy and pest-prone growth and can reduce flowering. It's worth getting your soil checked by a laboratory – you'll recoup the fee by saving on the cost of fertilizer. If there is something lacking in your soil, first consider how soil improvers might help. There is a range of organic, plant- or animal-waste-derived fertilizers available too, which are less damaging to the environment than inorganic compounds.

Soil improvers (above left) such as grit, mineralized straw and garden compost are ideal for the layer-cake method.

Garden compost (above centre) will break down through a combination of weathering and the action of soil fauna.

Organic matter (above right) adds nutrients and structure to the soil; the fauna present in compost and manure also help to keep soil healthy.

Checklist: Understanding your soil

1. Use the research you have done on soil texture, pH and type, along with macro- and microclimate, to inform the next steps.
2. Refer to your soil-profile test pit to look for subsoil structural problems, and check the top soil for possible surface problems such as capping.
3. Consider sending a soil sample to a laboratory for nutrient and mineral testing.
4. Before planning to cultivate your soil, carry out a trial dig to see if it is in a suitable condition.
5. Choose the right soil improver for your soil and climatic conditions, and choose plants suitable for your garden.
6. Apply layers of soil improver to a maximum of 10cm (4in) on existing plantings, and up to 20cm (8in) on bare earth.
7. Be patient if possible: allow soil fauna and weathering to do some of the work for you before you start to dig.
8. Keep digging to a minimum to preserve soil moisture, reduce the risk of damaging soil structure and avoid disrupting essential soil fauna.

Respecting your soil
Clearing and 'no-dig' regimes

Soil-improvement is all about working with nature not against it. If you are starting your garden with a completely blank canvas you will need to clear away any vegetation – grass or weeds – before you start. This can seem a daunting affair, so it is hardly surprising that herbicides have become a popular and convenient choice. But respect for soil starts with how the ground is cleared and progresses to how it is maintained, either through 'low-' or 'no-dig' regimes.

Ground clearance

The choice here is between physical clearance and chemical clearance. The former includes:
• *Digging out* *This is a time-consuming method but very effective providing it is carried out thoroughly, taking care to remove root and top growth.*
• *Covering with plastic* *At least a season is needed to exclude light and kill off vegetation.*
• *Using a mechanical device* *Examples of these are turf-strippers or flame-throwers. The latter may be one of the more exciting methods of ground clearance, but check thoroughly for wildlife before you begin.*

In some instances, where, for example, pernicious, deep-rooted weeds are present, or if the area requiring clearance is dauntingly large, there may be a case for using herbicide. Although I do not use chemicals of any description at home, at work we use a systemic herbicide called glyphosate, which is carefully applied by trained staff to areas where there is a serious weed problem. Systemic herbicides are taken up by the whole plant and kill both roots and shoots, and glyphosate is recognized as one of the safest available. If you think you need to use herbicides, consider first:
• *Is there* *an alternative to chemicals, such as cultural or mechanical removal?*
• *If not, apply the correct measure of glyphosate at the correct time. It must be used when plants are in active growth, otherwise the chemical is wasted. Don't be tempted to increase the dose: it won't work any more effectively if you do.*
• *Follow* *the instructions to the letter. Herbicides should never be used on or near water.*
• *Dispose* *of chemical containers responsibly. If you can, buy a pre-mixed product with built-in applicator.*

Using the cover-up method to suppress weeds

Rather than resorting to chemicals to remove weeds, especially on new, unplanted beds, use the 'cover-up' method. Not only will this kill off existing weeds and prevent new ones from germinating, it can also be used as an opportunity to improve the soil – and it helps to retain moisture too. Once you have covered the bed, you leave it until autumn. In the intervening months the compost mulch will have broken down into the soil and the weeds will have died off, leaving behind soil that should require little improvement before planting.

1. In mid-spring, apply a 30cm (12in) layer of mulch to the weedy area, ensuring all the foliage is covered. Use the appropriate soil improver for your conditions – in this case garden compost. If you wish, hoe off the weed foliage before applying the mulch.

2. Cover the weeds and mulch with a membrane – this can be plastic sheeting, tarpaulin, old carpet or, as in this case, a purpose-made, semi-permeable woven-fibre fabric. Weigh it down with stones to keep it in place, and then wait until autumn.

CASE STUDY 'No-dig' regimes

A 'no-dig' system of soil-improvement can work well on unstable, poor or heavy soils where excessive digging can adversely affect the soil structure. In essence it is similar to the 'layer-cake' method of surface application of soil improvers, whereby soil fauna and weathering do the work instead of digging. The key to a successful 'no-dig' regime is to ensure that any problems with drainage are resolved first. Do this by digging in grit and organic matter. Thereafter, maintain soil health by applying surface dressings of organic matter and allowing them to break down.

Raised-bed systems (above left)

Sometimes, if all else fails, you either concede defeat or you bend the rules. If your soil is basically builders' rubble, or you live in an area where the water table lurks just beneath the surface, or if you have limited mobility and find bending a problem, raised beds may provide the answer. Raised-bed systems bend the 'new gardening' rules somewhat because they rely on imported top soil, something to be wary of unless you have a reputable supplier. I have bought in soil in the past and been very disappointed. When it arrived it looked as though it had been scraped off a building site and used as a test track for excavators for some months. It was denaturized, lacking any real structure and ready to turn to slop with the first drop of rain. But reputable suppliers do exist, and although their product won't be the cheapest available, it will cost less in the long run. A good alternative to pure top soil is blended loam, comprising top soil that has usually been mixed with green-waste manure, making a light, friable soil that needs little or no additional improvement. Once in place, a raised-bed system should be cultivated using a 'no-dig' regime.

The Woodland Garden at RHS Harlow Carr (above right)

The woodland garden at Harlow Carr extends to around 6 hectares (19 acres), consisting of a mix of native and exotic broadleaf trees, coniferous trees and ornamental shrubs such as rhododendron. Over the years the woodland had become very overgrown. It had little diversity in the ground flora, which reduced the range of habitats available. In 2003 we began the process of thinning the trees to create areas of dappled shade. These would be suitable for bulbs and native woodland perennials, and consequently improve the habitat and food potential for biodiversity. Improving the soil in this kind of environment can be very tricky, since tree roots extend out in all directions, making it almost impossible to dig. So every year from autumn to spring we applied 10cm- (4in-) layers of garden compost and leaf litter adding up to no more than 20cm (8in) at any one time. We allowed fallen leaves to remain. After three years we were ready to plant the first section, and a profile test pit demonstrated that an average of 25cm (10in) of good top soil and compost had built up. That was enough to ensure that our new plantings would thrive.

The advantages

Improving soil by applying layers of material to the surface has a number of advantages over digging in. It is much easier than digging and keeps soil disturbance to a minimum. And it also allows different types of soil improver to be applied according to how the soil needs to be improved; grit, compost, manure and so on. But perhaps most importantly, this method is the closest we have to the natural cycle of soil improvement, where deciduous leaves fall to the ground and are gradually broken down into the soil.

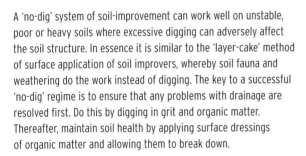

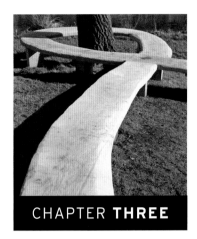

CHAPTER THREE

Reuse, Recycle, Sustain
Gardening with the future in mind

In recent years the people of the developed world seem to have woken up to the fact that the Earth is a finite resource. Our love of gadgetry, motor cars, international air travel and pre-packed foods all contribute to the inherently unsustainable position in which we find ourselves. The effect of human activity on climate change, and what we as individuals can do to address it, must constitute one of the most confusing aspects of modern life. The media is awash with phrases such as 'carbon footprint' and 'carbon trading', while big businesses talk of making their operations 'carbon neutral'. But what does it all mean? This chapter explains these ideas and shows how you can address them in your practical day-by-day approach to gardening. It looks at methods of watering your garden that don't use too much of this valuable resource, ways of recycling water, composting, how to purchase garden items wisely, which materials are sustainable and which are not, and the virtues and delights of using scrap material.

In this sustainable garden (left), designed by Kate Frey for the Chelsea Flower Show in 2005, the combination of direct-sown annuals, food plants and willow fencing is both beautiful and non-detrimental to the environment.

Sustainability
What does it mean?

I am neither a Luddite nor a flat-Earth exponent. I am writing this book on a year-old wireless laptop computer while my previous model languishes in a corner of the living-room. At four years old it is hopelessly out of date. Our love of all things new and shiny is mercilessly preyed upon by retailers and manufacturers, who build obsolescence into products from the start. But we all have more choices.

Carbon-neutral plants

We can all help towards reducing carbon emissions by taking greater responsibility for how we live our lives, the products and services we buy, the way we travel and so on. But our gardens offer something over and above what can be achieved through responsible citizenship. They can be more than just benign and non-detrimental, they can actively contribute towards carbon reduction and environmental enhancement in a way that few other activities can.

A garden planted with carbon-neutral plants (locally sourced, and which provide food sources and habitats for animals, and managed with minimal input and composted waste), is as close as one can get to virtuous living in our world of consumerism. Best of all, the pleasure to be had from gardening this way far exceeds any modest compromises that may have to be made to achieve it. It is the perfect virtuous circle.

What is a carbon footprint?

A carbon footprint is a measure of the impact that human activities have on the environment in terms of the amount of greenhouse gases produced, measured in units of carbon dioxide. Given that modern life would grind to a halt without the fossil fuels that power it, we all contribute towards climate change to some degree. It may be that the reasons for climate change are more complex than we imagine and are ultimately part of the climatic cycle of the planet. But this doesn't absolve the responsibility we have towards preserving the Earth's diminishing resources.

Opting for a 'push' lawn-mower (left) and trading in petrol- or electric-powered machinery is a simple way to reduce your carbon footprint as well as keep fit.

Using recycled scrap and found materials (below) in the garden is artistically liberating and the costs to the environment are much lower.

The 'S' word

It's a big word, sustainability, and one that requires a degree of explanation before we go any further. Short of becoming a hermit and living in a remote cave, it is hard to imagine a life in the modern world that is inherently sustainable. Because the predominant sources of fuel for heating, lighting, manufacturing and transport are fossil fuels, all of which are finite resources, the basis of modern life is unsustainable. But we can choose to reduce and offset our carbon footprint – the amount of carbon emissions that we generate – through simply living and being. Some scientists believe that carbon dioxide is responsible for 80 per cent of greenhouse emissions, which absorb infra-red radiation and thus change the balance between energy arriving from the sun and energy escaping from the Earth.

Improving the insulation in our homes, turning off electrical goods rather than allowing them to sit on stand-by, switching off lights, car-sharing, harvesting storm water, buying locally produced food, recycling waste – it is a long list that we can all engage with at one level or another.

But our manic modern lives lead us increasingly towards convenience, and convenience always comes at a price. Pre-packed salads have become a popular choice in supermarkets, offering out-of-season food in convenient portions. But they are often produced thousands of miles from the point of sale, packed in non-biodegradable plastic bags that are inflated with carbon dioxide before being shipped.

And because of the way in which nutrients break down in salad crops, they often have reduced nutritional value by the time they reach your plate.

Growing vegetables on an allotment (above) is a simple step towards a more sustainable way of life. If you don't have an allotment to 'grow your own', a container will do.

So the carbon footprint of a convenient bag of nutritionally deficient salad is huge, while the benefit to the consumer is questionable.

There is no doubt that leading a more sustainable life is less convenient. It requires research, planning and commitment. Historically, gardening is one of the most self-contained, sustainable activities on Earth. It may seem like a rather comical caricature today, but the old image of a gardener with trousers held up by baler twine and miscellaneous bits of rescued string in each pocket represents a paragon of sustainability. Nothing ever went to waste, from recycled materials to compost, plants grown from seed or swapped with other gardeners – the garden of old was a self-contained, closed-loop system that was almost entirely self-sufficient.

Lifestyle choices

Gardening today is a somewhat different affair, embracing interests and values that are more to do with lifestyle choice than the traditional gardening values. These were based primarily around the growing and appreciation of plants. So now we include within gardening such diverse features and activities as patio heaters, cooking on barbecues and building hard-landscaping structures. I'm not condemning it, if it means that gardening appeals, but the accumulation of knowledge borne out of observation and experimentation which makes gardening such a satisfying experience is in danger of being ignored.

Water, water, everywhere?
Good watering techniques

Water is one of our most precious resources, without which we would cease to exist very quickly. In the developed world we have become used to the convenience of clean, healthy water at the turn of a tap without really thinking about where it comes from, or our responsibility to use it wisely.

Ineffective watering

During my four years as curator at RHS Hyde Hall in Essex, I learned a great deal about water from the experts at the local utilities company. Essex is not only one of the driest counties in Britain – the average annual rainfall at Hyde Hall is lower than Jerusalem, Beirut and Tunis – but it also has to import a large percentage of its water from out of the county, through a system of rivers, pumping stations and canals. This might be okay if our climate wasn't changing and the population of Essex wasn't growing, but on both counts it is, casting doubt that a regular supply can be guaranteed. And the more water that is abstracted from rivers, the greater the effect on the creatures and plants that rely on fresh-water ecosystems.

But water use in gardens makes up a comparatively small percentage of the total used through human existence, so is it really that wrong to water our gardens? In principle no; the effective application of water at the right time and to the right place is okay if restrictions in the form of hosepipe bans are not in place and if you are making every effort to harvest and recycle water. But in practice it's easy to get it wrong.

Standing in your garden on a sunny day with a thumb over the end of the hosepipe waving a fine spray over everything in sight isn't doing your garden, or the planet, any good at all. And watering the plants as soon as the first green shoots appear doesn't help them either. In fact it's detrimental, because watering early in the season encourages lush, sappy growth that is a magnet for sap-sucking pests – and this growth will require continuous watering to prevent wilting and even total collapse and death in really hot weather.

Effective watering

The key to reducing water use is to understand the microclimate and soil type in your garden, and use the appropriate soil-conditioner and plants. If your climate is arid, the microclimate in your garden sunny and hot and your soil fast draining, there is simply no point in filling the beds with thirsty plants – especially when there are literally thousands of plants that can survive with the minimum of water. And if you do have to

A leaky-hose system (right) delivers water to where it is needed – the roots – with minimal waste. Many leaky hoses are made from recycled car tyres, and biodegrade safely after a few years.

Flooding (far right) works well when borders have become dry through cultivation and planting and need a lot of water to rehydrate the soil.

water parts of your garden then use good water husbandry – store storm water in water butts, apply water only when plants really need it, and only to those that require watering, and use a watering can rather than a sprinkler, to ensure that your watering habits are as sustainable as possible.

In order to gain anything from irrigation, plants need water at their roots, and in quantities that actually benefit the plant by getting down into the soil rather than just damping down the top layer. Little and often is anathema to plants, because it encourages roots to make for the surface in their quest for moisture, where they become even more prone to drought. It's far better to irrigate the plants thoroughly in your garden that really need it, when they need it and in the cool of the evening, rather than indiscriminately watering everything every day.

Sprinkler systems

One of the most common ways of applying water to a garden is through a sprinkler. Easy to set up – and let's be honest, great fun for kids and pets – sprinklers throw an arc or jet of water over the garden and can cover a large area in one go. They are undoubtedly convenient. Unfortunately, sprinklers can be appallingly wasteful, watering everything within their range rather than just those plants that actually need the water. On a hot, sunny day as little as 10–15 per cent of the water applied through a sprinkler will ever reach the roots of the plants – the rest simply evaporates in mid air or on contact with the soil. And their consumption is prodigious; it is estimated that they use as much water in one hour as a family of four would in a week – regardless of what time of day they are used. Ultimately, it is hard to recommend the use of sprinklers as an effective and sustainable means of irrigating your garden.

Leaky-hose systems

For a great way to deliver water directly to the plant roots, try leaky-hose systems. Many are made from recycled materials such as car tyres, and biodegrade safely after a number of years. Leaky-hose systems are laid out at regular (usually 50cm/20in) intervals over the border, and pinned in place with bent wire directly on the soil. As water is pumped through the hose it leaks out, gradually soaking into the soil and down to the plant roots. The efficiency of leaky hoses is increased by mulching over them after installation to hold the moisture in – it looks a lot neater too.

A lawn sprinkler (above) is a convenient way of watering, but if you want to make a really positive contribution to reducing water wastage, recycle it – having first rendered it useless.

Leaky hoses aren't without their faults; in hard-water areas they can 'fur up' with limescale within a couple of seasons, but then if you use rain and grey water rather than mains water this becomes less of an issue.

Flooding

An effective way to irrigate a border deeply, or part of a border, is flooding. It's best used only as an emergency measure to rehydrate seriously flagging plants, and involves laying a hose directly on to the soil and, with the water at low pressure to avoid washing the soil away, leaving the water running until the soil is saturated to a depth of at least 20cm (8in).

Watering cans

The least technically advanced methods are sometimes the best, and a watering can has many advantages. The act of lugging heavy cans around the garden leads us to discriminate between the plants that really need watering and those that don't. And a well-aimed can-full of water will usually get down to the roots of the plants far better than a spray from a hose. Lastly, a watering can makes you really think about the water you're using because each plant is looked at, rather than a whole bed.

Recycling water
Collecting and storing

The most obvious way to reduce the use of mains water in a garden is to harvest and store rainwater in butts for use during times of drought. The trouble is, unless you want to fill your garden with dozens of water butts, it is unlikely you will ever be able to store enough water to fulfil the needs of even a modest-sized garden during prolonged hot and dry weather. However, that shouldn't put you off the idea of installing a water butt or three. Connecting a butt to the gutter downpipe of a house or garage enables much larger volumes of water to be harvested than just by collection through the open aperture at the top of the butt. Once connected, even a modest amount of summer rain will soon replenish the supply.

Storing water
There are a number of methods of mass storage, including above- or below-ground water tanks that harvest storm water from rooftops and drain outfalls. The technology involved in large-scale water harvesting will be well known to the inhabitants of arid countries, where it is a fact of daily life. The cost of installing this equipment goes way beyond that of a few water butts, but should be considered for anyone building a new home or with space to retro-fit the tanks. There are grants available in some countries, and in the future it may be that such installations become mandatory for new buildings, even in temperate countries.

Recycling grey water
Recycling grey water – from baths, showers and water-using appliances such as dishwashers – provides an opportunity to harvest and reuse comparatively small amounts of water throughout the year, removing the need for bulk storage. Again, there are systems available that will capture all the grey water from your home and process it for re-use, although you should only collect as much wastewater as you need for your garden – the rest should go into the sewer or septic system. Current advice is that grey water shouldn't be used for watering food crops, because of uncertainty over the take-up of the bacteria present in grey water. Just as important as recycling and harvesting water is conserving moisture in the soil, and we'll look at this in 'Don't add water' (see p.142).

Water storage systems (above) can be both practical and aesthetically pleasing, as Cleve West's 2006 Chelsea Flower Show garden demonstrates.

Checklist: Watering

1. Carry out microclimate and soil assessments to establish what will grow best in your garden without relying heavily on irrigation.
2. Plan your planting so that plants requiring little or no additional irrigation are grouped together, preventing indiscriminate watering.
3. For new borders, consider a leaky-hose system at the start when it is easiest to install.
4. Consider installing water-harvesting and recycling systems. Just one water butt, correctly installed, can make a difference.
5. If you do have to water, make sure you do so as efficiently as possible. Water in the cool of the evening, don't use sprinklers if you can avoid it, and check all irrigation equipment for leaks.

Water storage (above) combined with a water feature brings the benefits of sound and movement, and a ready supply of harvested water.

Grey water (left) can be transported to the garden in a number of ways, the most basic being to bucket the water from the sinks and baths and carry it to the garden. More sophisticated systems involve siphoning or pumping water from the bathtub or other deep basins (sumps) through a garden hose, or removing the trap from the bathroom sink drainpipe and putting a 23-litre (5-gallon), or larger, bucket beneath the sink. If you decide to adapt your plumbing system to allow you to get the grey water to the garden, make sure you involve the local water authority.

The pleasure of composting
Different types and methods

Successful composting constitutes one of life's unsung pleasures. Taking raw waste material and turning it into the stuff from which plants grow is tremendously satisfying. Some of my happiest moments have been spent sniffing handfuls of sweet-smelling compost (I really should get out more). Composting is, after all, one of the oldest means of recycling.

Almost all biodegradable household waste can be composted. An open heap can take everything from shredded paper and cardboard to grass clippings and annual weeds. Closed composting vessels, such as wormeries, can process food waste that should not be put on an open heap. The key to good composting is to understand how the raw ingredients are broken down and to manage the way those ingredients are mixed and added.

The open heap
The traditional compost open heap relies on the activity of soil fauna (principally compost worms and earthworms) to turn fresh waste into compost. A healthy open heap may well generate reasonable levels of heat, caused by the activity of bacteria as they break down the waste, but bacterial decomposition isn't the primary cause. An open heap can be truly open with no retaining front and sides, or the waste can be held in a bin constructed from timber, recycled plastic, metal sheeting and so on. You can purchase compost bin kits if you don't fancy making your own.

Wormeries
Increasingly popular because of their relative ease of use and small size, wormeries are closed vessels that rely completely on a resident population of worms to break down waste. Unlike an open heap, it is safe to put cooked vegetables and waste fruit products into a wormery. A constant and consistent supply of waste is essential to maintain the worm colony once established. Wormeries are the ideal method of composting if you don't have much space and have only limited amounts of green waste to recycle.

Black sacks
Black or dark-coloured refuse sacks are perfect for breaking down the fallen leaves of deciduous trees, the resultant leaf litter (or leaf mould) being one of

A simple leaf bin (top) is easily made from chicken wire and canes, or by filling black sacks with leaves.

Food scraps (bottom) and other household and kitchen waste are best composted in a wormery and should not be put on an open compost heap.

the best soil-conditioners available. The process can take anything up to two years, so an out-of-the-way location for the sacks, preferably in shade, is advisable.

Leaf bins

If you have the space, and plenty of leaves to compost, you may want to consider making a leaf bin. This can simply be a pit in the ground, into which the leaves are loaded, or a chicken wire and fence post enclosure.

Liquid feeds

Some plants make excellent liquid fertilizer when steeped in water for a few weeks. Stinging nettles and comfrey are particularly good, especially when the foliage is young and fresh. The leaves and stems should be chopped up or crushed into a watertight container, ideally one with a tap at the base such as a water butt, and then covered with water and stirred every three or four days until the water thickens and turns a peaty black colour. This liquor can be diluted (1 part liquor to 30 parts water) and used as a liquid feed, or watered on to a compost heap as an accelerant.

Shredding waste

Shredding waste before composting helps to speed decomposition and produces a more uniform end product. Larger woody stems can take years to rot away if they aren't shredded first, but green waste also benefits from a buzz through a shredder. Unfortunately most domestic shredders are pretty feeble and require considerable patience to use, especially if you have a lot of waste material to work through. If you have gardening friends or neighbours you might be able to justify the expense of hiring a heavy-duty shredder and sharing the cost between you.

A modular timber composter (top) can be built up in layers to accommodate more waste.

This recycled plastic composter (middle) has a clear plastic pyramid that acts like a lens, warming the waste and accelerating the composting process.

The colony of worms (bottom) in a wormery processes waste into rich, dark compost.

The perfect compost
Making a successful open heap

Open heaps need a mixture of waste materials (but not cooked food or meat), applied in layers, to work well. To get your heap 'cooking', the layers are best built up quickly, but because the supply of 'compostable' waste can be erratic this often doesn't happen in practice. If you store material in black sacks until you are ready to build the heap, you can ensure the availability of the right amount of waste. A multi-bin system can be another efficient solution. Three bins provide one 'holding' bin for fresh waste, a 'working' bin where the material is breaking down and a 'ready-to-use' bin.

What to compost on an open heap
You can use the following on an open heap: grass clippings, vegetable peelings, spent stems from thin woody material (less than 1cm (½in) diameter), annual weeds, spent annual plants and bedding plants, fallen leaves, shredded paper and cardboard, old turf and top soil, hedge clippings, spent potting compost, manure.

Do not compost the following:
- **Perennial weeds** These can often persist in the compost, so that when you come to use it you are, in effect, spreading weeds. Dispose of these via local authority green-waste collection schemes.
- **Meat products** Although these do compost, they smell and can cause rodent problems – in some countries it is illegal to use them in an open compost heap. They can, however, go into a wormery.
- **Diseased material** The spores of blackspot, rust, mildew and so on can often survive composting. Dispose of these through the local-authority green-waste scheme.
- **Woody material** If it is more then 1cm (½in) in diameter, this can take too long to break down, unless it is shredded before being added to the heap.
- **Inorganic matter such as plastics** Even biodegradable plastics can take too long to break down for compost, though they can be safely buried.

Building the perfect compost heap

A successful compost heap requires a mixture of materials built up in layers. As a general rule, compost should be moist enough to hold together when formed into a ball, but not so wet as to ooze water when squeezed. The speed at which the compost is ready to use will vary depending on the material used, the degree of maintenance and the weather conditions, but it can take up to a year. At this point the compost should be evenly decomposed, light and friable and have a 'sweet' smell. Anaerobic conditions (where little or no oxygen is present) will result in very slow decomposition and an unpleasant smell, similar to woollen socks left unwashed for a few days.

1. If you want to house your compost in a bin, the ideal size is 2m (6½ft) square and around 1.4m (4½ft) high. It can be made of timber, and either be open at the front or have a removable section. The floor should be of bare earth, lightly turned over with a fork – this is essential because it allows worms and insects to get in.

2. Start your compost heap with a layer of material, perhaps grass clippings or perennial stems, filling the bin to a depth of 20–40cm (8-16in).

Checklist: Composting

1. Consider the best form of composting for you, based on the waste you produce, the space available for composting and how and where you will use the processed waste.

2. If you are unable to compost, make sure you take advantage of green-waste recycling schemes run by local authorities.

3. Depending on the method of composting you select, use the appropriate means of sorting and storing waste from the start - especially if you are using the open-heap method.

4. Don't 'spoil' your compost by adding non-biodegradable waste, perennial weeds or diseased material.

5. The speed at which the compost is ready to use will vary on the material used, the degree of maintenance and the weather conditions. It is usually between eight months and a year. At this point the compost should be decomposed, light and friable and with a 'sweet' smell. Anaerobic conditions (where little or no oxygen is present) will result in an unpleasant smell.

A three-bin system (right) allows waste to be stored 'raw' in one bin (far right), 'worked' by turning in another (left) and used as compost in the third bin (middle).

3. Add a second layer of material, again to a depth of 20-40cm (8-16in). Partially decomposed leaves are an excellent addition to the compost heap.

4. Once you have a reasonable depth of layered green material, perhaps 80cm-1m (2½-3ft), the decomposition process should be under way and the heap will warm up as aerobic bacteria get to work. Monitor the heap to make sure it doesn't become excessively dry or wet. Be prepared to water and use a breathable cover on the heap - an old piece of carpet is a favoured choice, as above.

5. Once the green material has been decomposing for about a month, turn the contents of the bin over, using a dung fork or digging fork. Having two or more bins helps, as the contents of one bin can be turned into another. Continue the process of adding, turning and monitoring. Remember to water when dry, and cover when wet. Uncover as soon as good weather returns to allow drying.

Purchasing power
BLOOM logic

While it's relatively straightforward to establish whether or not a gardening activity or practice is sustainable, choosing materials can present more of a challenge. For one thing, there are conflicting opinions regarding what is or isn't sustainable. I try to base my purchasing decisions on logic by considering: **B**eneficiaries, **L**ifespan, **O**rigin, **O**rnamental value and **M**anufacture - the acronym of which is BLOOM.

Beneficiaries can include the manufacturer, retailer and customer, but also biodiversity, either as part of the production process or once in situ, or both.
Lifespan considers not only the life of a material in its intended role, but any future uses too, and whether or not the material is biodegradable when it reaches the end of its life.
Origin reminds me to question where something has come from, and how many carbon miles it has used to get to the point of sale. It also covers whether or not it has come from a protected or threatened environment.
Ornamental value is simply the aesthetic consideration of one choice against another. It may be worth sacrificing a degree of ornamental appeal in favour of sustainability, although sustainable materials are often the more attractive.
Manufacture takes in the processes required to make something and whether that itself is polluting. This includes the conditions under which manufacturing takes place, and how they affect the workforce.

The pit, the flag and the patio
When I began redesigning my own garden, I included a 3 x 6m (10 x 20ft) patio area adjacent to the house. The garden at that time was pretty much a blank canvas consisting of lawn, a small flower bed and a concrete flag path from the back door to the garage. The concrete flagstones were of the type best described as 'industrial, heavy duty, landscaping to the outside of public conveniences for the use of'. My initial reaction was to grab the nearest sledgehammer, break them up into small, sub-industrial-sized pieces and replace them with something prettier. But I resisted, and instead had a bit of a BLOOM moment to consider what the effect of recycling the flags would be.

My bank balance would certainly benefit from not replacing the flags, which still had years of life left in them. And although I couldn't say where they had originated they were now very much where they were needed, so no additional carbon miles would be expended. Ornamental value is always in the eye of the beholder, but once plain concrete begins to age and weather it takes on a rather attractive patina. And since the manufacturing process of concrete is considered to be polluting and the damage had already been done making the flags in the first place, why make matters worse by replacing them?

So the flags were lifted and re-laid, spruced up with the addition of some second-hand burnt stock bricks. I cannot claim that the patio is carbon neutral, since I used cement and quarried sand in its construction, but it's better than it could have been.

Of the alternative materials I could have chosen, the most controversial would probably be quarried stone.

Offsetting carbon emissions

Let's be clear on this: BLOOM may be a useful guide but I've no doubt that many of the purchases I make are not from sustainable sources. In such cases the only thing to do is offset the resulting carbon cost. You can find out how big your own carbon footprint is by logging on to a website that has a carbon calculator. You can then begin to make choices about how to offset your carbon emissions by direct action, by responsible shopping and by supporting local traders or suppliers who have a proven carbon-reduction policy. Trade carbon against other resources; for example, growing vegetables takes more water and fertilizers than ornamental plants but the trade-off is that your vegetables will only have travelled a few feet to get to your plate. Supermarket veg will have been packaged, transported by road and then displayed in chiller cabinets in a heated, lit supermarket. The trick is to use common sense in how you apply carbon trading. Buying and planting trees and shrubs in your own garden is good, and contributing to forestation schemes (established as part of a supplier's or manufacturer's carbon-reduction policy) in other parts of the world is highly worthwhile. But don't be afraid to think creatively about how to reduce your carbon footprint - you may find some inspirational opportunities close to hand.

For some the idea of quarrying is inherently wrong, but applying BLOOM logic on a visit to my local quarry pit threw up some different results. Potential beneficiaries abounded, not least the workers employed in a shrinking industry and, in this case, in an area of economic decline. And as quarried stone is already several million years old you can't really argue on the lifespan issue, not least as good-quality stone flags can be used over and over again. As the pit is just 32km (20 miles) away, delivery wouldn't be too serious a problem. Real stone is about as ornamentally pleasing a product as you can find and has a long tradition of use in Yorkshire, where dry-stone walls have stood for over a thousand years, rebuilt by successive generations.

Good manufacturing

The manufacturing process is probably the bit that gets people most agitated, but I was impressed that 98 per cent of the water used in the process was filtered and recycled on site. Fossil fuels are undoubtedly used to power the machinery, but a good proportion of the stone is still worked by hand. And the input required for a product that will

Using Christmas trees (below) that have been felled may seem controversial, but they are a crop, just like wheat or barley, and benefit the environment during production.

By recycling the existing concrete flagstones (above) in my garden I have made a modestly beneficial impact on the environment.

outlast several generations is actually remarkably small when put in context. I would certainly have far fewer qualms about using real stone from a local source than replacing my mobile phone for the umpteenth time.

On a recent visit to a local retailer I noticed a rather natty set of teak garden furniture at a low, low price. Picturing it on my new patio, the temptation to buy

was almost overwhelming. But something was missing. A search of the packaging revealed no mention of whether or not the teak had come from a sustainable source. Responsible retailers will usually take advantage of one of the certificated schemes, such as that administered by the Forest Stewardship Council (FSC). The FSC works in more than 80 countries to help guarantee that timber comes from a sustainable source. This furniture may well have come from a managed forest, but I couldn't be sure, and the sales assistants were stumped too. As tempting as the low price was, without that clarity I couldn't be sure that the furniture hadn't actually come at a big, big cost.

Illegal timber

The clear felling of exotic hardwoods (where every tree in the vicinity is felled) is among the most heinous of environmental crimes. It causes massive and irretrievable damage to fragile ecosystems and leads to mass extinctions. The larger tropical and subtropical forests are often referred to as the lungs of the Earth, but are shrinking so rapidly we are at risk of suffocation. According to the Environmental Investigation Agency (EIA), rampant illegal logging is being carried out in

The mobius loop (left) is used to indicate that an object is capable of being recycled. The loop on the right denotes an object contains x per cent of recycled material.

Indonesia at three times the sustainable level and far in excess of legitimate production. Much of this illegal timber is 'laundered' through other states before making it on to the market in the US, Europe and so on. And the primary use for all this illegal wood is garden furniture. Are you sitting comfortably?

Properly managed forests can and do produce exotic hardwood products, which although coming with a high carbon-mile deficit have the same advantage as stone flags; that is, they last for a very long time – a lifetime if cared for properly. But rather than buying hardwood products that have traversed the globe, why not look into what is available locally?

A rammed-earth wall (right) can be used for ornamental plants or, as here, vegetables, salad leaves and companion plants. The 'waste' soil used to make the wall around the raised bed might otherwise have ended up in landfill.

Using a rammed-earth wall to make raised beds

This low, 30cm (12in), rammed-earth raised bed is perfect for vegetable or herb growing. Given that soil has been a principal building material for humans since pre-history, it seems strange that it is now considered rather 'way out'. But earth-built structures include some of the most magnificent buildings on the planet, including temples, citadels and fortresses. Using the subsoil from, say, the construction of a pond to make a useful garden feature is a great way of recycling what would otherwise be waste material. If you want to make a taller wall consult an expert, as the structural and design issues that affect conventional building are no different when using rammed earth.

1. Create a timber frame – known as form work – using milled softwood or plyboard, in this case the dimensions are 30cm x 10cm (12in x 4in). Drive square cut pointed stakes into the ground around the frame and fix them to the form work with screws. It's essential that the stakes are firm in the ground so the form work doesn't move.

2. Dig a 30cm (12in) deep footing inside the outer form work. This will help the earth wall to key into the surrounding soil and provide greater stability and strength. The soil excavated for the footing can be used to fill the raised bed on completion, so either put this to one side or place it in what will become the centre of the bed.

3. Create a second form-work frame inside the outer frame, 30cm (12in) parallel all the way round. Using the same methods as in step 1, drive in pointed stakes to secure the frame and fix these with screws. To improve strength, fill the centre of the frame with the soil excavated for the footings.

4. Apply the earth in layers of around 20cm (8in) at a time, and consolidate them with a tamping bar (pictured) or a small pneumatic ram, which can be rented from a plant-hire shop. Each 20cm (8in) layer should be rammed to approximately half that depth. Continue the process by ramming successive layers around the whole length of the raised bed.

5. Once the rammed earth has been applied and rammed to within 5cm (2in) of the top of the form work, wait approximately 1 hour and then carefully remove the outer form work. The internal form work can either be left *in situ* or removed after a couple of days once the earth is completely dry and it has the consistency of concrete. Reuse the timber to make further raised beds.

Keeping it local
Supporting your community

Throughout these last few pages the word 'local' has cropped up more than once. Once upon a time even the smallest of towns would have had a variety of shops. Now we have the freedom to travel granted by the car, and desire a greater variety of products at cheap prices. Big retailers can fulfil those desires through massive purchasing power, but this has all contributed to the decline of the small, local shop.

But local crafts and skills still exist, as do neighbourhood suppliers. By going local you are not only reducing your carbon footprint but also supporting local business, thereby ensuring they are there for the future. It can be pretty difficult to build up a good relationship with a sales assistant working in a busy superstore, but by dealing with local suppliers you can ask BLOOM questions (see p.56), tailor products to your needs and respect the local vernacular, while doing your bit to save the planet.

Choosing your supplier
If you cannot find the services you require locally then try to seek out suppliers that have environmental and ethical policies for their products and services. Many companies now carry out environmental audits of their operations, or produce clearly defined statements relating to their activities and how they do business, and these can either be found on the company website or requested by post.

There are some excellent mail-order companies that, although they rely on postal delivery with inevitable carbon cost, have strong environmental credentials, employ local people to manufacture their products and only use sustainable materials.

Increasingly, companies are engaging in schemes for offsetting carbon, many of which are of significant importance to the communities they benefit. But beware – some schemes are little more than public relations stunts with limited benefit to the environment, so it's worth asking a few questions about how the scheme is run and who it benefits.

Under your nose...
When seeking out a supplier for two curved benches at Harlow Carr, we wanted a local craftsperson who would use traditional and modern methods of manufacture and locally sourced timber harvested from sustainable woodlands. The search took me no further than the

In a sustainable forest in Eastern Europe (below left) loggers pull logs from a woodpile to load them on a horse-drawn cart for transport. This forest, a huge ancient tract of woodland on the Polish-Belorussian border, is strictly managed and only designated areas may be logged.

Clear felling (below) of irreplaceable rainforest for timber extraction or agriculture is devastating parts of southeast Asia, such as the Malaysian rainforest, and South America.

other side of the road from my home. When completed the two benches had travelled fewer than 112km (70 miles), from the wood to sawmill, sawmill to workshop, workshop to garden.

Lifetime of use

At around 100 years old, the oak tree that was felled to make the benches would have processed pollution and carbon, produced oxygen, provided food and habitats for wildlife and generally enhanced the planet just by being there.

Using local craftspeople (below left) such as Richard Taylor from where I live, makes environmental sense, as the end product doesn't need to be moved across the country.

Locally sourced timber (below right), harvested from managed woods and forests, is environmentally sound. During their lifetime the trees help to remove pollution, reduce carbon and provide food and shelter for wildlife.

The finished bench (bottom) is not only beautiful, tactile and comfortable, but has come at minimal cost to the environment, while supporting local crafts and skills.

Get creative with scrap
Reusing building waste in the garden

The throwaway society in which we live is a very recent phenomenon. In the not too distant past, humans survived perfectly well without generating vast amounts of waste. Industry and business may well be the main culprits, but, according to the Organization for Economic Cooperation and Development (OECD), domestic homes in Britain today produce more than 35 million tonnes of waste per annum, while in the USA the tonnage exceeds 200 million tonnes.

And all that waste has to go somewhere. Towed out to sea and dumped offshore, burnt in incinerators or buried in vast landfill sites, the environmental consequences range from toxic pollution to the squandering of finite natural resources. And, of course, the processing, towing, burning and burying of waste produces even more carbon dioxide. As much of this waste is comprised of modern materials we have no clear idea of the long-term effects of its production and disposal.

Getting creative
Even in the picturesque part of the world in which I live (Yorkshire), the reality of our consumption isn't far away, as within 3.2km (2 miles) of my home is a landfill site of some 5 hectares (12 acres). And the greatest tragedy is that much of that waste could be recycled or reused, and much of the rest not generated in the first place. Aside from composting and reusing existing materials such as hard landscaping products, we can also buy long-lived products with built-in reuse like natural stone or hardwood from sustainable local woodland, grow some of our own food and choose gardening products and plants with minimal packaging (or, failing that, packaging that is recycled, recyclable or biodegradable). And we can creatively use materials in our gardens that others throw away. The thought of this might sound tacky, but with imagination it is possible to use scrap in a way that is just as aesthetically pleasing as purpose-bought material.

The possibilities are endless...
Building waste provides plenty of opportunity for inventive reuse in the garden, and if you don't want to hover suspiciously outside building sites you can always ask the site manager for first refusal on scrap, which will usually be agreed providing you remove it on time. You might be surprised at what you can find.

At Harlow Carr, soil-pipe u-bends have been turned into alpine planters – as have the toilets that were once connected to them – and pig-iron fence posts and concrete reinforcing mesh have found new life as plant supports. There are seemingly endless opportunities to reuse waste timber. These range from the utilitarian – my compost bins are constructed from old pallets, while the staging in my greenhouse has been made from cut-down display tables that were thrown out of a plant centre – to the ornamental; all the timber cladding used to transform a range of summerhouses at Harlow Carr has had a 'previous life'.

And if you're not keen on hanging out with a bunch of construction workers, why not sign up to a free recycling network? These web-based networks – the one I use is called Freecycle – offer the chance to allow somebody else to reuse items that you no longer have a use for, or for you to reuse another's waste. Recent items up for grabs on Freecycle have ranged from garden sheds to spare onion sets.

A simple collection (left) of 'found' objects can create interest and bring a little drama and individuality to your garden.

Scrap does not need to be rubbish (top left), as Dennys Henessey's garden in Solihull, near Birmingham, UK demonstrates. With imagination, a raised deck and balustrade of gracefully curving spars can be made from waste timber.

This stone pillar (top right) rescued from an exhibition hall and wrapped in a length of exotic looking material, is also waste. Here it becomes a fun, irreverent installation.

Patio materials (bottom left) can be expensive and detrimental to the environment. This galvanized-steel patio has been recycled from the inside of an articulated lorry.

Metal screens (bottom right) of recycled corrugated metal, cut at the same angle but at different heights, make a stylish backdrop to architectural foliage plants such as *Chamaerops humilis*.

Using permaculture to improve sustainability

The term 'permaculture', a contraction of 'permanent' and 'agriculture', was first coined in the 1970s by David Holmgren and Bill Mollison. Its meaning has shifted slightly over the years, and today permaculture is considered as a lifestyle ethic for seeking sustainable ways of living, incorporating social systems, organic gardening, architecture, agroforestry and ecological economics. Central to permaculture is the observation of the systems and patterns that exist within nature, and then learning how to apply these observations to daily living. Permaculture provides a framework for those who aspire to live in a way that is less damaging to the planet. Making informed choices over what we buy and consume is a good way to start the permaculture process.

CHAPTER FOUR

The Wildlife Hotel
How to attract wildlife into your garden

Gardens and garden plants can be seen as hotels for wildlife, providing food, water, shelter, warmth and safety. In some parts of the world, gardens are the last bastion of species that find their home range either diminished or destroyed, such as the common frog and house sparrow. But, the stereotypical view of wildlife gardening as being messy, only planted with native species and full of stinging nettles has had a detrimental effect on encouraging gardeners to allocate space for wildlife. In fact, the term 'wildlife gardening' is something of a misnomer, as it suggests that gardens can only be of value if gardened in a certain way. The reality is that even gardens that appear superficially to have nothing to offer can benefit certain species – but, when appropriately managed, gardens can make an important contribution to the preservation of wildlife. For example, just putting in a pond will attract wildlife. Mammals, birds, insects, and frogs, and even small fish will appear – the latter can become attached to the legs of birds or to the moist skin of a frog.

A garden pond (left) is a great way to attract wildlife. Lush planting at its edges and an irregular shape, both of which mimic natural pools and lakes, will help to provide the best environment for wildlife.

From dragonflies to golden eagles
Gardening with wildlife in mind

Gardens don't have to be messy to be good for wildlife, nor do they have to be full of introduced habitats. A wide variety of plants that provide food sources at different times of the year, allied to sensitive management, can greatly benefit biodiversity. If you want to be even more proactive in encouraging wildlife by installing artificial habitats, then so much the better. But it is the encouragement of natural cycles that are beneficial to all biodiversity, including the ornamental garden, that have the greatest impact. This is why 'new gardening' embraces the concept of the garden as part of the wider, wilder environment, rather than hermetically sealed from it. A time-consuming and environmentally costly battle against wildlife in the garden is futile – it is a battle that can never be won. But a partnership built on knowledge and understanding where 'pests' are controlled naturally as part of the natural balance in the garden is an achievable and sustainable goal.

Connecting with wildlife

In any street it's possible to find a range of gardens, from those that are densely planted to those bereft of plants altogether, and all stages in between. It is this diversity that is all important to wildlife. An unplanted garden with a mown lawn will suit species of birds that predate worms, a garden left to run wild may well be full of small, scurrying mammals enjoying the cover of tall grass and weeds, while a planted garden can provide food sources in the form of pollen, nectar and fruit. Add a few additional features – a pond, nest-boxes, decaying wood, feeders, etc. – and a garden can become a veritable wildlife hotel.

Gardens can also provide environments that are otherwise missing locally. If, for example, there are no natural bodies of fresh water in your area, a well-designed and planted garden pond can make a huge difference to the survival of native pond fauna. Best of all for plant lovers, is the value that ornamental plants provide for wildlife. Pollen- and nectar-feeding insects get pretty short shrift in winter from native flora in countries such as the UK which have comparatively few indigenous species, but there are plenty of cultivated plants that flower during this period and provide sustenance. Ornamental plants

that produce berries, nuts and fruit will feed on everything from mammals to insects, and, of course, not only will these exotic plants help our wildlife they will also fill our days with colour, form and fragrance.

The reasons why I garden with wildlife in mind, both at home and at work, are far from altruistic. I know that by encouraging a healthy, balanced garden I will have far fewer 'pest' problems, but I also think of the wildlife in my garden as being as important and beautiful as the plants themselves. A freshly emerged dragonfly clinging to an iris leaf at the edge of the pond has an iridescence and depth of colour that few plants can match. And the birds that visit my feeders or take advantage of the various nest-boxes provide a constant supply of colour and sound, especially during the cold winter months. Gardens are fantastic places to get to know wildlife because they make it so accessible, especially for children.

The ebb and flow of life

I know that I will never get a golden eagle in my garden, no matter how hard I might try, but out there among my *Miscanthus* and *Rudbeckia*, the pursuit of life, death and, maybe, happiness are in full flow. And although a golden eagle may well be more beautiful and impressive than, say, a shield bug, having an understanding of the life of a shield bug is more likely to help us to understand the natural world than focusing on a rare bird of prey. Embracing wildlife as an integral part of our gardens is a hugely rewarding experience that enables us to connect with life at its most fundamental level.

Biodiversity – what on Earth is it?

Simply, biodiversity is biological diversity: the complex web of organisms and ecosystems that make up all life on Earth. Everything from the largest living organisms on the planet – fungi – to the tiniest micro-organism, including the species of mammals, birds and insects that visit our gardens and the plants that we grow in them. The greatest threat to biodiversity on Earth is posed by human activity and the manner in which we live our lives, the pollution and waste we generate and the natural resources we consume.

A garden shelter can be as homely for animals as it is for humans. The timber can provide the building materials for invertebrates such as wasps, while the warm cover can be an ideal hiding place for numerous bugs, including beneficial insects such as ladybirds and lacewings, that need dry places in which to over-winter. If situated in a peaceful place, an open-fronted shelter might even be used by nesting birds.

Water is the stuff of life for most animals, and a well-balanced pond can soon become a magnet for a whole range of creatures. As well as providing water for visiting mammals and birds there are hundreds of species of invertebrates and amphibians that either rely on water for part of their life cycle, such as spawning frogs, or that spend their entire lives in the deep. Without water, these creatures will never visit your garden.

Plants aren't just pretty, they are also vital for animals. Although some species rely solely on indigenous plants as food sources (primarily invertebrates), nectar and pollen-rich ornamental plants can provide a bountiful harvest when no natives are in flower. Similarly, the bountiful harvest of fruit, berries and nuts that exotic plants produce can feed animals and birds for many months, especially important during winter when food can be scarce.

Generous planting at the pond edge provides a 'rope ladder' by which animals can get in and out of the water. This is particularly important for species of invertebrates, such as dragonflies, that spend their larval life in water before emerging as adults. Pond-edge planting also gives cover for vulnerable animals like baby frogs or small mammals that come to the water to drink, and the shade cast by the plants will help to keep the water temperature stable in summer.

Why aphids can be good
Encouraging natural cycles and beneficial animals

One of the best reasons for encouraging greater diversity is that you will find the need for human intervention to control what we consider to be pests becomes markedly reduced, as beneficial predators discover that you have put up the equivalent of a neon sign for them.

The first step in the journey is, and always will be, a leap of faith. I remember a time – shortly after the planting of Hyde Hall's dry garden – when a plague of aphids descended on every freshly planted *Artemesia* in the garden, encrusting the silvery stems and foliage with their plump, black, sap-sucking bodies. The temptation to spray them with chemical pesticide was strong. However, I resisted, and within two weeks they had vanished – the result of predation by insects and birds but perhaps also the natural life cycle of aphids, which tends toward sudden population explosions followed by periods where they are absent.

Good guys, bad guys

What makes a garden pest a garden pest? We do. The various invertebrates and vertebrates that nibble and suck our garden plants are just animals, neither good nor bad, just predators, prey or both. It is us that give them the good guy, bad guy tags. All predators are controlled by the availability of prey, whether on the plains of the Serengeti or the back garden of 17 Laburnum Drive. Aphids may seem a controversial choice for garden heroes, but without them we wouldn't have ladybirds, lacewings, species of hoverfly, beetles, birds and so on – up and up the food chain. If you kill every aphid in your garden on sight then the good guys will never appear, for there will be nothing for them to eat. But if you accept these prodigious breeders as part of a balanced garden then that is what they will become, controlled by their own boom-and-bust life cycle and the many and various predators that will come, and stay, in your garden.

Establishing natural cycles

The successful establishment of natural cycles in your garden is affected by many factors, such as the size of your garden and the manner in which it has been previously managed, and how your neighbour's garden and the local environment is managed. An urban garden, surrounded by buildings and roads, is likely to be attractive to a slightly different range of species than a rural garden surrounded by fields, woodland and hedgerows.

The size of your garden and its interaction with neighbouring gardens is important too, because larger gardened areas (either your own plot or the combined area of several gardens) are likely to have a greater diversity on offer. The next few pages will show you how to encourage natural cycles in your garden.

Coping with slugs and snails

It is really very difficult to love slugs and snails, thanks to the devastation they can wreak in the garden. The truth is that molluscs are difficult to control without intervention, but it needn't be to the detriment of other species. There are now organic slug pellets on the market that don't poison other animals. Or, try laying a plank of wood on the grass or next to a planted area in your garden. Molluscs love cool, damp places to hide in, and by daybreak they will have migrated to the underside of the plank – from whence you can dispose of them as you wish. Gravel mulches, upturned grapefruit, beer traps and crushed eggshells have been put forward as possible controls, but all they have given me is an exotic-smelling garden!

When to step in and use control methods

Reducing the level of intervention in your garden and encouraging natural cycles will certainly help to engender a better balance between 'good' and 'bad' creatures, but there will always be occasions when the only way to save the life of a plant is to intervene. However, rather than resorting to using chemical sprays, consider first natural or organic alternatives: companion plants, such as marigolds and onions, that may deter pests by masking the smell of plants you want to protect; garlic barrier sprays that make plants unpalatable for aphids and other sap suckers; biological controls in the form of predatory insects that either eat or parasitize their prey; and soap-based sprays that clog the spiracles (breathing holes) of sap suckers and thereby cause them to suffocate. With chemical controls now subject to increasing legislation, the manufacturers of organic products have really got their act together and now offer a huge range of alternatives.

In towns and cities (right) gardens form vital corridors to and from the countryside that wildlife can exploit.

Snails (below) are a vital food source for species, such as frogs and birds.

An aphid infestation (above) can be a real worry, especially on young plants. Intervention in the form of organic controls may be required.

Companion planting (right) is a non-invasive and environmentally sensible way of deterring 'pests'. Here marigolds are planted with chard.

Life within the decay
Enhancing existing wildlife habitats

The most intensively managed garden will have a variety of habitats available for wildlife, even if we aren't aware of them. A small pile of leaves, the dead flowering stems of a perennial, a tiny crack in the mortar of a wall – can all provide homes for animals. While we can proactively introduce new habitats, as we shall see on the next few pages, we can also improve existing habitats by knowing what is there and why.

Living together
A few summers ago I had the pleasure of observing a leafcutter bee building its nest beneath my bedroom windowsill. Back and forth it flew for three days and more, each time bringing back a perfectly cut segment of fresh rose leaf that the insect placed together to make cells into which her eggs were laid. The gap beneath the windowsill was no more than a few millimetres wide, but that tiny aperture provided the space required for the next generation of leafcutter bees to be brought into the world.

But the recent trend for home improvement and changes to the rural landscape, such as the conversion of old barns into homes, has reduced the number of wildlife habitats, which can often be incredibly fragile, as well as remarkably discreet. Bats use echo location to detect their food, and often follow the routes of hedgerows to hunt for their prey in much the same way as we use a specific route to reach a destination. Removing a hedgerow, or even a section of hedgerow, can be disastrous for the bats that rely on it.

Decay and its benefits
It has been estimated that as many as 20,000 animals can be supported in and around a single mature oak tree, taking advantage not just of the living wood and foliage, but also the dead and decaying wood for food and shelter. Decaying wood, in fact, can be home to some of the most interesting and rare invertebrates on

Fallen autumn leaves (below) attract soil flora and fauna. These, in turn, help the leaves decompose, thus enriching the soil.

Earth, as well as to larger, more obvious animals such as nesting birds. The lignin and cellulose in wood can be difficult to digest, so the insects that carry out this invaluable task are highly specialized and often found in small numbers and in localized communities. Many species of fungi live on dead and decaying wood, hastening the process of reabsorption into the soil.

Soil improvement

Amphibians find the warm, dry environment beneath and within fallen trees perfect for overwintering. Small mammals will make nests in dead wood, while the carnivorous ones will predate the invertebrates that are attracted to it. Species of bat often live in the holes left by long-dead branches, as do species of birds, including nocturnal predators such as owls.

Decaying leaves also provide natural habitats for the invertebrates that help in the process of decomposition, and, in turn, the predatory animals that feed on these insects. This process improves the structure and health of the soil, and enriches it in preparation for the growth of the tree again the following season.

Fungus forming (left) on a carved wooden head is part of the natural cycle of decay that happens to all natural materials.

Cycle of life

Gardeners often fear decay because it comes from death, and who wants a garden full of dead plants? But death and decay are part of the cycle of life, and shouldn't be feared or tidied away too quickly. There are simple ways in which decaying matter can be accommodated in the garden – leaving fallen leaves and branches and not filling every crack in the garden wall, for example. And though bagging up leaves is a great way to obtain free soil-improver, and insects will make their way into these bags, leaving a pile of untouched leaves in a corner of the garden will be of more benefit.

Many species of bats (below left) rely on holes in trees for either temporary or permanent roosts, as do numerous bird species.

The decaying area inside this cavity (below) provides a food source for invertebrates and building materials for species such as wasps.

Creating new habitats
Building log piles to encourage biodiversity

One of the simplest ways to create a habitat for the biodiversity that thrives on, in and around decaying wood is to create a log pile. At its simplest a log pile is precisely that, but it is possible to create something that is aesthetically pleasing, even practically useful, from dead wood.

A traditional log pile, made from wood destined for burning as fuel, is stacked for ease of access rather than biodiversity but will still make the ideal habitat for

small mammals, amphibians and the numerous insects that either feed on wood or predate the bugs that do. Stacked in a manner that looks more like a tepee, the log pile can become suitable for larger animals such as hibernating hedgehogs.

Even a single log stuck into the ground vertically can be of benefit, especially if it is drilled with a number of holes of varying sizes – these provide a suitable nest hole for some species of solitary bees, and also will make a warm shelter for other insects including beneficial predators.

Paths and benches

Felled logs can be used to make path edges, simply laid on the ground in parallel lines to form a route, the space in between filled with bark or chipped wood. This is effective in woodland gardens, shaded corners or gardens with a wilder look, where the gradually decomposing wood will eventually green over with moss and lichen, which, when combined with the rotting wood, will make a suitable growing medium for other plants to seed into. The effect of this gradual decline can be quite beautiful, as nature reclaims the raw materials back into the soil.

Another use for felled logs is as a retaining device on banks, where they can be stacked to make terraces that are then filled with soil for planting. Again, the best application for this is in a shaded spot where the effect will be more natural. But perhaps the easiest log-pile object to accommodate in a garden – apart from a pile of logs – is a log bench.

Unless you have an endless supply of trees in your garden the best way to obtain the materials you need to make a log bench or a single log or path edging is to order the timber from a local saw mill. Or you could exchange a day of volunteering for a conservation trust involved in woodland management for the logs you need. Whatever you do, never collect fallen timber from the countryside; in doing so you might unwittingly destroy an existing wildlife habitat.

A basic log pile (left) can be made by stacking logs in a pyramid shape. Start with around five or six at the base and stack another three to four layers on top.

Making a log pile bench

A good way to incorporate a log pile in your garden is to create a bench in a spot where you like to sit. Ideally the bench will be partially shaded or fully shaded for part of the day to benefit animals such as amphibians – here the back of the bench is in full shade all day. The logs have been obtained as part of the regular cycle of woodland thinning in the garden, but could be obtained from a timber yard. The only non-biodegradable, manufactured parts of the bench are the chicken wire and nails.

1. Start with the largest diameter logs at the base, laying them directly on to the earth. Soil contact is important, as it will hasten the decomposition process. Once the bottom layer is in place start to build up the pile with logs of decreasing girth until the logs have been stacked to knee height.

2. Cover the top and sides with a layer of chicken wire. Then select some shorter logs, about a third of the width of the base, to form the backrest to the bench. Nail some thin timber laths to the seat and back to provide strength, and then fix the planks on to these laths with countersunk screws.

3. At the same time as building up the backrest, continue to build up the sides of the bench with full-sized logs. Once the backrest has reached a comfortable height for sitting, complete the sides and apply a second layer of chicken wire.

4. Cover the sides and back of the bench with a 40-cm (16-in) layer of top soil, working the soil into the cracks. Cover the layer of top soil with turf, bringing the edges right down to ground level. This can be planted with wild flower plug plants or left simply as turf.

Habitat boxes
Providing homes for beneficial wildlife

Perhaps the most manageable way to enhance the wildlife potential of your garden is to install habitat boxes. The bird nest-box is perhaps the most obvious and well-known, and many of us will have one or more in our gardens. But habitat boxes can be made or bought for wildlife as diverse as bees, ladybirds, bats, hedgehogs and species of birds with specific needs, all of which are beneficial to the health of the garden. It's possible to maximize the advantage of these creatures by installing boxes where they are needed most – insectivorous-bird boxes close to borders prone to aphid infestation, for example.

At Harlow Carr, the Rose Revolution Borders are home to six ladybird and lacewing boxes, with the same number of bluetit boxes fixed to nearby trees. Last summer I watched families of recently fledged bluetits and their parents working their way through the borders, devouring juicy aphids on the way.

Make your own
There are now many suppliers of artificial habitat boxes, all with a wide range of products to encourage greater diversity in the garden. But if you don't wish to go the expense of buying habitat boxes, many are easy to make, and there are simple alternatives to manufactured boxes. A bundle of bamboo canes

pushed into a crack in a sunny wall will benefit ladybirds, lacewings and species of solitary bee; an upturned clay pot filled with moss and partially buried in the soil may become the ideal nest for a bumblebee. Keep an eye out too for opportunities that arise naturally in your garden. A shed door left ajar in autumn will allow hibernating butterflies to take advantage of the dry shelter, and a crack in a wall may become home to any number of species of insect. Even a wooden post – providing the wood hasn't been treated with preservative – drilled with holes of differing sizes and 'planted' in a sunny spot in the garden can be of use to species of bees, which will lay their eggs in the apertures and then plug the holes with mud or chewed up leaves.

Fallen acorns (above) are a favourite food of small mammals. You can even make your own wildlife feeder, such as the one above.

A bundle of bamboo canes (left) will provide a nest for solitary bees to lay their eggs in. A variety of other insects will also overwinter in the dry, warm habitat it provides.

Making a habitat box

The range of habitat boxes available to buy has never been greater than it is today, with birds, mammals, insects and even amphibians all catered for. But you can easily make your own boxes for the creatures in your garden. Here is an example of a really simple way to make a habitat for bumblebees. These insects nest in holes in the ground, usually at the foot of trees or hedges, and often take over old vole or mouse holes. A simple bumblebee pot in the right location may well be used as an alternative to taking over a mammal nest.

1. Fill a small clay or terracotta plant pot with dry leaves, straw or dry grass. It's essential that the material you use is really dry and not decomposing, as wet or rotting material may harm the bumblebees that the pot should attract.

2. Line the middle of the leaf nest with a little moss, feathers or cotton wool, enough to cover the middle of your palm. Don't ever collect moss from the wild, and only use it if you have an abundant supply and can justify harvesting a small amount each year.

3. Find a sheltered, warm location at the base of a hedge, shrub or tree or near the foot of a wall and overturn the bee pot. If there is a risk of the pot being upended, push a cane through the drainage hole. Rest one edge of the pot on a stone so there is easy access for bees at soil level.

The garden that never sleeps
Plants as winter food sources

Gardeners sometimes talk of putting the garden to bed in winter. However, apart from plants that are grown specifically for their winter interest, there is so much to be gained from leaving perennials and grasses standing for as long as possible, for our own pleasure but also for biodiversity.

Summer- and autumn-flowering perennials take on an entirely different character in winter, their stems turning to the colour of straw, often topped with blackened seed heads. The low sun illuminates and magnifies their stately decline, and on a crisp winter day, especially following a hoar frost, they glisten with the frozen droplets of water, cobwebs strung from stem to stem like icy tightropes.

Food and shelter

The benefit to biodiversity comes in the form of food and shelter. The seeds of many species of perennials are rich in fatty oils, making them perfect for all types of birds and omnivorous and herbivorous mammals. Their survival through the winter months in turn assures the survival of other species that depend on them as prey. The standing stems of perennials can provide winter homes for a surprising number of invertebrates, both beneficial predators and their prey, while the basal foliage can give cover for small mammals as they scurry through the garden in search of food.

There will always come a time when standing plants need to be cut back, either in readiness for the next growing season or because rain, snow or high winds have levelled everything, leaving an unsightly mess. But even then it is possible to keep habitat disturbance to a minimum, by leaving the cut material in a pile close to the border or bundled near the base of a hedge or other sheltered spot where invertebrates can migrate to. In this way at least some of the beneficial insects and prey will have the chance to relocate and will be there, keeping your garden balanced, when spring comes around. In my own garden, and at Harlow Carr, the big cut-back begins in January with spring-flowering plants, and finishes two to three months later with autumn-flowering perennials and grasses,

Illuminated by the low, diffused winter light (below), the benefit of leaving plants standing through winter is obvious aesthetically. In pleasing the eye we are also helping wildlife by providing food sources, habitats and safe foraging cover for a wide variety of species.

Seedheads (top) of *Echinacea purpurea* 'Magnus' are covered with closely packed seeds that are rich in fatty oils. Finches are particularly attracted to them.

The teasel (middle) is a statuesque plant that lends architectural presence and a wilder feel to plantings. The prickly seedheads contain hundreds of energy-packed seeds.

Seeds of *Centaurea macrocephala* (bottom) are gradually parting company with the head, perhaps with the help of birds and small mammals.

ensuring the plants are ready for a new season but also that wildlife has been able to make the most of them for as long as possible.

The argument in favour of pre-winter clearance is based on sterilization, i.e removing the 'bad' insects from the garden. But the sterilization is just as indiscriminate as the blanket deployment of pesticides since it removes the 'good' insects too. It isn't unusual to hear gardeners talk of the need for a really hard winter to kill off the pests. This, of course, is something of a double-edged sword, as a really hard winter will kill indiscriminately.

The argument against pre-winter clearance is based on maintaining a healthy balance in the garden, but with the added benefit of so much beauty to enjoy. For me, gardens never go to sleep. They can be as vibrant and exciting in the depths of winter as they can in summer, especially when full of wildlife.

Nectar bars

Undoubtedly the easiest way to attract animals to your garden is through the plants you select. Winged invertebrates and birds are usually the animals most often seen in gardens, partly because of their mobility, but also because they are among the most conspicuous. Animals that feed on pollen and nectar can be especially well catered for in a garden, and moreover are essential in many instances – imagine what would happen without them; no apples, pears, apricots, cherries, the list could run for pages.

Ornamental plants are available that flower throughout the year. This means that a garden well-stocked with the right selection of pollen- and nectar-rich plants can be a veritable nectar bar, potentially benefiting dozens of species.

Berry buffets

Garden plants can also provide a rich harvest of food in the form of fruits and seeds, providing, of course, that the plants concerned are fertile and have been pollinated. These food sources can be invaluable to wildlife, especially if they are formed late in the season and persist into winter, when the fruits of native plants may have been exhausted. Birds can often be seen taking the fruit from ornamental trees and shrubs such as *Cotoneaster*, *Malus*, edible cherry and *Sorbus*, but there are many other animals that benefit. Insects will sup on the flesh of rotting fruit as readily as they will nectar, and small mammals will quickly harvest fallen fruit.

The good food guide
Native plants as food sources for wildlife

During the latter part of the 1800s, the enthusiasm for 'florists' flowers' – plants bred for their unusual flower colour, structure or size, but often at the cost of their sterility – meant that many popular garden plants didn't produce nectar or pollen, and so were of no consequence to wildlife as food sources. In recent years the fashion for more natural-looking plants has brought pollen- and nectar-rich species, as well as cultivars, back to the forefront of garden design, to the benefit of gardens and wildlife. Indeed, many of the most popular plants in our gardens are, in fact, wild plants, native to another country, that have been deemed worthy enough to be cultivated and therefore propagated and then moved from their home range to our plots.

Fussy eaters?

For all of the benefits of these ornamental plants to indigenous wildlife they cannot take the place of native flora in certain key situations, principally as food sources for the larval stages of invertebrates. In some species of invertebrates the relationship between their larvae and the food they require is highly specific and has no doubt evolved over long periods of time. In the UK, several species of butterfly rely on particular food plants for their young; the caterpillars of the orange tip feed on lady's smock and hedge mustard, while those of the brimstone – one of the loveliest of all butterflies and usually the first on the wing of the new broods – will only eat the foliage of elder buckthorn. Stinging nettles provide food for more than one species of butterfly, and so are invaluable native plants. And then there are the insects that have such specialized diets that they are, and have always been, highly localized and often extremely rare. While adult butterflies and moths will happily feast on a plant that originated in China, often their young cannot.

The importance of native plants goes well beyond those animals that rely on them for food as it affects every other creature in the food chain thereafter.

The relationship (right) between native plants and wildlife is often specialized and intimate. Ladies smock (*Cardamine pratensis*) is one of the primary food sources for the caterpillar of the orange tip butterfly.

Moths are a favourite food of larger animals, particularly bats, but many moth species require native grasses on which their young are born and fed. If these grasses are absent, or not sensitively managed, the moths and the bats suffer, as do the predators of the bats, such as owls.

A complex relationship

Having said that, it needs to be remembered that the relationship between food plants and the animals that feed on them is complex, and simply having the plants doesn't guarantee that they will be fed upon. On our allotment there are a lot of stinging nettles (in fact, too many), yet every year only one small clump is used by small tortoiseshell butterfly caterpillars. It may be that the presence of a large metal sheet behind the clump provides shelter and reflected heat, but nowhere else on our large plot do the nettles get nibbled, suggesting that butterflies are either very choosy or that the abundance of nettles is such that there are simply more nettles than there are butterflies to lay eggs and therefore caterpillars to eat them.

If you can plant native species in your garden then do so, providing they have been purchased from responsibly and legally grown stock. Many native species are the rival of any ornamental plant in terms of beauty, and if the plants are absent in the countryside around you then you may well be providing an invaluable service for the wild animals who feed on them.

Leave it to the experts

Don't feel, though, that native plants must take precedence over ornamentals, especially in a small garden where longevity of interest is paramount. In my own garden I have a few natives and many ornamentals, but I support the protection of wild plants and animals through involvement in local conservation organizations, that are better placed to protect them in the wild than I am in my tiny garden. It's back to the golden eagle again – I can enhance the biodiversity that I know does or could make use of my garden, but I cannot make a home for every species.

Spanish bluebells (below) have been hybridizing with native British bluebells ever since their introduction in the Victorian era.

A bluebell wood (below right) is hard to improve upon, so avoid invasive aliens and preserve the genetic diversity of native plants.

Alien invaders and plants from the wild

From the early 1600s a fad struck the wealthy and ennobled of the then known world. Able men were sent to far-flung places to collect and send back plants to adorn their gardens, and by the 1800s the fad had become a fever. Among the many beautiful plants collected that have greatly increased the enjoyment of our gardens, a few bad apples were unwittingly gathered. Today there is hardly a country in the world that isn't battling invasive alien species, or translocated native species gone wild. From *Agapanthus* in Australia to Spanish bluebells in Britain, the fight goes on. Worst of all, though, are the non-native invasive aquatic plants that spread like wildfire and play havoc with waterways and aquatic animals. So when you are purchasing plants, it is important to bear in mind the following points:

- Carry out some research to be certain you know which plants constitute a problem in your area, and make sure you never buy them. Local or national conservation organizations and government environmental agencies can provide this information.
- Purchase native aquatic plants from reputable dealers, and when buying exotic aquatic plants make sure they are safe to use and are not considered detrimental to the environment.
- If you are buying native plants make sure they have been legally sourced and propagated from local stock, thus ensuring that they have the same genetic characteristics as those found in the local countryside.

Water for wildlife
The benefits of a pond

Of all the elements that can be created in a garden, the one with the greatest benefit to wildlife is water. The wildlife hotel isn't complete without it. The range of creatures that will benefit from a supply of water is immense, from those that live in or on the water for all or part of their lives to providing a watering hole for the animals that visit your garden.

A pond was one of the first things I created when taking over my garden, and although it is not large, it has already become the hub of wildlife activity. Birds love to drink and bathe in it, mammals benefit from the reliable source of drinking water in summer, and in just a few short months the pond has become the home for myriad aquatic life.

A well-planted pond (below left) should have shallow and deep water and up to two-thirds of the surface covered with plants.

Candelabra primroses (below right) thrive in the boggy ground at the edges of ponds but will seed into quite dry ground too.

A wildlife pond doesn't just benefit the many species that visit it or dwell within it, but it also enhances our lives, providing us with a glimpse into an underwater universe full of fascinating animals. Pond-dipping (using a net to carefully investigate the life in a pond) is one of the best ways to engage children in the wonders of the natural world. Perhaps this is partly to do with the small scale of ponds and the animals within, or maybe it's the thrill of the unknown!

A balancing act

If you can find the space for a pond then so much the better as the diversity of creatures and plants that can be accommodated will bring a new dimension – and new dynamic – to your garden. But if you can't, then even a plastic tub sunk in the ground can fulfil a need. I've seen common frogs spawning in water-filled tractor tyre ruts, so a sunken plastic tub must seem luxurious in comparison.

For a pond to be as beneficial as possible to the maximum number of species you need to think carefully before introducing any ornamental fish. They may be lovely to look at but they have a tendency to eat their way through the contents of a pond, and can entirely denaturize a body of water. The koi carp pond at Hyde Hall became so overstocked that when visiting RHS entomologists surveyed the water they found, to their amazement, nothing at all – not even the odd water bug. It is possible to have fish in a wildlife pond but keeping their numbers manageable involves periodically removing excess fish to a new home. Consequently, it is simpler to exclude fish from the start and allow aquatic wildlife the maximum benefit.

Which plants?

A wide range of plants is really important. Pond plants can be divided into three groups: bog dwellers that thrive in permanently moist soil at the edge of water, marginal plants that enjoy having their roots just below the water surface and true aquatic plants.
Bog plants such as *Darmera peltata* and *Ligularia japonica* create the kind of lush, leafy edge to the water that is typical along streams and lakesides. They also provide plenty of cover for creatures that need to get in and out of the water, such as amphibians, and are also useful for such land dwellers as voles and shrews that will benefit from having fresh water.
Marginal plants, including *Caltha palustris* and *Lythrum virgatum*, are perfect for softening the transition between the water's edge and the bog plants, and will be used as a ladder by the emerging larvae of dragonflies and damselflies.
Submerged plants include those that are either fully submerged in water or that have leaves that float on the surface, such as water lilies. The submerged plants help to oxygenate the water while those with floating leaves shade the bottom of the pond and provide cover for wildlife.

A well-balanced pond will consist of one-third open water and two-thirds covered with floating plants, oxygenators or a mixture of both. Creating a balance between the bog and marginal plants will also help to ensure a natural appearance in and around the pond.

Aquatic plants (below and left) require thought when purchasing. Below is the North American native *Ranunculus aquatilis*, while on the left is *Hippuris vulgaris,* a scarce native in the UK. Not all exotic aquatics are invasive, but by sticking to solely native plants you can ensure there is no risk of introducing a damaging plant.

An aquatic habitat
How to create a wildlife watering hole

Ponds can be created in a number of ways depending on where you live and how large or small you want the pond to be. Traditionally, ponds were made waterproof by 'puddling' clay – applying smeared layers of clay until the whole pond was covered and waterproofed. To achieve success with this method requires a good supply of pure clay, and while it can work very well on a large scale – all of the ponds at Harlow Carr are puddled clay – it isn't always successful on a small site.

Getting started

Pre-cast fibreglass liners can be bought and installed in a prepared hole, but they are limited in size and you may not be able to find one of the right shape. Concrete can also be used, but it isn't a particularly sustainable material and can be a nightmare if it leaks. My preference is for flexible liners, either butyl or plastic, which can be used for ponds of different sizes and shapes. Neither material is especially sustainable but the trade off is big; the 20 plus years of benefit to wildlife before the liner needs replacing more than offsets the manufacturing processes.

A good wildlife pond will include a number of features aimed specifically at benefiting different animals. At least one side of the pond should comprise a shallow slope, lined with rocks or pebbles. This is essential if visiting mammals are to be allowed safe access and egress without risk of drowning, and it also provides an area where the water is shallower and therefore quicker to warm up in spring, making it ideal for spawning amphibians. The pond should be at least 1m (3ft) deep in the middle, as at this depth and below, the water will maintain a steady temperature just above freezing point in even the coldest weather – vital for those species that inhabit the pond all year round.

This barn swallow (below) is collecting mud at the edge of a lake. It will use the mud to build its nest. By creating your own wildlife pond, you are giving birds such as this the means to survive, since many of their natural habitats are disappearing.

Building a wildlife pond

Ponds are best sited in full sun on a level site, and ideally not beneath deciduous trees whose leaves can reduce the available oxygen as they break down. During the first few months, the pond can be affected by blanket weed, a fast-growing algae that can quickly cover the surface of the water. Use a forked stick to wind the weed out of the water and then leave it at the pond edge so that any trapped animals can escape. There are also organic treatments that can help to reduce blanket weed.

1. On a level site, mark out the pond using a hosepipe or sand, and view it from every angle, including upstairs windows. Wildlife ponds tend to be organic in shape with plenty of curves, but can just as easily be geometric. Decide where the shallow end and deep end will be before digging.

2. Dig down by at least 1m (3ft) at the deepest point. It's a good idea to create a shelf around the deepest part of the pond, approximately 30cm (12in) down from the eventual water level and 30cm (12in) wide. This will allow you to place marginal plants in baskets around the water's edge.

3. Liners need protection from stones and roots to prevent puncturing. Old newspaper, sand or a woven pond underlay can be used. Once the liner is in place fill the base of the pond with a little top soil, on a layer of underlay.

4. The almost finished pond shows the liner protected by woven fabric on to which top soil has been placed. This will encourage pond plants to root. The 'deep end' has been filled with water to stretch the liner.

CHAPTER FIVE

Planting
Putting it all into practice

Armed with an understanding of the microclimate and soil type in your garden, and having undertaken the appropriate soil-improvement – all with the aim of reducing your carbon footprint, enhancing biodiversity and lowering inputs of water and the like – you'd be forgiven for wondering if there were actually any plants involved in this book. Fear not: this chapter looks at how to maximize the advantages of all that accumulated knowledge through the employment of 'correct' planting, alternative planting techniques for specific situations (such as mound planting on heavy soils or where the water table is high) and aftercare, including mulching. It also looks at lawns and the alternatives to a conventional green sward, the basic principles of plant growth and the adaptability and versatility of plants and tips on how to ensure that your garden flourishes without excessive intervention.

Direct-sown annuals (left) bring beauty and biodiversity to the garden with almost no intervention at all; demonstrating just one aspect of the amazing versatility of plants.

The plant powerhouse
What plants need to thrive

All terrestrial plants need water, light and nutrients to thrive and achieve their full potential. Think of them as green skyscrapers, rising up from the ground. Just as a skyscraper has secure foundations and a basement for the essential stuff like boilers and generators, plants have root systems that enable the take-up of water and nutrients but also ensure that plants are anchored to the ground. Roots can often be combined with specialist organs such as bulbs, or adapted into rhizomes, all of which have a specific function adapted to the needs of the plant and the environment in which it grows.

Plant structure

As a skyscraper has windows to let in light, plants have leaves, and sometimes flattened stems, to absorb sunlight and therefore enable photosynthesis – the process by which plants create the food they need to grow. These leaves and flattened stems also function as the air conditioning units of a plant. They allow water to escape via a process called transpiration, which keeps the plant cool. And in the same way as opening windows allows air to circulate, so the plant can breathe in oxygen and breathe out carbon dioxide. This process is known as respiration and helps convert food into energy.

Thin grass-like leaves (below) and silver leaves that reflect the sun are just two of the clever adaptations that plants use to survive hot and arid conditions.

If roots are the substructure, then the stems are the superstructure, housing the vessels that transport water and nutrients, supporting the leaves and flowering parts and making the plants desirable for growing in a garden. And on top of that, these wonderful structures benefit an enormous workforce: the insects, birds, mammals and humans who depend on them, and on whom plants also depend, by and large. This is a simplification of the complex life of plants, of course, but from a gardening perspective it is about as much as one needs to know. The trick when it comes to growing plants is not just to know what they want but also to know which plants are suited to your garden, either through what is already there or what can be created through sustainable soil-improvement and microclimate manipulation.

Plants are marvellous, even miraculous, things. They provide us with the materials to make our homes and an incredible variety of other structures and tools, from broom handles to bridges – to the extent that often they still usurp the synthesized compounds designed to replace them. And, of course, they provide the raw ingredients from which this and every other book has been made.

Adaptability and hardiness

Plants also feed us, remove pollution from the air, generate huge amounts of oxygen for the planet and form the basis on which almost all modern medicine has been, and continues to be, developed. Through adaptation they can distribute themselves over vast distances, colonizing barren lands, making them habitable for humanity and preventing the land from disappearing into the sea or sky by anchoring the soil. They are the reason why we, and most other forms of life on Earth, have survived.

Everything that we know about plants comes from human observation. Even then, plants continue to catch us out, by growing in places where they shouldn't, by surviving at latitudes that seem inherently unsuitable and dying in locations where they should thrive.

But we shouldn't be surprised if plants surprise us. They have an amazing ability to adapt. Although gardens are contrived environments, the plants that we put in them were derived from the wild at some

Phormium tenax from New Zealand is a great architectural plant with impressive evergreen, grassy foliage that is resistant to wind damage and water loss. Used for rope making in its home range, it is perfectly adapted to dry climates.

Eschscholzia californica (the Californian poppy) thrives in the arid climate of south-western North America by sending down a tap root that stores starch and water and also helps to anchor the plant in exposed conditions. It produces abundant seed, to ensure the species survives.

Santolina chamaecyparissus or cotton lavender is a compact Mediterranean sub-shrub that uses a combination of tiny leaves and light-reflective silver colouring to reduce water loss. Its small size prevents it from being wrenched from the ground in windy, exposed sites.

Salvia x *sylvestris* 'Mainacht' is a hardy garden hybrid of two tough wild plants that employ a mixture of adaptations to cope with drought - tiny hairs on the leaves trap moisture from mist and fog and the light-green colouring is less light-absorbing than darker hues.

time in their long-distant past. Indeed, many of our favourite garden plants aren't cultivars or varieties at all, but translocated wild plants.

Another, perhaps more pertinent, example of this ability to confound us is plant hardiness. Regardless of the causes, climate change is a reality, and this means that plants which may have been considered tender in one part of the world in, say, 1970 might now be thought of as hardy. When microclimates are added into the equation it becomes even more unpredictable. For example, the Dry Garden at Hyde Hall (pictured above) contains more than 6,000 plants with origins in every continent except Antarctica. These plants share the ability to thrive in the prevalent conditions: dry, hot and exposed to desiccating winds. Drought resistance is only one example of the range of adaptations that plants have undergone in order to conquer almost the entire terrestrial world.

Potting and planting
What are the best techniques?

Until around 50 years ago the vast majority of garden plants were 'field grown'. In this process, seedlings are started off protected by a glasshouse or polythene tunnel. They are then planted and grown on outdoors before being lifted and sold 'bare root' in bundles, or potted up for immediate sale. This is still the principal method of production for young trees and hedging shrubs, but back then it applied to many other types of plants, including perennials.

Optimum growing

Provided you bought locally, the main benefit to the gardener was that there was a good chance that the soil and climatic conditions in which the plant had been grown would be similar to those in your garden. This increased the chances of good transplantation. Availability of plants during spring and autumn meant that planting took place during the optimum seasons. Since field-grown plants have an obvious 'nursery mark', it was also easy to see the correct planting depth showing which part should be below the soil.

For the plant nursery owners, this arrangement meant that their business was truncated into just two seasons – spring and autumn – when plants could be lifted from the field and sold in a dormant state ready for planting. With tight profit margins to work to, this made life extremely tough for nursery owners.

The advantages of peat

Salvation for the industry came in the form of peat-based compost. Loam composts had been developed by the UK plant-science research centre, the John Innes Institute, and had been around for a long time, but peat offered a number of advantages over loam. The cost of shipping peat was low, it was light and easy to handle when dry and such a light material made the use of mechanized potting machines a reality, leading to significant increases in productivity. Peat-based composts were also cheaper to buy. And when plants started to be produced and grown on in pots under protection, the whole process from start to saleable product became much quicker. And, of course, plants could be offered for sale throughout the year, removing some of the risks associated with an entirely seasonal business.

This was a big improvement for the plant nursery industry and one that I benefited from personally.

Irises (below left) should be divided every four to five years in late summer. Carefully dig and divide the clumps using a shovel or fork, taking care not to damage the rhizomes.

Replanting the rhizomes (below right) will give you a fantastic display of flowers for the next few years, especially the second through to the fourth year (see p.91).

Correct planting technique

What could be easier than planting? Well, quite a lot actually. In the course of my working life I have seen many plants that have been badly planted. Most were planted too deep, many were planted in inadequately prepared soil, and others - seriously - were planted while still in their pots. All the plants suffered as a consequence. Taking the time to cultivate a good planting technique is well worth the effort. It takes no longer to put into practice than a bad technique and the rewards will speak for themselves. As your plants establish more readily, they will flower more freely, require less looking after and live for longer.

1. Gently ease the plant from the pot, taking care not to damage the root system. The top layer of compost in a potted plant usually contains weed seedlings and seeds, so scrape this away very gently. This will prevent the weeds establishing through your plant, and then becoming impossible to remove.

2. Some gardeners swear by root-teasing, the gentle loosening of the roots from the root ball. Certainly if the root-ball is congested, it is well worth teasing out some of the roots. If the plant is root-bound (the roots congested into a solid mass in the pot) then it will be necessary to free up the roots by pulling them away from the root-ball.

3. The ideal planting pit should be no deeper than the root-ball of the plant but up to twice as wide in diameter. This will ensure that the soil around the root-ball has been loosened, will encourage root penetration and prevent a sump effect, whereby water sits around the absorbent compost, which can cause the roots to rot.

4. Place the plant in its planting pit, making sure its neck is level with the surrounding soil. Backfill around the plant with excavated soil. As you do so, firm the soil around the plant with your hands or, if it is a larger, woody plant, with your heel.

5. As you move away from your beautifully planted specimen, use a fork or hand rake to lightly cultivate where your hands or feet have been. Not only will this look tidy, it will massively benefit the plant by reducing the risk of capping, which occurs when rainfall causes the surface soil to bind together so preventing water from reaching the plant roots (see p.37). Water the plant thoroughly.

My parents ran a cut-flower and pot-plant nursery in Kent, and I can remember the arrival of our first potting machine in the 1970s. Various cams, chains and conveyer belts chuntered and clattered, spewing out neat peat-filled pots at the end. It reduced staffing costs and made my parents' working life a little easier.

The downsides of peat

But there were and are negative consequences associated with the use of peat-based composts. The sensitive management of peat bogs, including a degree of extraction, can work, and indigenous people have been caring for bogs while extracting fuel and building materials for centuries. However, industrial peat extraction is inherently unsustainable and involves the destruction of pristine ecosystems that have taken millennia to form. In the light of such a serious issue it seems churlish to mention the negative impact on the gardener, but for all peat's attractiveness to the nursery industry it also has some inherent faults in the garden, especially on heavy soils. These arise from its light, water-retentive qualities. Transplanted into a heavy clay soil, a peat root ball can act like a sump, filling rapidly with water and drowning the roots of the plant as the water around it heads for the point of least resistance. Another unfortunate phenomenon is root

girdling. This is where the plant roots grow round and round the soft, peaty root-ball rather than venturing into the cold, damp soil. I have witnessed this first hand with trees that had been planted on clay soil in peat-enriched pits. Twenty years on, their roots hadn't ventured beyond the pit but had continued to circle the peat until the tree died. Nowadays the nursery industry is working hard to reduce peat quantities in compost by using sustainable alternatives such as coir fibre. But this doesn't solve the transplanting problem on heavy soils, since coir is as light as peat.

Planting at the correct depth

A thousand *Geranium psilostemon* are produced in small pots by a plant nursery and sold wholesale to a retailer in good time for spring. In spring, the weather turns nasty and sales are slow, so by summer

Matthew's parents (above) My father (top and middle) and mother at our nursery in Kent during the early 1970s and late 1950s respectively.

Nursery mark (left) The nursery mark on potted plants is usually visible as a dark 'stain' on the stem. The stain should be above ground on planting.

400 plants remain. The retailer pots these unsold plants into bigger pots for an autumn sale. The lads doing the potting are not quite as thorough as they should be, so the potted-on plants are all 3cm (1in) deeper in their pots than they should be. That autumn, visit the retailer and see rows of plants with lovely, dark-centred magenta flowers set off against spectacular autumn foliage – how can you resist?

At home the plants go into the garden, planted just a little too deeply – but never mind. And to suppress weeds and keep in the moisture you add a good thick layer of mulch on top. So now the nursery mark – that vital bit of the plant that should be above ground to allow it to breathe – is anything from 6–15cm (2–6in) below ground. In effect, the plant is drowning in soil.

Some perennials can cope with being drowned under compost and mulch; others, such as clematis, actually benefit from being planted rather more deeply than other plants. But most plants cannot cope, and for woody plants, especially trees, deep planting almost always spells an untimely death.

The trade magazine *American Nurseryman* conducted a trial where 100 trees were deliberately planted too deep and then 100 others were planted at the correct depth. All of the correctly planted trees grew well but none of the trees that were planted too deep survived.

Mound planting

Mound planting is an ancient technique used in areas where a combination of heavy soil and a high water table can have adverse effects on plant establishment. Although it is a practice that has been around for centuries, it is unusual to see mound planting employed today but it is well worth considering in gardens with heavy, poorly drained soil.

The technique involves raising the soil level by incorporating additional soil-improver or top soil. This can be done either locally to benefit individual plants or across an entire border. For it to work properly, the mound should be at least 30cm (12in) high and four times the width of the plant pot or root-ball. Following this ratio will enable the plant to establish good root growth within the mound, while excess water is shed to the sides. Mound planting has been employed to good effect at both Hyde Hall and Harlow Carr, especially with trees and shrubs.

Dividing plants to make more

Plant division of flowering perennials and ornamental grasses is a long established method of maintaining plant vigour (perennials become woody and flower less freely after a few years) and 'making' new plants. Carried out in spring or autumn, it simply involves digging the clump from the ground and splitting it into smaller clumps for replanting or potting on.

Mound planting in heavy soils

This planting technique is ideal for heavy, poorly drained soils such as clay. Before you start, it is a good idea to mix some well-rotted organic matter and some sharp sand or grit into the top soil, being careful to leave the clay pan more or less intact. This provides a reasonable depth of soil for the plant to root into, while the water runs away without puddling around the collar. Take care not to let the plants dry out during the first summer by using a good thick layer of mulch on top.

1. Make a mound by heaping up loose soil. It is preferable to work with mineral soils such as clay, as peat dries out too quickly. The mound should be 30cm (12in) high, so that the tree roots will be above the level of the badly drained soil.

2. Firm the mound as much as possible by treading. Using a trowel, make a slit in the top or side of the mound then insert the plant at the correct depth. Firm the plant in by treading.

Mulching for life
Conserving soil moisture

Even though nature has provided gardeners with a bountiful supply of plants for different growing conditions, they still require appropriate soil cultivation and management techniques to thrive. Good drainage is essential for all plants except those that have adapted to being in boggy soil or watery margins. For the majority of plants, conserving soil moisture is just as important as good drainage. Time and effort put into cultivating and improving the soil with appropriate additives will greatly aid moisture retention, but without suitable mulch it will all be in vain.

How mulch works

Mulch acts as a permeable blanket, allowing water to seep through without eroding the top soil, preventing desiccation by the wind and keeping soil temperatures noticeably cooler than the air temperature, thereby preventing plant roots from drying out or 'cooking'.

Mulches also suppress weed growth, removing the competition for water and nutrients and, in the case of biodegradable mulches, helping to improve the health, structure and nutrient levels in the soil. Applying annual mulch is no different from the soil-improvement method in a 'no-dig' system, as during a season most of the mulch will be drawn down into the soil by earthworms, other soil fauna and weathering.

Which mulch?

The range of organic material suitable for use as mulch is largely the same as those used for soil-improvement (see p.38). By varying the mulch material each season, it's possible to improve soil structure or nutrient levels accordingly. For example, composted bark adds little in the way of nutrients to the soil but aids drainage and

Gravel and pebble mulches (top right) don't add nutrients to the soil, but are very effective at suppressing weeds and keeping plant roots cool. They are best suited for use in hot, sunny borders.

Low-growing, mat-forming plants (middle) such as herbs, succulents and alpines, create their own mulch and cool root run.

Mulching (right) is as applicable and important to vegetable growing as it is to ornamental plants.

Mulching newly planted plants

There are few pitfalls with mulching, but the one serious risk is that the 'neck' of the plant, the nursery mark, which needs to be at soil level, can be drowned in mulch, restricting plant growth and exacerbating rot. The way to avoid this is to leave a clear space around each plant where there is no mulch, or to plant a few centimetres proud of the soil level, with the difference made up by the mulch. Follow the steps below for the best way to keep mulch away from newly planted plants.

1. After planting, invert a pot over the plant. This will protect the neck and crown from getting swamped with mulch.

2. Carefully apply the mulch to a depth of 15-20cm (6-8in) using a shovel - in this case the mulch is mineralized straw (see p.39).

3. Remove the pot carefully, ensuring that the neck/crown is still clear of mulch. Water thoroughly.

soil structure, whereas garden compost or manure is usually nutrient rich. There are other mulch materials that are largely static and act solely as weed suppressors and moisture conservers such as gravel, slate and pebbles. These are appropriate for drought-tolerant plants that require little in the way of nutrients. They have the added aesthetic value of setting the plants off in something akin to the conditions that might be found in arid environments in nature. Mulching is probably the single most important gardening activity for soil moisture conservation and health. It brings with it subsequent benefits for the plants in your garden: strong growth, drought tolerance and good flowering.

After mulching

It is important to give plants a good drink after mulching - 3-4 litres (5-7 pints) for a 2-litre (3½-pint) potted plant - to settle the soil and the mulch and improve root-to-soil contact. By watering after mulching you will reduce the need for further irrigation and give your plants the best possible start.

Why bare earth is bad

It seems as if some gardeners define neatness by the amount of empty, weeded soil around their plants rather than maximizing the interest in their garden with extra plants. Bare earth loses moisture rapidly and is prone to erosion and capping (see p.37), and even more so when it is constantly being weeded by hand or hoe. This turns over the soil, exposing any moisture, which in turn dries out further. The constant disturbance can also have a detrimental effect on soil fauna, so vital in keeping the soil healthy but unlikely to hang around if their 'home' is being constantly unsettled.

In terms of soil-moisture conservation there is nothing worse than bare earth. You can easily test this yourself by checking the temperature and soil moisture content at the base of a well-furnished perennial - even in the heat of summer it should be cooler and more moist than any bare earth around it. This is the reason why animals such as amphibians and molluscs are often found lurking at the base of plants in hot weather.

It's far better to have a garden that is richly planted and thoroughly mulched than one where the plants sit in sterile soil ghettos. Frankly, it looks weird and it isn't healthy.

Are lawns sustainable?
Grass lawns and other options

There is no doubt that a really good lawn can be great for setting off a garden and showing plants to their best effect. A lawn can create a space from which various elements can radiate, it can highlight a vista or draw the eye away from something we would prefer to hide. As lovely as a closely clipped sward of lush green grass may be, it is one of the most challenging aspects of gardening, and with hotter, drier summers becoming the norm in most temperate countries, it's questionable whether maintaining a traditional lawn is sustainable.

High-maintenance care
The species of grass most commonly found in lawn seed or turf mixtures require regular moisture to remain green. Grass roots rarely penetrate more than a few centimetres into the soil, so they are more prone to drying out than border plants and trees, leading to the foliage quickly turning the colour of straw during prolonged drought. Luckily, beneath the soil the roots can often remain viable for some time, and even a really desiccated lawn can quickly recover its greenness with a good downpour of rain.

We want our lawns to be green during the summer and the temptation to irrigate during dry spells can be overwhelming – but keeping grass lush and green takes a huge amount of water. To keep a lawn in tip-top condition takes more than just water however, and a traditional care regime will include regular mowing, aerating to improve drainage, scarifying to remove dead grass, moss and weeds at the root zone (thatch), and regular feeding in autumn and spring.

The turf industry is now advising a different approach to the traditional care regime. By reducing the amount of fertilizer, overly lush growth in spring is avoided. By not watering at all in spring the grass plants develop deeper root systems, which then help to keep the grass greener for longer. And leaving the grass longer (up to 8cm/3in) and allowing clippings to mulch back into the sward reduces water stress and boosts nutrients.

Low-maintenance options
Traditional lawn maintenance demands a sizeable investment in terms of time and resources, but by altering the way we manage our lawns we can still have a green sward for much of the year, which should stay a little greener for longer, even in searing heat.

The turf and grass-seed industry is also fighting the effects of climate change by looking into new strains of grass and altering seed mixtures to find those that are most resistant to drought. By taking on board their advice, rather than following outmoded traditions, we may still be able to enjoy the pleasures of a green lawn.

In the meantime, there are ways to reduce the effort that lawns require and alternatives to the traditional lawn. The most obvious is simply to reduce the size of the lawn, but another option is to introduce groups of plants – such as herbs and *Sedum* species – that can be used to create the effect of a lawn but without the need for mowing, feeding and spiking.

Alternatively, you can turn the lawn into a meadow or bulb-planted area. The growing interest in native wild flowers is encouraging many gardeners to experiment with mini meadows. They aren't always easy to achieve without practice and experience, but are well worth the effort. There are even ornamental perennials and grasses that can be established in turf, creating the effect of a miniature prairie, as we shall see in the section on prairie planting in Chapter 7.

Flashing blades – choosing a mower

If you want to have a turf lawn, you'll need to have some means of cutting it. Prior to the invention of the pedestrian lawnmower, that meant scythe-cutting by hand. With today's technology the choice comes down to mowers with two different types of cutting mechanism: cylinder or rotary. Cylinder mowers produce a high quality of cut but have more moving parts and engineering involved in their manufacture, so are more expensive to buy and maintain. They won't cut grass that is longer than about 8-10cm (3½-4in), either. Rotary mowers are inexpensive, will cut short or long grass and have fewer moving parts, but the quality of cut isn't as good as that of a cylinder mower.

A well-proportioned lawn (right) can help to set off flowering plants, define views and create space. But the effects of climate change may require us to reconsider the type, size and composition of our lawns.

Cutting it down
Alternative lawns

The simplest way to reduce the workload of a lawn is to reduce it to a size that is right for you. If you have pets and children and no access to public green space then you may well need your lawn to be as large as possible. But if you only need somewhere to park a chair for an alfresco post-work drink, then you may want to consider a smaller, more manageable lawn that you can keep looking good in most conditions without a massive amount of effort.

Herb and sedum lawns

Herb and sedum lawns make interesting alternatives to grass but can't be considered as a replacement for turf – it would take sublime footballing skills to make an accurate pass on a patch of herbs, although the ball would certainly be fragrant by the end of a match. Where these lawns excel is in really small areas where there is a need for open, green space as a design feature, rather than a hardwearing leisure area.

One of the best herb alternatives to grass is wild thyme (*Thymus polytrichus*). This non-deciduous creeping perennial has horizontally growing branches that reach only about 1cm (½in) high. Plant about eight plants per 1m (3ft) squared to ensure a dense carpet the following year. Once the plants are joined together, the thyme lawn can be walked on, releasing a lovely scent as you do so. Wild thyme also has the advantage of small bunches of white or pink flowers in the summer which gives it a spectacular appearance.

Creating an alternative lawn

In many respects the process of creating a herb or sedum lawn is much the same as making a green roof (see p.180), albeit without the need for a frame in which to plant, and the benefits are similar too.

First, ensure that the ground is level to avoid the soil getting waterlogged. If the soil is soft from cultivation,

Tiny lawns (top right) can be a real headache to maintain in a small garden, while a herb or sedum lawn can make a low-impact, easy-to-care-for and attractive alternative.

Acaena microphylla **(right)** will quickly colonize thin, well-drained soils, but with burr-like seedheads that stick like Velcro™, this plant is best avoided if you have pets.

tread the whole area and rake to restore the required level. Don't plant into loose soil – roots need firm ground to establish themselves. You will also need to weed the area thoroughly. Dig a large enough hole to enable the roots to be spread out evenly and loosen the soil at the base of the hole so that water will not collect there and kill the plant.

Herb and sedum lawns require much less aftercare than grass. Some plants (such as chamomile) may require a light mowing occasionally, but most plants, including sedum, can be left to their own devices.

Low-growing culinary herbs (left) such as thyme, oregano and chamomile are hard-wearing but have the added benefit of providing a fresh supply of flavouring for the kitchen.

A beautiful tapestry (below) of colourful foliage can be created with drought-tolerant spreading plants such as *Sedum acre* and *Sempervivum* cultivars.

Mini meadows
Create a wild-flower haven

The idea of creating a mini meadow in the garden is a seductive one; a species-rich wild-flower meadow must be among the most beautiful sights nature can offer. Unfortunately, meadows are notoriously difficult to recreate, because of the complex nature of the relationship between wild flowers and grasses, the soil, soil fauna and fungi and human intervention.

We don't know anywhere near as much as we could about how these interactions actually work. What we do know is that the most diverse wild-flower meadows are often centuries old and have been managed in much the same way throughout their known history. Consequently, the soil is 'unimproved', neither manured nor fertilized nor disturbed by ploughing, enabling the symbiotic relationship between flora

Wild-flower meadows (right) aren't easy to re-create but are worth the effort. Direct-sown annual meadows are a colourful, low-input alternative that can also benefit biodiversity.

How to plant a mini meadow

The quickest way to establish a perennial mini meadow is by using wild flower 'plug plants' – very small plants grown and purchased in cellular trays or 'root-trainer' pots. On a larger scale (above 3m/9ft square) this is likely to be prohibitively expensive, in which case it is better to establish a meadow from seed. In both cases the steps are the same until the last one. Remember that when purchasing seed or plug plants you should always try to find locally sourced material to preserve any genetic variation in local wild-plant populations. And don't ever take wild plants from the countryside, or 'improve' the wild by planting – in the UK it's illegal.

1. To create a naturally flowing sinuous edge to a mini meadow – or indeed any border – lay a hosepipe along the ground, adjusting its position until it looks right. Cut the turf along the edge of the hose to a depth of 10cm (4in) using a half-moon turf cutter or spade.

2. In autumn use a turf iron or spade to cut and lift the turf inside the marked out area, to a depth of between 10cm (4in) and 15cm (6in). This top layer of turf and soil is usually the most fertile and least suitable for wild flowers and grasses, so it's essential to remove it. Recycle the turf in a log bench, compost heap or turf stack.

Terrestrial orchids (right) are one of the great highlights of a really well-established meadow.

and fauna to thrive and become increasingly diverse. A hugely varied, species-rich meadow is probably beyond the reach of most gardeners – unless your garden was once unimproved grazing pasture and the seedbed is just waiting for the mower blades to stop in order to reappear, in which case I urge you to stop mowing now. It is possible, however, to introduce some of the more robust wild-flower species into a garden, and then manage the resulting mini meadow in such a way as to provide the best possible environment for wild plants to thrive, which in turn might lead to a greater diversity of plants. Mini meadows do take an amount of effort, but they are worth it; everything from moth larvae to small mammals and amphibians will benefit from a little wildness in the garden.

The very helpful yellow rattle

Yellow rattle (*Rhinanthus minor*) is a semi-parasitic annual plant of old hay meadows that helps to maintain the balance between flowering plants, less vigorous grasses and potentially invasive spreading grasses. The common name derives from its seeds, which rattle inside the seedheads and in bygone days were a favourite children's toy in rural communities. Yellow rattle germinates as grass species get into growth, absorbing some of their water and nutrients and thereby ensuring they don't overwhelm weaker plants. Including the seeds of yellow rattle in a new meadow can help the establishment of wild flowers and grasses. In time it can form large, self-sustaining colonies, but in the first few years it may require repeat sowings in late winter.

3. Fork over the soil to a depth of around 20–30cm (8–12in), removing the roots of any vigorous weeds such as docks or thistles. Break up the clods using the back of the fork to get them down to about the size of a watch dial. If this is carried out in early autumn the soil can be left to weather down further until late winter.

4. In late winter or early spring, rake over the forked soil, which by now should be weathered and easy to break down to a fine tilth – a crumb-like structure. This should only be done when the top layer of soil is dry enough to walk on without it sticking to your boots or forming clods.

5. In very early spring when ground conditions are neither wet nor frosty, plant plugs of native, locally sourced wild flowers and grasses approximately a trowel-head apart. If using seed, sow at the recommended rate directly on to the prepared soil and then lightly rake in.

Bulbs in grass
Spring and autumn colour

If you still want to reduce the size of your lawn, and a mini meadow is out of the question, you can create areas of naturalized spring and/or autumn bulbs. Planting part of your lawn with spring-flowering bulbs will bring colour at a time when many garden plants are in their dormant state. Later, as the grass in which they are planted grows long around the dying foliage, it provides additional habitats for animals until it is mown down, usually in midsummer.

Choosing bulbs

If you choose your bulbs carefully it's possible to plant spring- and autumn-flowering subjects together, bookending the season with colour. There are many species and cultivars of bulbs that are vigorous enough to thrive in turf, indeed some grow in similar conditions in the wild and are perfectly adapted to the competitive conditions associated with grasslands. Given a good head start and the appropriate maintenance these tough little plants will quickly bulk up and provide increasing colour every year with almost no

intervention. The key to achieving a successful look with naturalized bulbs is to concentrate on wild species or cultivars that look wild. These are generally smaller in stature than 'border' bulbs, simpler in flower structure and altogether less flamboyant. Big, blowzy flowers are to be avoided as they can look pretty ridiculous, and are often less suited to naturalizing anyway. By selecting appropriate plants it is possible to have a succession of flowers for weeks, if not months.

An ideal spot for naturalized bulbs is in an area where a little shade is provided by deciduous trees. The grass here tends to be poorer due to the demands of the tree roots, giving less competition and also remaining a little shorter at the time the bulbs are flowering.

Planting calendar

Naturalized spring bulbs can start with snowdrops just a few weeks after Christmas – the common *Galanthus nivalis* being perfectly suited to naturalizing. If you are lucky enough to have suitable growing conditions, patience and are willing to spend a bit of cash then you could have colour even sooner with the highly desirable daffodil *Narcissus* 'Cedric Morris'. Tough, hardworking crocuses follow, then the main body of daffodils that flower in succession from late winter to late spring, my favourites being the dainty *Narcissus cyclamineus* and robust yet compact *N.* 'Hawera'. In between, the colour can be enhanced with dog's tooth violet, *Erythronium dens-canis*, white-flowered *Ornithogalum nutans* and the beautiful snake's head fritillary (*Fritillaria meleagris*).

Autumn bulbs suitable for naturalizing include *Crocus kotschyanus*, a lilac-flowered form that spreads readily through seed and offsets (small bulbs that form at the side of the main bulb), rich purple-flowered *Crocus goulimyi* and several species and cultivars of colchicum. Between the spring bulbs dying back and the autumn bulbs coming into flower the lawn will need to be cut several times. Gradually lower the height of cut, rather than cutting it short straight away, so that the grass can recover gradually.

Naturalized spring bulbs such as daffodils (left) are a highlight of spring when grown in clumps at the foot of deciduous trees.

How to plant bulbs

There are almost as many methods for planting bulbs in grass as there are suitable plants. Small bulbs – *Crocus, Scilla, Chionodoxa* – can be quickly planted with a trowel or by using a digging fork to make shallow (10cm/4in) holes into which the bulbs are pushed. Larger bulbs can be trowel planted or, if planting in quantity, using a long-handled bulb planter as in step 3. If you are planting bulbs by the thousand you may wish to lift the turf (to a depth of 20cm/8in) with a turf cutter. Place the bulbs on the soil and re-lay the turf over the top.

1. Spring-flowering bulbs, such as *Narcissi*, should be planted the preceding autumn to ensure good establishment and flowering the following season. You can usually place your order with suppliers from late summer – it is worth doing this to ensure you get what you want.

2. To create a natural effect when planting in grass, throw a handful of bulbs on to the turf and plant them where they fall. Don't be tempted to fiddle around with the composition too much – the object of this exercise is to create a random, unevenly spaced effect.

3. Long-handled bulb planters take the strain out of planting bulbs, especially when planting in quantity. They also ensure the bulb is planted at the correct depth of three times the bulb depth. Push the planter head into the soil using the boot plate then twist to remove the plug of soil.

4. Place the bulb in the hole checking that it is the right way up – I've made that mistake, more than once – with the roots down and the tapering top uppermost. Bulbs with offsets – as in this case – are best planted complete rather than split.

5. Remove the soil plug from the planter head and replace it in the hole, covering the bulb. Use your foot to firm down the soil. If I am planting lots of bulbs I tend to leave this till last so that I can see where I have already planted. This prevents planting bulbs on top of other bulbs.

Meadow maintenance
A centuries-old technique

Maintaining a diverse, flowering sward of wild flowers, bulbs or perennials is largely the same process. In all cases, the timing and methods you employ are vital. Even if you simply choose to leave an area of long grass to benefit biodiversity the time will come when some form of intervention is required.

The basic principles of maintaining a mini meadow or bulbs in grass derive from the centuries-old techniques employed in a hay meadow, albeit on a much smaller scale and using different equipment. Although agricultural hay-meadow management is now largely superseded by intensive silage production, there are still a few species-rich hay meadows that are managed in the traditional way for the benefit of both livestock and biodiversity. Maintaining perennials in grass is a similar process but it is done much later in the season.

Mosaic mowing

The key feature of meadow maintenance is the removal of the spent stems and seed heads of the grasses and flowers that make up the meadow. Unfortunately, this can have dire consequences for the wildlife that relies on the food and cover the meadow provides. The animals affected can range from amphibians to small mammals, and the disturbance caused by the annual meadow cut is not without casualties.

In order to maintain some cover and food through the autumn and winter months for the wildlife, it's advisable to leave at least part of the meadow uncut. To ensure that this doesn't affect the long-term diversity of the sward this is best done on a rotational basis known as mosaic mowing. This means leaving an uncut area for one season, then cutting it at the right time – late summer or early autumn – the following season and leaving a different area uncut.

Mosaic mowing (top left) is a technique that allows areas of uncut meadow to be retained, so maximizing habitat potential for wildlife during winter.

Cutting garden meadows (left) can be delayed until autumn. In farming, however, meadows are cut the moment the main flush of flowering has passed.

Looking after your meadow

Traditionally, meadows were cut in mid- to late-summer to provide hay for livestock. Over centuries the timing of this activity became intrinsically linked with the breeding patterns of many species of ground-nesting birds, a pattern now broken because of the switch to intensive silage cultivation. As a garden mini meadow doesn't exist to produce hay it can be cut a little later on, in autumn, thereby maximizing the benefit to wildlife in the form of cover and food sources.

1. During dry weather in late summer or early autumn, brush through the mini meadow with a rake or besom broom to flush mammals, insects and amphibians from the long grass and to help shake off any dew. Take time to really look for wildlife – it's part of the fun of having a mini meadow!

2. An important part of mini meadow maintenance is the collection of seed. In a large hay meadow the seed is allowed to fall from the cut plant material and shed into the soil, but in a mini meadow the compact size allows the careful harvesting of seed from individual plants. Collect seed by rubbing the seedhead between thumb and forefinger.

3. A small mini meadow needs no specialist equipment or machinery to cut, just a pair of hedge shears or, for slightly larger mini meadows, a strimmer/brushcutter fitted with a metal blade. Cut the stems back to within 30cm (12in) of the ground, working back and forth in lines. Don't ever cut in concentric circles; any wildlife you have missed will end up in the middle, with nasty consequences.

4. After cutting a large hay meadow the material will usually be left to dry for a week or so, to enable seed to be shed and to aid the baling process. With a mini meadow, the material can be immediately raked into rows – known as windrows – and then collected up and composted.

5. After removing the cut material run a lawn-mower with its grass box attached over the mini meadow on a high setting to collect clippings. Then use a spring rake to scarify the meadow, removing the thatch (the dead grass at the root zone), which can impede seed germination.

CHAPTER SIX

The Kings of the Earth
The importance of trees

Trees are among some of the most magnificent and longest-lived organisms on Earth – not as old as fungi perhaps, but far more visible. As impressive as many treeless landscapes are there is something disconcerting about them too. This may be because the association between trees and humans is as old as the history of our species. When our ancestors spread across the world, much of it was entirely covered in trees. As we evolved, timber provided us with fuel, building materials, utensils and weapons. Depending on the tree from which it is cut, timber can be as hard as iron or flexible as plastic, light as a feather or heavy as a stone. It's also surprisingly resilient. Human intervention has reduced trees to a fraction of their original range, yet if we vanished from the face of the Earth tomorrow they would soon recolonize every suitable bit of land. This chapter explains the new gardening approach to their care and introduces techniques for pruning and planting.

This magnificent acer (left) in the full beauty of its autumn foliage reminds us that we should all be in awe of trees, not just because of their sometimes great size and age, but also because of their vital contribution to our planet and human existence.

The key to a healthy planet
Why we need trees

Trees play a vital role in the health of the planet by producing huge amounts of oxygen, filtering out pollutants and providing homes for millions of species of animals and plants.

The absence of trees in the landscape can have a profound effect on ecology and biodiversity. Without the extensive root systems of trees, soil can quickly erode in the wind and rain, and the animals that are reliant on trees for food and shelter vanish as well. The enriching effect that fallen leaves have on soil flora and fauna is one of the most important aspects of soil health, but this also disappears if there are no trees. The beneficial effect of trees on macroclimate and microclimate can be keenly felt – open, treeless country is typified by strong, desiccating winds.

Alive, dying or dead, we need trees to help maintain a healthy planet. In our towns and cities they help to bring a human scale to rows of uniform buildings and

are an integral part of parks and other green spaces that are essential for our well-being. At the same time, they absorb pollution through their leaves and bark and provide important habitats and food. Trees tolerate the worst abuses we can mete out, including the lopping of branches and the ghettoizing of root systems behind concrete kerbs, and they are extraordinarily resilient, capable of regenerating even when they have been blown over.

Longevity and adaptability

We know far too little about trees, but modern science is beginning to unlock their secret world with some staggering results. For example, at Westonbirt Arboretum, Tetbury, UK, DNA testing on a group of small-leaved limes (*Tilia cordata*), thought to be a grove of young trees, shows that they are actually the suckers from a single long-dead tree. Speculation suggests that the tree may be as much as 6,000 years old – more ancient than any other tree in the country, as far as we know. Trees are just as adaptable to different environments as other plants. The giant

This fallen willow (below) is producing numerous new shoots from its trunk. Trees have an incredible capacity to regenerate, even when toppled by winds.

sequoia, *Sequoiadendron giganteum*, one of the largest trees on earth, has adapted perfectly to the forest fires that periodically ravage the dry hills of southwest USA. Not only is the thick, spongy bark able to withstand the flames, but the fires provide the ideal conditions for the sequoia seed to germinate. Because the inferno clears all the surrounding scrub and feeds the soil with ash, the seedlings have the best possible start in life.

Today our respect for and understanding of trees has diminished as modern materials have filled the roles that timber once held. Yet it could be argued that we are missing the point; carefully managed forests can provide us with much of the material we need, just as they did our ancestors, but benefit the environment and biodiversity at the same time.

In the garden, planting new trees with attention and forethought, and investigating ways to preserve rather than remove old or damaged ones, is one way in which we can make a small, yet positive, difference.

The giant sequoia (left) has developed thick, fire-resistant bark, but also relies on fire to help its seeds germinate and to clear the forest floor of competing vegetation.

Lime trees (below) are well-known for their longevity and hardiness. A group of small-leaved lime trees at Westonbirt Arboretum, Tetbury, UK is thought to be 6,000 years old.

Tree care
Cutting and pruning for preservation

The techniques used to care for trees have changed at a dramatic rate in recent years. There was a time when the principal role of a tree surgeon was to fell trees, whereas now the emphasis is firmly in favour of preservation and saving the habitats that trees provide for the benefit of biodiversity. The following are some of the modern tree-care methods employed by enlightened tree surgeons.

Coronet, monolith and standing

Coronet cuts ape the natural shredding that occurs when a branch snaps from a trunk. Instead of leaving a neatly cut stub, the chainsaw is inverted and used to shred the stub, which then forms hardened deadwood, protecting the living wood and providing a rich habitat and food for invertebrates and the animals that feed on them.

Monolith pruning preserves the main trunk of a tree that has become inherently unstable. It's pretty dramatic as it involves removing all the side branches and lopping the top, but if the tree is being used as a nest site or roost for birds and bats it ensures that a habitat is preserved for as long as possible.

Standing dead wood may seem a tricky proposition, but many trees can remain stable for years when dead, and it's recognized that standing dead wood is of the greatest benefit to wildlife. If a dead tree poses a limited risk it is allowed to stand, but if it is unstable it is felled and then the trunk is strapped to a living tree.

If the bulk of the tree is too great to strap to another, unstable trees can be felled in large sections and laid down. At Harlow Carr a large, hollow ash became home to a honey-bee swarm, but was very

Leaving a stub (top) is a modern cutting technique, which allows a callus to form naturally over the wound.

Coronet cuts (middle) simulate the natural tearing and shredding that occurs when a branch falls. The dead wood provides food and habitats for wildlife.

Pruning (bottom) while a tree is still young will help to prevent long-term structural problems such as twin leaders and crossing branches, which in turn can create health problems that may shorten the life of the tree.

unstable and had to come down. The long sections were laid down in a stack and the bees have remained.

A tree's life can be seriously shortened by structural problems that develop while the plant is quite young and grow into major faults if left untreated. Among the most common is the development of a twin leader, often caused by damage to the main stem, where two equally vigorous shoots compete to be the dominant stem. In so doing, a deep fork can form in the trunk, which can further weaken because of settling water and subsequent rotting. Invariably, the combination of the rotten split and the weight of the two leading stems eventually cause the tree to split in two.

A little judicious pruning at a young age will keep a tree healthy long into the future by ensuring a single, strong trunk develops. It is equally important to prune out crossing branches at an early age as these can rub together and the consequent damaged wood may become diseased. Thinning out unnecessary branches also helps to create an open, well-balanced crown.

Healthy roots, healthy shoots

Taking care of the root zone of a tree is of paramount importance if the plant is to thrive. Tree roots extend to at least the diameter of the crown, often further, and although the main roots that help to anchor the tree to the ground can be substantial in size, those that take up water and nutrients can be as fine as human hair and easily damaged. Applying an annual mulch of organic matter over the root zone will help to protect and feed the roots, and simple steps such as keeping footfall over the roots to a minimum will reduce compaction. Terraventing and mycorrhizal injection is technology employed by tree surgeons that is still in its infancy, but may help to extend the lives of old trees by de-compacting the soil in the root zone and re-establishing a relationship with introduced beneficial fungi.

An old wound (top) that is almost completely covered by a hard callus, keeping out diseases that might affect tree health.

Monolith ash trees (middle) that have been made stable by the removal of side branches. The monoliths that remain still play an important environmental role as they are full of bird and bat nest holes.

A clean cut (bottom) on a new tree made with sharp secateurs requires no treatment or wound painting - a practice that has proven to be detrimental to tree health.

Trees for life
Selecting and planting out

Trees can be purchased and planted as bare root or root-balled (where the roots and accompanying soil are bound in hessian and wire) in winter, or as containerized plants all through the year. A new development employed by some nurseries is to grow trees on in woven bags. This encourages the development of a fibrous root system without causing the roots to 'girdle' – in effect, go round in loops – a problem that can afflict container-grown trees.

Trees in the garden (above) are long-term additions so time spent in planting them well is essential, and will be repaid with rapid establishment and healthy growth.

Seedlings, whips and planting methods

Trees are available in a range of sizes from one-year-old seedlings, whips (usually two years old and the most common size for mass woodland planting schemes) and a variety of 'standard' sizes that are referred to by their girth (trunk) measurement as well as height. Multi-stem trees have been deliberately coppiced at a young age to encourage numerous stems rather than a single trunk, which is especially effective for plants with good stem colour such as *Acer griseum*.

Just as tree-care methods have evolved, so have planting techniques. It's now recognized that a wide planting pit, the same depth as the root-ball or nursery mark, is of far greater benefit than a deep but narrow pit. This is because a wider pit provides a bigger area of disturbed ground which encourages the spreading roots of trees to penetrate further into the soil.

Soil-improvers have also come into question, especially the use of a lightweight improver on heavy soil. The lightweight compost can act like a sponge and absorb water from the surrounding heavy soil to create a sump. If this occurs, the effects can be serious, as it leads to rotting and root disease.

Plant small, grow big

It is perfectly understandable that we want our gardens to look as mature as possible as quickly as possible, and at times I have felt impelled to plant large trees for instant effect, or purchase an oversized perennial for a bit of 'wow factor'. But there is no doubt that the best way to plant is with young, small specimens. If a plant has sat in a pot for a few years, cosseted in a wind-proof tunnel and regularly fed and watered, what chance does it have when shoehorned into a windswept hillside or damp, frosty valley? Trees planted as one- or two-year-old 'whips' of about 1m (3ft) in height may grow by as much as 5m (16ft) in the same number of years, while a 2.5m (8ft) 'standard' tree might put on just a few centimetres or an inch or so of growth.

The reasons for this are to do with acclimatization and root disturbance. The larger the plant, the more likely it may have suffered root disturbance as part of the production process. Imported woody plants are often protected in covered tunnels, making it much harder for them to acclimatize to tough conditions.

How to plant a tree

In recent years the techniques for tree planting have changed considerably. Instead of planting in a circular pit, a square pit is thought to be more beneficial for trees because it allows more space for the roots to spread laterally into the soil. Tree staking has also been reconsidered and it is now recognized that a short stake is better than a tall one because it allows the tree trunk to flex and strengthen in a similar way to a human muscle.

1. Prepare the soil by adding soil-improvers according to your soil type and needs. Do this over an area that extends beyond the tree-planting pit if possible to prevent a sump effect. Dig out a square pit that is at least twice the width of the tree root-ball but no deeper than its depth.

2. Place the tree in the pit, still in its container, to check that the nursery mark is level with the surrounding soil (unless you are using the mound-planting technique). Remove the tree and fork over the base of the pit to loosen the soil. Take the tree out of its container and place it in the pit.

3. Before backfilling the pit, drive a stake at an angle of approximately 45° over the root-ball and into the surrounding soil. Fix a rubberized tree tie and spacer to the stake and attach it to the trunk of the tree – I'm attaching it to the thickest stem of this multi-stemmed *Amelanchier lamarckii*. Next, secure the tie to the stake with tacks.

4. Backfill the planting pit by firming the soil in layers with the heel of your foot. Don't be afraid to firm the soil really thoroughly. This will greatly help to stabilize the tree and aid establishment by ensuring better contact between the roots and the surrounding soil.

5. Irrigate the tree thoroughly – a specimen of this size will require four or five watering cans-full – to further settle the loose soil around the roots. Then apply a layer of mulch to seal in the moisture. Larger trees such as this one will require the same amount of water each week during dry weather for the first season.

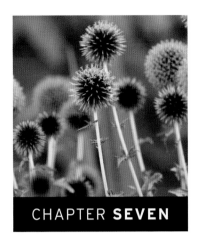

CHAPTER SEVEN

Planting Styles
Sustainable choices for today

Gardening is as vulnerable to the vagaries of fashion as most other areas of life and influenced by the same pressures for change. So if we accept that the need to garden in a more sustainable and environmentally friendly way is, or soon will be, a given, how will this affect planting styles? Accepting that the observation and knowledge of microclimate and soil are the cornerstones of 'new gardening' and inform our plant choices, will this limit our options? This chapter introduces a range of alternative planting styles that can help to reduce or completely remove the less sustainable 'interventions' in gardening; feeding, watering, tying-in and so on. This is made possible by creating plantings that work harmoniously as communities rather than disparate individuals that have been combined in the garden on looks alone. As an added bonus, many of the plants that are most suited to this approach are also especially good as food plants for wildlife and so have the potential to enhance biodiversity in the garden.

Drifts of alliums and echinacea, ornamental grasses and other drought-tolerant plants contribute to Piet Oudolf's prairie planting at RHS Wisley Garden, Surrey, UK.

Naturalistic planting
The case for cultural harmony

In recent years the terms 'naturalistic planting' and 'naturalistic perennials' have been bandied about with increasing regularity. Confusingly, they can mean different things depending on your point of view. The reality is that there is no single way of implementing naturalistic planting – individual gardeners and garden designers interpret it in a variety of ways.

Aesthetic planting

It might be easier to define naturalistic planting by looking first at what it isn't. The plants in a traditional mixed border are selected primarily on aesthetic grounds – their ability to cope with the microclimate and soil is considered, but it is expected that regular intervention will be required. So a mixed border might comprise a plant such as *Canna indica* that thrives in a sheltered spot, with nutrient-rich soil and a good supply of water, alongside thrifty, drought-tolerant *Artemisia arborescens*. The primary reason for planting them side by side will be aesthetic, as clearly they are culturally incompatible.

Cultural planting

Naturalistic planting relies on grouping plants that have very similar cultural needs in largely self-sustaining 'communities' that are suitable for the prevalent conditions with minimal intervention. Often these are species that occur in the wild, or cultivars that have been bred to enhance the flowering or foliage qualities of the plant without compromising its toughness. Simply, 'naturalistic perennials' are plants that have a wild, rather than a highly cultivated look, and require less in the way of watering and soil improvement to get by. The 'naturalistic movement' has been typified by the expansive plantings of grasses and flowering perennials by designers such

Piet Oudolf's prairie meadow (below left) at Scampston, North Yorkshire, UK, demonstrates the versatility of the naturalistic style.

The structural qualities of perennials and grasses (below) are self evident in this small garden, as is the colour and texture they impart to a planting.

as James van Sweden and, latterly, Piet Oudolf, but in reality a naturalistic planting can just as easily be a small grouping in the shade of a tree or within a discrete area, such as in Beth Chatto's highly variable yet essentially naturalistic garden in Essex, UK. The key isn't the scale, it's the reduction of intervention through appropriate plant selection.

An unnatural approach?

For some gardeners, the naturalistic movement is the antithesis of what gardening should be; they argue that manipulation is a key tenet of gardening, allowing for more expression through the widest possible variety of plants. Another argument is that this style is unsuitable for small gardens, needing scale for impact.

Those in favour of the naturalistic approach cite the environmental benefits and point to the aesthetic value of plants that look 'at home' in the wider landscape. And they believe that the principles of naturalistic planting can be applied in smaller gardens. It is an argument that has been going on since William Robinson published *The Wild Garden* in 1870, a time when high horticulture was at its peak with millions of bedding plants and monocultural rose gardens being tended by thousands of gardeners up and down the UK. *The Wild Garden* was a plea for the planting of mainly exotic ornamental plants in the garden in a natural state, delivered in Robinson's highly opinionated style.

A modern ethos

If naturalistic planting is just a style, it is easy to see that it can go out of fashion. But naturalistic planting is more of an ethos than a style – the modern expression of one of the oldest horticultural adages: right plant, right place. Although typified by the planting styles associated with the naturalistic movement of recent years, it embraces all garden plants.

Assuming that environmental concerns will have an irreversible effect on the way we garden, the concept of naturalistic gardening seems a logical way to sustain ornamental horticulture. It doesn't mean abandoning some plant groupings, rather to question how they are currently used and whether that can be applied differently and in a more sustainable way.

The brilliance of plants and their adaptability to the different conditions found in gardens makes it actually quite easy to utilize a more natural approach to planting styles, all we need to do is learn.

James van Sweden's work (below) utilizes hard landscaping with soft, billowing perennials and grasses.

Naturalistic drift planting

Drift planting employs single species or cultivar groups in numbers large enough to have impact, rather than plants in small numbers 'dotted' through a planting. These drifts are usually arranged in interlocking patterns to create a more natural look – one group giving way to another.

The term 'drift planting' was first coined over 100 years ago by the hugely influential English garden designer Gertrude Jekyll. She embraced many of the ideas promulgated by her contemporary, William Robinson, and developed them, using her training as an artist to group plants according to colour, foliage and growth habit. Most importantly, her work was designed for the burgeoning market of the middle classes and so the impact was far-reaching.

Whereas Gertrude Jekyll tended towards subtle colour themes and was happy to utilize ephemeral bedding and half-hardy plants, naturalistic drift planting uses only permanent plantings of hardy plants that require minimal intervention. One of the best examples of naturalistic drift planting in the UK is Piet Oudolf's Millennium Garden at Pensthorpe Park in Norfolk, UK, where bold, blocky drifts of flowering plants and grasses create a dramatic effect.

Matrix planting

Matrix planting uses plants in entirely the opposite way to drift planting. Rather than grouping large numbers of the same plant in big blocks, matrix planting uses large numbers of a limited range of species and cultivars in what appears, at first glance, to be an entirely 'thrown together' fashion. In reality, this haphazard appearance is usually the result of careful planning on the part of the designer.

The aim of matrix planting is to give the impression of an entirely natural community of plants, as one would find in the wild. In nature, plants often intersperse with one another at different densities over a given area. This variation is due to the prevalent conditions and the manner and rate at which different plants spread. In an ornamental matrix the plants are set out at different densities to mimic this natural variation, so that one species will appear dense in part of the scheme but then fade in numbers to nothing,

A hot, dry slope at Lady Farm in Bristol, UK (left) has been transformed by a matrix planting.

The main borders at Harlow Carr (below) combine robust perennials and grasses with roses, shrubs and trees,

with a few scattered subjects that have seemingly 'seeded' distantly. A good example of matrix planting exists in the Steppe Garden at Lady Farm near Bristol, UK. Designed by Mary Payne and Judy Pearce, the scheme comprises grasses and flowering plants at different ratios on a sunny bank that is steeply sloping and dry, with thin and dry soil (see p.120).

Prairie planting

The great prairies of North America must have constituted one of the most impressive natural scenes. Now reduced to a fraction of their original range, even the fragments that remain are remarkable in their beauty and diversity. Prairies are essentially species-rich grasslands, the equivalent of the British unimproved wild flower meadow (see p.98), and as British meadows have declined so have the prairies.

If the predicted model for climate change impact in the UK proves correct, it may be that prairie plants will become even more widespread in use, given their inherent ability to cope with both dry summers and wet winters.

Piet Oudolf's expansive borders (above) at RHS Garden Wisley, Surrey, UK, comprise bold ribbons of grasses and perennials that flow like streams through the planting.

Ornamental perennials

Many ornamental perennials are in fact grassland species, including some that have become established garden favourites. At Harlow Carr in Yorkshire, UK, trials of perennials grown from seed in grass in a facsimile of a prairie have been conducted by Sheffield University. The aim was to assess the potential for such sowing as an alternative landscaping technique for low-value 'brownfield' sites and areas where ornamental plantings were unsustainable.

Flowering perennials in grass make an unusual and beautiful alternative to a traditional lawn, especially when they are preceded by spring-flowering bulbs. Their maintenance and establishment is exactly the same as for the mini meadow: seed is sown in unimproved soil during late winter/early spring and yellow rattle is a key component in reducing competition from the grass.

Naturalistic drift planting

THE MILLENNIUM GARDEN AT PENSTHORPE NATURE RESERVE
Situated near Fakenham in Norfolk, this is one of Piet Oudolf's most successful drift planting schemes in the UK.

Garden aspect: Open and sunny, some shade along the boundaries

Soil type: Variable, gravel and sand (the site is a former gravel pit)

Microclimate: Sheltered, high light levels

1 *Persicaria amplexicaulis* 'Firedance'
The long, dark red flower spikes of this handsome bistort dominate the foreground in this plant composition. The cultivars of *P. amplexicaulis* are particularly robust and, once established, need almost no aftercare. The flowers are highly attractive to bees and are borne over a long period, from mid-summer right up until late autumn. Oudolf repeats this plant further up the curving path to help create a sense of rhythm and unity.

2 *Lythrum virgatum*
Here Oudolf deploys an interesting colour shift; the dark red flowers of *Persicaria amplexicaulis* 'Firedance' are deep enough to stand out against the purple blooms of *Lythrum virgatum* but at the same time compliment each other. A brighter red may well have created a colour clash. The shapes of the inflorescences are complimentary too, both being narrow flower spikes. *Lythrum virgatum* requires moist soil to thrive, and will tolerate marginal conditions at the edges of water where the roots are permanently submerged.

3 *Deschampsia cespitosa* 'Goldtau'
The golden inflorescences of this mid-sized grass form a billowing backdrop to the *Persicaria* and *Lythrum*. The introduction of another colour here might well have saturated the scheme, but Oudolf avoids this by opting for a fairly neutral colour – which is picked up in the gravel surface of the path. *Deschampsia* tolerate full sun or semi-shade, and prefer moist soils.

4 *Astilbe chinensis* var. *taquetii* 'Purpurlanze'
A broad drift of *Astilbe* strikes right across the path in the middle of this composition, linking the two sides of the planting but continuing the theme of the dominant flowering plants in the scheme; red/purple colouring and vertical flower spikes. The effect is such that even though the *Persicaria*, *Lythrum* and *Astilbe* are all different plants, they seem to be a continuation of one another. This particular *Astilbe* is noteworthy in that it grows in drier soils than other species and cultivars.

5 *Scutellaria incana*
The spiky blue flowers of *Scutellaria incana* are borne in late summer over felty, grey-green leaves. In this composition it acts as a cooling foil for the darker purple-flowered plants, and as blue is a component of purple there is also a complimentary element.

6 *Festuca mairei*
This beautiful yet totally underused and underappreciated fescue is quite unlike the more familiar compact, blue-leaved forms. Evergreen grey-green foliage is topped with very narrow flower panicles. In this planting scheme it links naturally to the similarly coloured *Deschampsia*.

7 *Panicum virgatum* 'Strictum'
Yet to come into flower, the foliage of this late summer-flowering ornamental grass acts as a neutral backdrop for the rest of the planting. It too is repeated further along the path, this time on the opposite side (just above

the *Echinacea purpurea* 'Rubinstern') to ensure that the rhythm of the planting is consistent right through until autumn. *Panicum* are tolerant of all but very dry soils.

8 *Gaura lindheimeri* 'Siskiyou Pink'
Although at a distance it is hard to see any colour consistency between the dark pink flowers of *Gaura lindheimeri* 'Siskiyou Pink' and the predominant purple/red flowers elsewhere, there is a subtle connection in the purple-pink colouration of the flowering stems. Located on the inward curve of the path this drift exaggerates the line of the path and also picks up on some of the lighter foliage and inflorescences in the planting, primarily of the grasses.

9 *Sedum* 'Matrona'
This sedum is in bold contrast to the dominant flower colour, and also the dominant flower shape in the planting. Rather than vertical spikes, this plant holds its flowers in broad, flat cymes. But even here there is a connection; the foliage and stems of *Sedum telephium* 'Matrona' are tinged a dark metallic purple colour. Sedum are very robust, tolerating a range of conditions including dry, nutrient-poor soil.

10 *Echinacea purpurea* 'Rubinstern'
Yet more purple/red, this time in the rich, wine-coloured blooms of *Echinacea purpurea* 'Rubinstern'. Unlike the vertical flower spikes that predominate in the composition, this plant has broad, daisy-like flower heads dominated by a large, bristly central disc.

Matrix planting

1 *Salix exigua*
Growing at the edge of the lake, this silver foliage willow provides an appropriate colour backdrop for the drought-tolerant planting within the Steppe Garden, even though it is not a drought-tolerant plant and requires moisture at the roots. This is a great example of transitional planting, where a theme is continued across quite different growing conditions by using plants that appear have the same cultural needs.

2 *Miscanthus sinensis cultivar*
Miscanthus dislike really dry conditions, so the placement of this plant near the lake edge is deliberate. As the season progresses and the miscanthus comes into flower it will become dominant in this corner of the planting, providing interest through into winter until pruned back ready for the new season. The *Miscanthus*, *Salix* and pine (behind) create a screen from which the lake appears as progress is made along the path.

3 *Coreopsis verticillata*
Scattered through the planting like droplets of sunshine is the cheery and charming *Coreopsis verticillata*. Prairie and matrix plantings are built around the notion of plants appearing to be self-sown in natural communities, and this plant will do just that given the right conditions, as here, of well-drained soil and a sunny site. Thereafter the success of a planting such as this is based on deleting unwanted seedlings to maintain an open effect.

4 *Stipa tenuissima*
Another prolific self-seeder, *Stipa tenuissima* creates a sense of movement in this planting, while also adding texture and colour to the silvery/gold effect that dominates the ground cover planting. Seedlings of *Stipa tenuissima* can be allowed to grow on and then be replanted. It's a more reliable way of propagating the plant than division, which can sometimes lead to premature death.

5 *Stipa gigantea*
This highly popular grass has been a favourite of garden designers for some years now, and rightly so. Here it demonstrates its two finest qualities; the light and airy golden inflorescences and the translucent quality of its thin flowering stems. *Stipa gigantea* is not known to set seed in the UK so the seemingly random placement of the plants is entirely deliberate.

6 *Verbascum olympicum*
This is perhaps the most transient plant in this composition due to its tendency to die after flowering. However, *Verbascum olympicum* usually sets reliable seed so, once it is established, it will create an ever changing scene in the garden. Here the vertical flower spikes repeatedly strike through the scheme, creating a loose, almost wild effect.

7 *Kniphofia* 'Royal Standard'
The dominant plant in this composition by dint of its very strong colour, there are numerous groups of *K.* 'Royal Standard' and other forms of *Kniphofia* in the Steppe Garden, which create splashes of intensely hot colour in what is otherwise a fairly muted scheme. Using really strong colour in this way is a bold move, but here it is what makes the planting work.

8 *Onopordum acanthium*
Another wandering plant, *Onopordum acanthium* will seed around easily, just like *Verbascum olympicum*, *Coreopsis verticillata* and *Stipa tenuissima*. The challenge is then to decide which seedlings to keep and which to delete. This is primarily a foliage plant, grown for its intensely silver leaves and stems, which are armed with rather fearsome spines.

9 *Eryngium bourgatii* 'Picos Blue'
Almost lost among the bold red, silver and gold colours that dominate the Steppe Garden, this little sea holly is positioned close to the path that cuts through the planting so it can be properly admired at close quarters. With blue-grey stems and flower heads there is a subtle reference to the big, bold *Onopordum acanthium*, and it is also the perfect foil for the bright colours of *Coreopsis verticillata*.

10 *Achillea* 'Moonshine'
Achillea 'Moonshine' has one of the most subtle flower colours of all the achillea cultivars, being a lovely soft, silvery yellow. Here it merges with the similarly coloured *Stipa tenuissima*, the contrast coming in the shape of the flower heads, which are flat, horizontal umbels against the vertical stems of the grass.

Off with their heads!
The Chelsea Chop

Naturalistic plants may have the ability to thrive with lower levels of intervention but that doesn't mean they are completely intervention-free. One of the main chores with perennials is staking and tying-in – a task requiring good timing and sympathetic treatment if the plants are not to look trussed-up. An overly rich diet and excessive watering can turn the most robust perennials into sappy flops, and such pandering should be avoided with naturalistic perennials if you want to bring out the best in them.

However, there are tricks of the trade that can be used on a wide range of perennials that obviate the need for tying-in. For example, using cut hazel or birch stems as natural supports is a practice that has been around for centuries and works perfectly well without being visually intrusive. But there is another intervention that can help to improve flowering, reduce the need for staking and enable the flowering times of plants to be manipulated – namely, the 'Chelsea Chop'.

Timely pruning

The Chelsea Chop is one of those interesting practical tips that has been around for a long time but tends only to be utilized by those in the know. The American garden writer Tracy de Sabato Aust has written almost an entire book based on her experimentation with the technique, which suggests using it on a far wider range of plants than has hitherto seemed possible.

   The Chelsea Chop is suited to perennials that come into flower from late summer to autumn. It consists of cutting back the foliage and stems of growing perennials by a third or more in order to create a more compact, free-flowering plant. The name derives from the timing – about the time that the RHS Chelsea Flower Show takes place (the last week in May) seems to be the optimum, although this can vary depending on the weather and the size of the perennials, which should be around a half to two-thirds full size.

Prolonging flowering

Deploying the Chop should reduce or negate the need for staking by making the plant more compact and less likely to flop, and should encourage more flowers by causing the main flowering stems to 'break' at the point of the cut and form extra buds. With planning, plants that have usually faded can be used with others that flower later, such as *Tricyrtis*, *Colchicum* and *Nerine*. Some of these will also make fine associations with shrubs displaying early autumn colour such as *Rhus*, some *Euonymus* and various Japanese maples.

Sedum are popular garden plants **(left)** but they have a tendency to flop when in flower. Deploying the Chelsea Chop encourages more flowers and robust stems.

Supporting plants

For plants that aren't suitable for the Chop, or if the weather conditions are so hot and dry that the procedure would cause undue stress to your plants, the timely installation of plant supports will prevent flopping stems and damaged foliage. There are many bespoke plant support systems available but if you can find a supply there is nothing quite like materials such as hazel or birch stems, which look natural, come at no carbon costs and can be reused or composted at the end of the season.

Hazel and birch should be harvested in early spring by cutting back 1.5m (4½ft) lengths – longer for really tall plants – with plenty of side shoots. If you don't have a supply in your own garden, and few of us do, contact a local conservation trust or forester, who may be able to help. In mid spring, when perennials are still in their emerging state and not too tall, push the hazel or birch lengths into the ground by up to one-third of their total length, forming a circle around each plant. The side stems will form a cage around the plant, through which foliage will grow. Providing the stems are solid in the ground there should be no need to tie them together.

In terms of bespoke supports, bamboo canes and metal rods and frames are widely available. Grid or grow-through supports and plastic and galvanized meshes can also be purchased. Three-ply soft twine is suitable for tying small plants, but use five-ply soft twine for larger specimens. It is not advisable to tie-in plants too rigidly; they should be able to move in the wind. Use rubber clips to hold supports together.

The Chelsea Chop

Employ this intervention to improve flowering. The timing is usually around the time of the eponymous flower show – the last full week in May. However, this will vary depending on micro- and macroclimate and whether or not it has been a warm or cold spring. Don't employ this technique though if plants are under stress through lack of water or extreme heat – wait till next year. Suitable plants include later-flowering perennials, especially those of the compositae (daisy-flowered) family, such as *Echinacea*, *Rudbeckia*, *Helenium*, *Leucanthemella*, *Monarda*, *Helianthus*, *Heliopsis* and *Eupatorium*.

1. As a rough guide, plants should be between a half to two thirds eventual size before chopping, and not already producing flower buds. Using sharp, clean secateurs, cut each stem back by one-third to a half as shown.

2. Make sure you have cut back to a bud or leaf joint as shown to ensure that there are no unsightly snags and to encourage new stems to form at the leaf joint. Water thoroughly and apply a deep mulch to the base of the plant.

Self-sustaining seed
Direct-sown annuals

The most common role for annuals in a garden is as pot-grown bedding plants, planted out seasonally in early summer and again in winter to provide changing displays of colour. It's a labour- and resource-intensive way of gardening requiring heating fuel to grow the plants under glass and plentiful watering throughout the growing season. Finally, the plants are discarded, the soil flora and fauna disturbed and the whole process starts again. Bedding certainly has its place but there are alternative ways of using annuals that use very few additional inputs and create a display that for many – myself included – far exceeds that of traditional bedding.

Direct-sown annuals are easy to establish from seed, cost-effective to buy, require little maintenance and provide rich sources of pollen and nectar. They thrive on a mean diet, so don't need feeding or the addition of organic matter before sowing. The ancestors of these plants are from arid areas such as Asia Minor (they were imported with grain seed and came into cultivation as field weeds by accident) and consequently they don't need artificial irrigation.

Field flowers

Cornfield annuals such as cornflowers, corncockles and corn marigolds have been used in gardens for years, along with wild annuals including *Eschscholzia californica* and *Nigella damascena*. Work carried out at the University of Sheffield in the UK has led to the development of strains of annuals with longer flowering periods in a wide range of colours.

The applications for direct-sown annuals are many, from giving quick cover in new gardens where the soil is poor to providing a genuinely sustainable alternative to summer bedding. They don't require a huge space to be effective – I sowed an area of about 1m x 8m (3ft x 26ft) in my garden that flourished from early summer to late autumn. They give instant cover when inter-sown between establishing perennials or provide a self-sustaining, dynamic addition to the garden that changes yearly as the plants seed around.

Direct-sown annuals at Harlow Carr (below) provide masses of colour for little cost, and require minimal aftercare. Being rich in pollen and nectar, they are great for invertebrates too.

How to establish direct-sown annuals

It is easy to establish direct-sown annuals in all but the wettest soils, and once established they will usually set viable seed each autumn and so become self-sustaining. Although cornfield weeds rely on annual soil disturbance to germinate, a direct sowing from modern seed blends will often germinate in spring from seed that has fallen the previous year. Unlike perennial and woody plantings only the minimum of soil preparation is required for direct-sown annuals - in fact they flower best and remain compact in quite thin and nutrient-deficient soil.

1. In late winter, fork over the soil to a depth of around 20cm (8in) and use the back of the fork to break up any large clods of earth. This should be done when the soil is dry enough to walk on, so an alternative method is to prepare the soil in autumn and then hoe off any weeds before you start the raking and sowing.

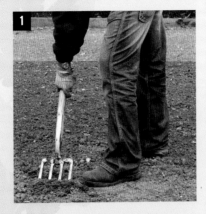

2. After forking over, tread the soil to break up any further clods and consolidate the seedbed by walking with 'pigeon steps' - that is, heel to toe - across the soil. Then use a rake to prepare the seedbed to a fine tilth - a crumb-like structure.

3. If you want to use more than one seed mixture to create different effects with colour combinations, or even mix up your own seed blends - which is great fun and can throw up some interesting mixes of colour and form - divide the border up using sand to mark where you want one mixture to end and the next to begin.

4. Sowing is best done when the surface of the soil is damp from rain or rain is expected. However, most modern seed blends can be sown in dry weather and will remain viable in the soil until rain arrives - so there is no need to water. Mix the seed with sand in a bucket to aid even distribution, using the instructions on the packet to work out the sowing rate.

5. For small areas, seed can be simply sown by scattering directly from your hand. For larger borders it is better to use the broadcasting technique; with the bucket of sand and seed under one arm, walk at a slow pace dipping into the bucket and then throwing the sand/seed mix in an arc on alternate steps. It takes a while to master but is a very rewarding and accurate way of sowing. Finally, lightly rake the seed into the soil.

Seed mixtures
Contrasting effects

The seed mixtures featured in these photographs are part of a range of themed mixes, selected for their long season of flower, originally developed at Sheffield University and now sold under the name Pictorial Meadows. However, similar effects can be created by mixing your own seeds, which can be purchased as single species packs, the only proviso being that the plants selected can be direct-sown outdoors *in situ*.

Both the mixtures – pastel and volcanic – comprise many of the same plants, but by adjusting the quantity of each plant and deleting a couple, you can see how a completely different effect can be created.

Pastel mix

This mix (below left) is particularly good when sown among roses, or used on its own against a dark green evergreen hedge, where the colours show to best effect. Even though the field poppy is deep red in colour rather than a pastel shade, it still creates a romantic, soft focus feel, that of bucolic summer afternoons and bygone days.

- **The lacy white flowers** of *Ammi majus* dominate this planting, creating a soft, slightly wild feel. The regularity of height and form of this plant creates its own repetition through the sowing, even though it is entirely random. In contrast, this plant plays only a background role in the volcanic mix.
- **The tall white flowers** are *Cosmos bipinnatus* which rise above the rest of the flowering plants in the pastel mix, and continue to flower until after *Ammi majus* has gone over. The finely divided light green filigree foliage of *Cosmos bipinnatus* is also evident here, adding to the frothiness of the sowing and creating interest even without flower colour.
- **Cool, blue tones** are provided by *Centaurea cyanus* which is very at home in this pastel mix and forms the second largest component after *Ammi majus*.
- **Splashes of red** are formed by the field poppy, *Papaver rhoeas* which doesn't seem at all out of place in this sowing, despite being a hot-coloured flower. Perhaps this is because of the emotional connection we have with this evocative plant, which evokes not just remembrance of those who fell in war but dates back to Celtic times, when the symbolism of a blood-red plant wasn't lost on the Druids.

Volcanic mix

This hot and spicy mixture (opposite) is dominated by purple, blue, red and yellow, creating a vibrant colour range that shows especially well in high light levels, where softer colours can 'burn out'. It can be used to great effect on a hot, sunny bank, at the edges of a gravel path or sown among established perennials in a drought-tolerant planting.

A **pastel-colour mix** (left) can combine white and cool, blue shades with splashes of red.

Centaurea cyanus, the common blue cornflower, is one of the prettiest and best loved of all cornfield 'weeds', and was once eagerly collected by watercolourists who made blue paint from the crushed flowers. Here it helps to cool down the hotter colours around it. Interestingly, the purple form of *Centaurea cyanus* has the opposite effect of its blue brother, and adds to the heat in the sowing.

Ammi majus, also known as the bishop's flower, has flat umbels of white flowers, rather like miniature cow parsley. Here it is a background component in the mixture, providing splashes of white against which the stronger colours show.

Cosmos bipinnatus is a popular annual bedding plant and is often bought as a pot-grown specimen. However, it is easy to grow from direct-sown seed and will usually flower a little later in the season when grown in this way. As shown here, the flower colour is variable from white through pink to lilac.

Coreopsis tinctoria has attractive, daisy-shaped yellow flowers with a conspicuous red blotch in the centre, and forms the primary component of this volcanic mix.

Release the rose!
Mixing roses with perennials

To my eyes, roses are among the most beautiful of all flowering plants, combining sumptuous blooms with fragrance and often attractive foliage. Admittedly, I am less enamoured by what I consider to be rather overblown roses, primarily the hybrid tea (bush) and floribunda (cluster-flowered) types which smack of the Victorian fashion for faintly ridiculous florists' flowers.

My real favourites are the shrub, species, climbing and rambling roses – plants that are as versatile and tough as they are lovely. And yet to many people the rose is a 'specialist' plant requiring lavish care and attention, a complex pruning regime and regular bombardment with chemicals.

Unhealthy groupings

Imagine a room full of healthy people, all with differing levels of resistance in their immune systems. Introduce someone with a full-blown case of 'flu into the room. Close the door and lock it. You don't have to be a genius to guess the likely outcome – a good proportion of the people, especially those with weaker immune systems, would soon catch the 'flu. Now take a garden border. Stuff it full of roses, making sure that a number of them are older varieties and more prone to pests and diseases. You get the point, I'm sure. So how can it be that we think it sensible to ghettoize roses in a

manner that is guaranteed to create the perfect breeding ground for pests and diseases? We have become conditioned to believing that the only way to grow roses is as a monoculture, bereft of any complementary planting. Roses are beautiful but I challenge anyone to suggest that they are lovely during the winter and spring, and a massed planting only exacerbates these shortcomings, as well as encouraging pests and diseases to spread.

In recent years, rose breeders began to address the shortcomings created by hybridization programmes that were focused primarily on flower colour, size and structure at the expense of disease resistance and, criminally, fragrance. The result is that today's new roses draw on the best characteristics of their parents, such as crisp, clean foliage and fragrant blooms, but with the added bonus of compact, disease-resistant growth and longer flowering. But there is still much to be said for old-fashioned varieties and species roses. Old roses such as *Rosa* 'Complicata' and *Rosa* 'Roseraie de l'Hay' combine all that is best and are pretty much trouble-free, while *Rosa glauca* and *Rosa rugosa* are tough enough to have become popular landscaping plants, adorning car parks and roadside plantings around the temperate world.

Leave well alone

So forget all the stories about roses being troublesome, sickly plants in need of constant attention. After all, roses in the wild – such as *Rosa canina* and *Rosa pimpinellifolia* do perfectly well without the constant attention of a gardener, or the frequent application of chemicals, and are among our loveliest wayside plants, decorating hedgerows and dry banks respectively with their flowers and hips. Roses are, after all, just flowering shrubs. We have made them weaker by over-breeding and unsuitable planting – surely now it's time to release the rose?

Roses in mixed plantings (left) look much more cool and stylish than those in the serried ranks of municipal borders.

With careful management, roses (right) make the perfect accompaniment for flowering perennials such as *Sanguisorba menziesii* and ornamental grasses.

Roses in the mix
How to combine roses with perennials

The benefits of mixing roses with flowering perennials, bulbs and grasses will become immediately apparent as your plantings establish. Perennials help to mask the less attractive qualities of larger roses – the tendency to become leggy and lack foliage at the base – plus they can be used to fill the gaps either side on the main flowering flush, which for 'one hit' roses (those that flower only once) is usually mid-summer. Perennials and grasses also help to form buffers

between roses, slowing the spread of black spot and mildew and encouraging greater diversity of natural predators to help keep aphid numbers at manageable levels. Perhaps most importantly perennials and grasses change the context of roses in the garden. Rather than looking old-fashioned and stodgy, roses become cool and stylish when used with other plants.

Managing roses in mixed plantings

Roses need a slightly different management regime to perennials. Most roses like to be fed, ideally with a good layer of well rotted farmyard manure in spring. So when planning to mix roses with perennials allow space beneath the rose where this rich mulch can be applied without affecting surrounding plants. Because they take longer to establish, this space also gives roses a head start, or you could even plant them alone for one season before adding in perennials.

Blue-flowered plants (left) such as hardy *Salvia* or *Nepeta* are particularly effective with pink- or red-bloomed roses.

Grasses (below left) contrast handsomely with roses, especially those with soft, billowing forms.

Interesting foliage (below) is one of the unsung virtues of roses, as *Rosa* 'Helen Knight' shows when set against a purple backdrop.

Rosa odorata 'Mutabilis' is an old China rose that has been popular in cultivation for decades. Its flowers, held on stems that have few thorns, change colour (hence the cultivar name 'Mutabilis') from light yellow through copper-pink to deep pink. It can be grown as a climber or, as here, a free-standing shrub.

A planting of mixed perennials and bulbous plants runs in front of and through the planting, helping to hide one of the less attractive features of shrub roses - their leafless, leggy stems - adding colour, especially before the roses have peaked, through the silver-pink *Geranium* x *oxonianum* 'A. T. Johnson', and after, with *Colchicum autumnale.*

Rosa glauca, a tough, drought-tolerant species rose, is not the most flamboyant rose in flower - the blooms are charming, small and shell pink - but it makes up for it with superb foliage. The leaves are dusky pink beneath and pewter-grey above, held on dark, purple-red stems - especially effective with silver foliage plants and white flowering plants.

Digitalis purpurea 'Alba', the white form of the common foxglove, sends out tall spires which form a vertical accent against the bruise-dark foliage of *Rosa glauca*, and help to link through the planting while lending an informal, 'self-seeded' appearance, as if they happened to be there by accident alone.

Ornamental grasses
Using grasses in mixed plantings

This is a group of plants that continues to divide gardeners. Supporters of grasses cite their well-known merits in a garden: structural presence, longevity of interest, textural qualities, as well as movement and sound when touched by a breeze. I suspect that the chief gripe of detractors is not so much the plants themselves but the way in which they have been misused in some plantings.

When ornamental grasses first came into widespread cultivation around 30 years ago there was a tendency – in the big public gardens at least – to lump them into monocultural borders with no accompanying planting. The effect can be striking on a grand scale, but does little to inform domestic gardeners about how to use ornamental grasses in mixed plantings in smaller borders, which is where they really come into their own as a group.

Seasonal interest

Ornamental grasses are often grouped according to their flowering time: cool season or warm season. Cool-season grasses such as the graceful *Calamagrostis emodensis* are usually in flower by mid-summer, often retaining their flower structures well into winter. Warm-season grasses, including the vast array of miscanthus cultivars and *Pennisetum orientale* 'Karley Rose', flower in summer or autumn and look good well into the following year. Grasses can be evergreen, as with *Anemanthele lessoniana*, semi-evergreen (*Stipa gigantea*) or die back in winter like *Panicum virgatum*.

The spent flowering stems (below left) of *Calamagrostis* x *acutiflora* 'Karl Foerster' create a vertical accent in the garden.

Ornamental grasses (below) come in a range of shapes, sizes and forms, from light and airy to dense and 'woolly'.

Positioning grasses

Grasses excel as a component of mixed plantings because of the qualities mentioned earlier. Unlike more ephemeral plants, they lend structure to borders over several months and can therefore be used in either a secondary role or as stars in their own right. As supporting plants they perform their task both literally and aesthetically. Thoughtfully positioned they can be used to prop up lax-growing perennials like *Boltonia asteroides* or *Sanguisorba officinalis,* and even annual climbing plants such as morning glory (*Ipomoea tricolor*).

Warm-season grasses can be used to 'fill in' the gaps left by early-flowering plants: for example *Miscanthus transmorrisonensis* can occupy the space left by *Crambe cordifolia.* Some of the larger grasses, such as *Cortaderia richardii,* have as much presence as a specimen shrub or tree and create real impact in a planting, while the vertical habit of *Calamagrostis*

The graceful, arching inflorescences (below) of *Miscanthus transmorrisonensis* look their best in low autumn light.

x *acutiflora* 'Karl Foerster' can be used as a punctuation point or to mark a landscape feature such as a flight of steps or bend in a path.

The movement and textural qualities of grasses are especially helpful when designing plantings: repeating the same grass throughout a border can create a sense of togetherness and rhythm. But perhaps the most attractive quality of grasses is the manner in which the inflorescences seem to catch and hold the light, which is especially evident in the winter when the sun is low.

Habitat plants

Grasses also have an important role in supporting biodiversity. Although they don't provide the rich quantities of pollen and nectar that flowering plants offer, they are important habitat plants, particularly during the winter months when they offer dry cover for a variety of invertebrates, amphibians and small mammals. Even when ornamental grasses are cut back in late winter/early spring, the remaining crown can offer protection for animals.

Grasses

DOVE COTTAGE GARDEN, WEST YORKSHIRE, UK

There is plenty of colour and form in this late-autumn scene, designed by Stephen and Kim Rogers.

Garden aspect: Open, north-facing slope

Soil type: Heavy clay

Microclimate: Exposed, cold in winter

1 *Eryngium* Dove Cottage Hybrid
Even though they have long finished flowering this drift of *Eryngium* demonstrates the interest that comes from dried flower heads.

2 *Digitalis ferruginea*
The spent flower spikes of the aptly named 'rusty foxglove' form vertical punctuation marks against the *Calamagrostis* behind. When in flower, the rust colour is a great foil for bright blues and reds.

3 *Eryngium giganteum*
This plant can be short-lived but often seeds around. It's one of the few garden plants that can be described as appearing white – it is in fact light green tinged with silver – a foil for hot colours.

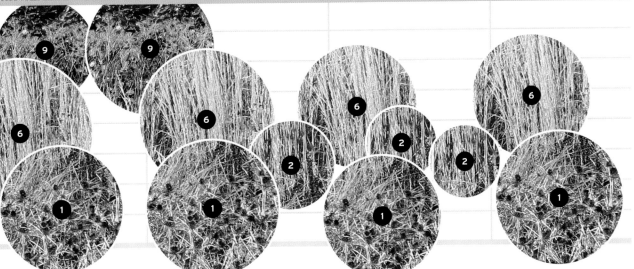

4 *Elymus hispidus*
This little blue grass is still holding its colour late in the season. *Elymus* are probably the bluest of all ornamental grasses, and they tend to be longer lived than festuca.

5 *Verbena bonariensis*
One of the best of all garden plants for wildlife, providing nectar, pollen and seeds. Its thin, wiry stems have a translucent effect and are topped with purple flowers.

6 *Calamagrostis* x *acutiflora* 'Karl Foerster'
The dominant plants in this composition, they act as a screen behind which the bench can be glimpsed. The trick in planting this kind of grass is to allow space between each plant, to create a see-through effect.

7 *Miscanthus sinensis* 'Silberfeder'
This *Miscanthus* is at its best now. Just a single clump is all that is required to add bold architectural structure to the garden.

8 *Miscanthus giganteus*
This is a big, bold grass that needs careful placement if its towering qualities are to be used to best effect.

9 *Thalictrum* 'Elin'
Another big plant, *T.* 'Elin' is the perfect accompaniment for grasses. Its tall, purple-black stems rise from the border, like bamboo.

10 *Sedum* 'Matrona'
The spent flowers of this plant are a rich reddish-brown in their autumn state, with a contrasting flat shape.

The winter garden
Planting for colour and fragrance

Colour in the winter garden is found in flowering plants but also in the bark and stems of trees and shrubs. Among the most colourful stems are the dogwoods (cornus), which come in an array of hues from blood-red through vivid orange, greenish gold and dark purple. During the summer, dogwoods tend to be rather inconspicuous, their bright stems largely hidden beneath their foliage. As autumn arrives, it's the first moment of glory for some varieties – in particular for *Cornus alba* and *C. sanguinea* cultivars as they begin to undress down to those lovely stems in spectacular style, producing some of the best autumn leaf colour of any woody shrub.

The willows are another genus that include plants noted for their colourful stems, including cultivars of the white willow *Salix alba,* of which *S. alba* var. *vitellina* 'Britzensis', with bright orange winter shoots, and *S. alba* var. *vitellina* 'Chermesina', which has carmine red shoots, are the most widely grown. Willow catkins also provide winter colour, from the reddish-black *Salix gracilistyla* 'Melanostachys' to acid-yellow, low-growing *Salix repens*.

The beauty of bark

Tree bark also comes to the fore in winter, especially white-barked birches such as *Betula utilis* var. *jacquemontii*, *Betula utilis* var. *jacquemontii* 'Grayswood Ghost', and the pink-tinged *Betula albosinensis* – all of which have peeling bark that further enhances their appeal. The Tibetan cherry *Prunus serrula* has glowing cinnamon-coloured bark while *Prunus maackii* has yellowish bark that peels off in slivers. With a height and spread of 10m (30ft), they are both suitable for a medium-sized garden, as is the slow-growing paper bark maple, *Acer griseum*.

In a small garden the contrasting effect of dark and light stem colour can be created by using white-stemmed shrubs like the ghostly *Rubus*

The colourful stems of dogwoods (top right) are a highlight of the winter garden. *Cornus sericea* 'Flaviramea' has beautiful golden-green stems.

Dwarf irises (right), such as *Iris reticulata* 'Joyce', establish easily in well-drained soil and tolerate full sun or partial shade.

thibetanus 'Silver Fern' or *Salix acutifolia* 'Blue Streak', contrasting with the almost black stems of *Cornus alba* 'Kesselringii'.

In order to get the best from stem-colour plants, whether trees or shrubs, locate them in a part of the garden where they catch the low rays of the winter sun. If you plant them near a pond their reflection in the water will amplify the effect.

Fragrant winter plants

Winter-flowering shrubs are among the most fragrant flowers in the garden. Their strong scent is designed to attract the few pollinating insects on the wing and can travel for considerable distances. Winter-flowering viburnum comprise several species and cultivars and *Viburnum* x *bodnantense* 'Charles Lamont', 'Deben' and 'Dawn' are easily grown. The evergreen shade-tolerant *Sarcococca confusa* and *Sarcococca hookeriana* var. *digyna* have small but powerfully scented flowers, and although they reach a height and spread of 2m (6½ft) they grow slowly enough to be considered for a small garden.

Perhaps the most spectacular of all winter-flowering shrubs are the witch hazels (*Hamamelis*). They bear their distinctive spidery flowers – which are fragrant and frost resistant – from mid-winter, on naked stems. Winter-flowering heathers were once the most fashionable of garden plants but have been in the doldrums for some time. Combined with plants chosen for stem colour and grasses – rather than the dwarf conifers that became their common bedfellows in the 1960s – they are enjoying a renaissance, and rightly so.

Colour variation

The hellebores are perhaps the finest of all winter-flowering herbaceous plants and are now available in a profusion of different colours, thanks to the introduction of new species and the breeding of cultivars, particularly those of the highly variable *Helleborus* x *hybridus*. Planted in dappled shade with snowdrops, *Cyclamen coum*, crocus and *Iris reticulata* cultivars, they can create one of the most beautiful sights in the garden, regardless of the time of year.

Stems of **Rubus thibetanus** (top left) are covered in a white bloom, which makes them especially distinctive in winter.

Cyclamen coum (left) creates splashes of colour in the garden from late winter into spring. It can create a carpet of colour under trees or shrubs.

The winter garden

A WINTER SCENE AT GLEN CHANTRY NEAR HALSTEAD, ESSEX, UK
Designed by Sue and Wol Staines, this garden is among the most seasonally interesting in Britain.
Garden aspect: Open, south-facing
Soil type: Free-draining gravel
Microclimate: Exposed to cold winter winds

1 *Juniperus communis* 'Hibernica'
Evergreen plants have year round presence but they really come into their own in winter, when the value of green foliage is most keenly felt. The spindle-shaped form of the common juniper strikes through this planting, providing both a vertical accent as well as a focal point.

2 *Stipa arundinacea*
The evergreen pheasant tail grass is at its best when adorned with metallic purple flowers in summer, but it still has plenty to offer in winter in the form of its attractively-coloured foliage, which is green tinged with brown and pink. *Stipa arundinacea* resents being divided and is best grown from seed.

3 *Viburnum farreri*
By keeping the planting relatively low through the whole scheme, the few shrubs in view have much stronger visual impact than they would if they were in competition with lots of other woody plants. The highly fragrant winter-flowering *Viburnum farreri* sparkles with small, pinkish white flowers, the colour of which is picked up in the scattering of delicate white snowdrops below.

4 *Luzula sylvatica* 'Aurea'
Coloured foliage is of particular value in the winter garden, and the golden form of woodrush is especially noteworthy at this time of year. This plant creates a welcome splash of colour that is a shade lighter or darker respectively than the hellebore seedlings and pheasant tail grass. *L. sylvatica* 'Aurea' is especially good in shaded conditions where it illuminates dark corners.

5 *Helleborus* seedlings
Hellebores are known for their ability to form new colour breaks as a consequence of seedling variability, which can lead to some really interesting – and in some cases, less handsome – flower colours. Running through the foreground of this composition is a group of primrose-yellow-flowered forms which link in with some of the foliage plants and also help to lighten the planting. Darker, wine-coloured hellebores add colour contrast.

6 *Euphorbia characias* subsp. *wulfenii*
Another plant that is renowned for its highly variable seedlings, *Euphorbia characias* subsp. *wulfenii* provides useful structure and form in the winter garden. It has striking blue-green evergreen foliage that is followed in early spring by sulphur-yellow flowers. In this garden, it provides repetition through the planting, as well as creating a backdrop against which the light-coloured hellebores and snowdrops shine out.

7 *Cyclamen coum*
A charming winter-flowering cyclamen that will tolerate deep shade, partial shade, or even sun with some midday shade, and it thrives in soils that dry out in summer. Its foliage is highly attractive too, often etched with silver markings. The low-growing plants in this winter scene appear to stud the ground with colour, a deliberate and beautiful effect.

8 *Cornus alba* 'Sibirica'
Tucked behind the winter-flowering viburnum are the colourful stems of *Cornus alba* 'Sibirica', an old favourite for winter gardens. However, it is noteworthy not just for its deep red winter stems but also its excellent autumn colour. As with all winter-stem colour plants it is best positioned to catch the low rays of the winter sun, so before you plant it, make sure you undertake some careful observation of where the sunlight falls in your garden in winter to get the most out of this beautiful plant.

9 *Arum creticum* 'Marmaris White'
A white form of the yellow-flowered *Arum creticum*, with conspicuous pure-white, sweetly fragrant spathes (flowers) in spring. During winter, however, it is its foliage that is of particular interest, being large, glossy and arrow-shaped. *Arum creticum* 'Marmaris White' requires full sun and well-drained soil.

10 *Galanthus* (in variety)
Snowdrops come in a bewildering number of varieties, some of which have such subtle differences that only real specialists can spot them. Glen Chantry boasts a huge collection of these iconic winter plants and here they form bright droplets throughout the planting, creating a natural, woodland floor effect.

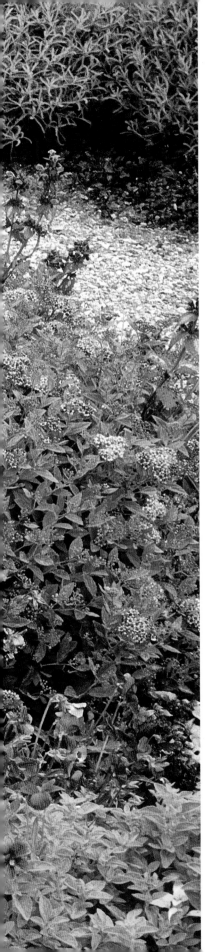

CHAPTER EIGHT

Don't Add Water
How to garden in a drier climate

With the effects of climate change becoming increasingly real, the impact on our gardens and what we will be able to grow will become more marked. The prediction that temperate countries will become hotter and drier in summer but milder and wetter in winter will make gardening all the more challenging, as most drought-tolerant plants – indeed plants in general – aren't well disposed to wet winters. So soil preparation and appropriate planting techniques, allied to suitable plant selection, and water harvesting and conservation, will all become vital for our gardens to continue to thrive and contribute positively to the environment. Fortunately, there is a bountiful supply of beautiful plants that can be used in gardens where summer rainfall is minimal to non-existent but which can also cope with shade and wet. Understanding these adaptations and how they fit with your garden, its soil type and climate forms the next step on the path to successful gardening.

The Round Garden at Sticky Wicket in Dorset, UK (left) contains many drought-tolerant plants that thrive without irrigation. The planting is designed to sustain bees and other beneficial insects by featuring herbs and nectar plants, including lavender and thyme.

Using water wisely
Watering know-how

Plants, like humans, need water simply to be. Their cells are full of it, supporting every part of the plant from the roots to the leaves. And no matter how cleverly adapted plants are, almost all need water at some point to carry out the functions that plants live for – to grow, flower and set seed – in order to ensure the survival of the species.

The extreme survival experts that thrive in desert conditions can wait for years, decades even, for enough rain to fall for them to carry out these processes. They get round the lack of water by making their appearances above ground fleeting, carrying out their business as quickly as possible before either dying or retreating below ground once more. Of course, this isn't much use in a garden, where we want the plants to grow and flower reliably every year, and stand above ground for much longer. Instead, to grow the plants we want, we have to use the water that we have wisely.

Maximizing water
Without doubt the most important time to apply water is immediately after planting, when a thorough drench will not only moisten the root ball and the soil around it but also help to settle the fine soil particles around the plant, ensuring good contact is made between roots and soil. When

followed with the application of a thick layer of mulch this can keep a plant going for a long time. If, however, you leave out the watering or the mulch, newly planted specimens can soon dry out and will begin to show the signs of water stress, such as wilting and scorching of the leaf edges, followed by the entire leaves.

Using the right mulch
At the time of writing, there has been no significant rain for almost a month. Yet despite this, the well-mulched borders in my garden still have plenty of moisture in them, and none of the plants is showing signs of stress. The story on my allotment is mixed, however. In early spring I decided to cover half the bare earth with well-rotted farmyard manure in readiness for planting potatoes and sweet corn. The rest was left without a manure covering for crops that prefer less rich soils.

The difference in soil moisture content six weeks on is extreme; the manured areas are moist from the top down, while the rest is as dry as dust. I have resolved to mulch the entire allotment from now on, using either a lightweight soil-improver such as mushroom compost, or chopped straw for crops such as onions and garlic that don't do well in soil that is too rich.

Allow water to settle
In order to ensure the maximum amount of water gets down to the roots of the plant, rather than simply rolling off the surrounding dry soil as often happens, you can try a technique that is used in a number of arid countries. By simply creating an earth 'berm' or dam around the base of a plant, water can settle where it is really needed without the problem of water run-off. I've seen this successfully used in Greek olive groves, where the earth is so dusty and thin that water run-off is a regular and serious occurrence, but easily redressed by ensuring enough water is available.

Grouping plants (left) that require the same amount of water combined with effective mulching is an efficient way of managing water use in the garden.

Building an earth dam to keep roots moist

An earth dam can work well for all plants, but is especially good when transplanting established woody plants and perennials, where the shock of losing part of their root systems must be redressed by ensuring that there is enough water available. A dam also works well for newly planted large trees which require regular and thorough irrigation during the first season after planting. When the dam is no longer needed – after a season or two – it can simply be levelled back into the surrounding soil.

1. Use a spade or trowel to scrape loose soil into a circular bank around the base of the plant, approximately 1m (3ft) in diameter for a large plant (such as this multi-stemmed *Amelanchier lamarckii*) down to 30cm (12in) for a medium-sized perennial.

2. Ensure the soil forms an even circle around the base of the tree. If the ground slopes, remember to build up the soil on the lowest side so that it is level all round. This will prevent water from escaping at the low point when the plant is irrigated.

3. Once the loose soil has been gathered around the base of the plant, use your hands to firm this into a circular dam, approximately 30cm (12in) wide at the base and 10cm (4in) wide at the top in the case of this 1m- (3ft-) diameter dam. Apply plenty of pressure to make sure that the soil is properly consolidated.

4. Once the dam is finished, irrigate the plant using watering cans. This 1m- (3ft-) dam will hold between four and five cans of water, which is the amount that the tree will need to thrive during dry weather. Apply the water slowly to prevent the dam from eroding.

5. An earth dam reduces water use by ensuring the water you apply gets to where it is needed most – the roots of the plant. There is no wasteful run-off and the water tends to settle into the soil slowly, rather than disappearing, ensuring the soil is thoroughly wetted. Apply a layer of mulch around and inside the dam to help seal in the moisture.

Drought-tolerant planting

DRY GARDEN, RHS HYDE HALL, ESSEX

Designed by Matthew Wilson and Chris Carter in 2000, this area has never been irrigated.

Garden aspect: South-facing

Soil type: Clay loam, heavily ameliorated with sharp grit

Microclimate: Hot, exposed to drying winds

1 *Chamaerops humilis*
Framing this composition to the extreme left is a compact, hardy palm, also known as the dwarf fan palm. Along with the *Euphorbia* to the far right, these two plants form an evergreen, structural frame.

2 *Verbena bonariensis*
The thin, wiry stems of this verbena have a see-through quality early in the season and are topped with panicles

of violet flowers from mid-summer to late autumn. It self-seeds easily.

3 *Eschscholzia californica*
Orange is such a useful colour in the garden; zesty, powerful and the perfect foil for plants with dark blue, purple or magenta flowers. *Eschscholzia californica,* or the Californian poppy, is an invaluable plant for dry gardens and easy to grow from seed *in situ*.

4 *Allium* 'Purple Sensation'
With their big, domed flower heads, repeated groups of *Allium* 'Purple Sensation' are an early highlight in the dry garden. The heads are a source of pollen and nectar, and give structure in winter.

5 *Artemesia schmidtiana* 'Nana'
This compact, low growing *Artemesia* has finely cut leaves of intense silver. In

the high light levels at Hyde Hall these appear as shimmering silvery white points of light among the surrounding planting.

6 *Chasmanthium latifolium*
Although this planting looks full to bursting point there is plenty more of interest to come - which is vital to a successful planting plan - including this group of spangle grass.

7 *Helichrysum italicum* subsp. *serotinum*
Perhaps the most exotically fragrant of all garden plants, the curry plant has silvery foliage with a pungently aromatic smell just like curry, hence its name.

8a *Cistus laurifolius*
8b *Cistus* x *dansereaui*
8c *Cistus populifolius*
These groups of *Cistus*, or rock rose, draw the eye from left to right by being the

only white-flowered plants on view, and also through their similar flower shape and habit. An offset tripod arrangement looks more natural than a line of plants.

9 *Salvia* x *sylvestris* 'Mainacht'
This flowering sage has real impact when planted in a generous group. The bright orange *Eschscholzia* also serves to heighten its dramatic flower colour.

10 *Juniperus horizontalis* 'Glauca'
This low-growing juniper provides colour, form and texture during the winter, but in summer acts as a foil for the surrounding colour.

11 *Euphorbia characias* subsp. *wulfenii* 'Lambrook Gold'
Providing early colour from its golden yellow flowers, this *Euphorbia* still has lots to offer as a foliage plant.

Life on the edge
Plant adaptations to arid conditions

Of all the climatic conditions that challenge the existence of plants, arid environments must rank as the most extreme. Baked by the sun during the day, often freezing cold at night, battered by wind and parched through lack of rain, arid lands seem to offer almost none of the essentials for plant growth. Yet even in the most barren desert it's possible to find species that take advantage of what little is on offer.

Although some of these plants are so specialized that their cultivation in a garden is nigh on impossible, there is a diverse range of other beautiful plants that fit the principles of 'new gardening' perfectly. These are plants which will grow in sunny conditions in a temperate garden, without continuous – and unsustainable – watering.

A low-maintenance dream

The brilliance of these plants lies not only in their adaptations but also in the fact that, when they are assembled in a suitable place, they look just right. The components that work so hard in keeping the plants alive in their native home are what make them so aesthetically pleasing in a sunny garden.

Ironically, many of these cleverly adapted plants are already commonly grown in our gardens, but when treated to an overly rich diet of compost, fertilizer and water they behave much as any other garden plant when things hot up. Plump and sappy from too much of everything, they can wilt and collapse in a trice. These are definitely plants for the more pioneering gardener; someone who is willing to cast off the shackles of double digging, excessive irrigation and over-feeding and instead embrace plants that like to live on the edge.

And there are other benefits that come with these tough, drought-tolerant species. Among them are fine architectural plants, lending structure and presence to a planting scheme. Many have strongly aromatic foliage, exuding essential oils that fill the garden with exotic fragrance. Others have flowers that are so rich in pollen and nectar as to be permanently smothered in bees, butterflies and moths. And they're a lazy gardener's dream, as not only are feeding and watering not on the agenda, nor are staking, tying-in or other forms of time-consuming maintenance.

Nine adaptations to arid conditions

Leaves

Leaf modification is one of the key ways that plants cope with arid conditions. Tiny leaves like those of thyme **(1)** help to cut transpiration simply by having a reduced surface area through which moisture can escape. Narrow or incurved leaves do the same thing in a different way, and are the reason why many grasses, including *Stipa gigantea* **(2)**, are so successful in dry conditions. The waxy leaves of *Cistus laurifolius* act like a seal, holding in water and defending the plant against drying winds. The thick fleshy leaves of the desert-dwelling *Agave americana* **(3)** are like a camel's hump, storing food and moisture in the form of thick, glutinous sap. And to reflect as much sun as possible, many arid plants have silver leaves, such as *Lavandula angustifolia* **(4)**, while a similarly large proportion have hairy leaves to trap any moisture in the air. This is especially important for *Pulsatilla vulgaris* **(5)** which can grow straight out of rock. Most extreme of all are those plants that have done away with their leaves altogether and instead have flattened modified stems, like *Colletia paradoxa* **(6)**.

Roots

The root systems of arid plants are just as well adapted as the leaves. Tap roots serve three purposes, questing deep underground for water and nutrients, storing food and moisture, and anchoring the plant to the ground in exposed conditions – as anyone who has tried to pull up *Eryngium x oliverianum* **(7)** will know. The open terrain found in arid environments is notoriously windy, so the low-growing *Rhodiola rosea* **(8)** is less likely to get torn from the ground than taller species. And if you can't stand the heat, summer dormancy is an option. Bulbous plants, including tulips **(9)** and alliums, flower and set seed either before or after the hottest part of summer.

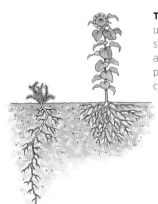

Tap roots (left) act as underground storage systems full of water and starch. They are the plant equivalent of a camel's hump.

CHAPTER NINE

Life in the Shade
Bright ideas for plants

Shade comes in many varied guises and depths, depending on whether it is created by solid, unchanging objects such as buildings or more changeable and transient features like deciduous trees. A shaded garden is often considered to be a tough challenge. But there are just as many opportunities for creating dynamic and interesting plantings in a shaded garden as there are in a sunny one. Varying levels of light and shade affect the way in which our eyes interpret flower and foliage colour, which can be exploited to great effect with careful plant selection. And shady gardens offer the chance to grow some very desirable plants: woodland flowers that thrive in leaf litter, spring bulbs that stud the ground with colour when few other plants are in flower, and shrubs with exotic blooms or fiery autumn colour. The key to success with a shaded garden is researching appropriate plants and soil conditioners, and improving soil and light levels, especially when establishing new plantings.

Shaded gardens (left) may seem like a daunting prospect but they can offer an excellent opportunity to utilize the textural foliage qualities of shade-loving plants such as hostas and alliums.

Making the most of shade
Get to know the conditions

Understanding the microclimate and soil conditions of the shady areas in your garden will help you to get the most from the site. If the shade in your garden is cast by immovable objects such as buildings, and its orientation is such that it receives only diffused or indirect sunlight, the plants that will thrive will be those that grow in deep shade, typically those found in coniferous woodland or in the shaded lee of hillsides and rocky outcrops.

Semi-shade

If, however, shade is cast by semi-permeable objects such as trees, or the orientation of your garden means that parts of it receive sunlight for differing lengths of time and at varying times of the day, then the range of plants opens up to include those that enjoy dappled shade and semi-shaded conditions. Plants suitable for shade cast by trees are those found in deciduous woodlands, where sunlight levels vary through the year. Many of these plants do their growing, and often flowering, when the trees above are dormant and the light levels more consistent.

Plants that love semi-shade tend to be those that dislike very strong light levels at particular times of the day, typically midday but sometimes at sunrise. This is often due to the plants having thin or light-coloured foliage that is prone to scorching – yellow-leaved or variegated plants are especially prone – or delicate flowers that prefer the ambient temperature to rise before the sun reaches them.

It's possible to manipulate the microclimate in a shady garden, of course, by crown lifting trees and including light-reflective surfaces, as shown in 'South by Southwest?', (see pp.24–25) but there are limits, especially if the shade in your garden is cast by surrounding buildings. Matching the growing conditions in your garden to those found in the wild will help you to navigate your way through the variety

Ferns (left) thrive in areas of deep shade and so can be planted in the shade cast by such objects as a house or garden wall.

Purple cyclamen and white snowdrops (below) are able to flower before deciduous trees come into leaf.

of plants on offer and match the right ones to your garden. And what a range of plants they are! From huge-leaved architectural plants that bring structural presence and stylishness to exquisitely tiny bulbous plants, the richness and variety of shade-tolerant species is matched only by their beauty.

However, to get the best out of these plants you must observe a few rules. The rate of establishment and ongoing health of all shade-loving plants – even those adapted to dry, deep shade – will be improved through enriching the soil with organic matter, especially leaf litter, applied in layers to the surface. And don't be tempted to buy big plants for an instant impact – shade-tolerant plants often have to work hard to succeed, so are better off planted as small plants, so they can acclimatize and fill out in their own time.

The light level in this shady courtyard garden (top) has been lifted by the light-coloured gravel.

Variegated hostas (right) and delicate-flowered plants thrive in the protection of a semi-shaded area.

Shade-tolerant planting
Plant adaptations to shady conditions

The foliage adaptations of shade-tolerant plants offer plenty of opportunities for attractive combinations in the garden. Having gardened in the dry heat of Essex, the prospect of being able to grow lush-leaved shade-loving plants was a major attraction for me when I began gardening at Harlow Carr. Shade-tolerant plants can provide almost endless variation in texture and colour too, and these features can lighten up dark spaces or create magical, jungle-like effects.

Fronds and foliage

Ferns are a group of shade-tolerant plants with tremendous variation in foliage, from the light-green filigree of *Onoclea sensibilis* to the tiny fronds of *Blechnum penna-marina*, the strap-like, glossy leaves of *Asplenium scolopendrium* and the extraordinary, silver and purple *Athyrium niponicum* var. *pictum*. In each case, the foliage is designed to reduce water loss and in some cases to gather moisture. The glossy fronds of *Asplenium scolopendrium* act like a funnel that traps moisture in the air and slowly drip feeds it to the roots. Contrast ferns with some of the larger-leaved plants – *Ligularia*, *Rodgersia aesculifolia*, *Rheum palmatum*, *Hosta* 'Big Daddy' – that have developed big foliage to absorb as much light as possible, and immediately the shaded garden becomes as interesting as one in full sun. Add some of the shade-tolerant grasses and the foliage effect becomes even more striking, especially with golden foliage grasses such as *Hakonechloa macra* 'Alboaurea' and the grass-like rush *Luzula sylvatica* 'Aurea'.

Planting combinations

Euphorbia are very accommodating plants in shade and their sulphur yellow flowers have an illuminating effect, as does *Smyrnium perfoliatum*, a stately woodland plant that will gently seed around, creating an ever-shifting golden tapestry in the shady garden. Self-seeding plants such as *Smyrnium*, *Digitalis* and *Tellima* are invaluable in this respect, as they are able to seed in dry, shallow soil areas. There is no reason to feel limited by shade – even a sunless garden offers opportunities for dynamic planting combinations. The sheer versatility of plants comes to our rescue and offers a huge range of plant types to choose from.

Five adaptations to shady conditions

In the wild, plants have adapted to shade just as readily as they have to hot and sunny conditions. These adaptations often completly oppose those of their sun-baked brethren. The tiny, light- reflecting silver leaves of a plant such as lavender are exchanged for the huge leaves and dark pigmentation of plants such as the imposing *Gunnera manicata* **(1)**. This plant is perfectly adapted to shade – its big, dark leaves absorbing as much light as possible, while the shade in which it thrives prevents the plant from wilting through excessive transpiration. In contrast, some shade-lovers use similar adaptations to sun-loving plants; many species of fern have small or dissected fronds (leaves) to reduce transpiration in dry shade where little moisture is available, while the pretty, spring-flowering woodlander *Brunnera macrophylla* **(2)** has hairy leaves to trap moisture. This feature is an ideal adaptation for plants growing in the understory that might get very little direct rainfall due to the dense canopy of leaves above. Although we may not think of plants as being particularly mobile, by developing roots that 'run', many shade-tolerant species are able to spread, seeking out areas where the soil is richer and more moist or light levels are higher. *Anemone hupehensis* **(3)** is one of many that employ this adaptation. Other plants have spreading stems and adventitious roots that enable them to branch out into new areas, or suckering shoots that can enable the plant to 'reappear' some distance from the parent. Some, like the common ivy *Hedera helix* **(4)** are just as happy scrambling over the soil as they are climbing up trees and walls, while the delightful wild strawberry *Fragaria vesca* **(5)** spreads by means of over ground running stems, which are known as stolons, and can colonize large areas with remarkable ease as a consequence.

Stolons (above) are overground running shoots that enable shade-dwelling plants to move to more accommodating areas.

Damp & dry shade
Plants in action

1 *Iris sibirica* 'Dreaming Yellow'
At the top edge of Streamside the conditions are dry and shaded, so the plants here are all suited to the conditions. *Iris sibirica* 'Dreaming Yellow' spreads slowly by rhizomes, but is never invasive. In midsummer it bears flowers with white standards (the upright part of the iris flower) and creamy yellow falls. The upright, grassy foliage acts as a marker edge to the path behind.

2 *Onoclea sensibilis*
The pale green, deeply divided foliage of this compact fern acts as a foil to the linear, grass-like foliage of the *Iris* 'Dreaming Yellow' behind. Although lower growing than the iris, the fall of the bank ensures that it can be clearly seen. *Onoclea sensibilis* requires moist soil and in the right conditions will spread indefinitely.

3 *Arum italicum* subsp. *italicum* 'Marmoratum'
Unusually for a deciduous perennial, this plant is interesting throughout the year. From winter until early summer it produces attractive leaves marked with cream in the veins, and then pale, greenish-white spathes (flowers), which are followed by upright spikes of bright orange-red berries that last through until winter. The dry soil in the root zone of the large oak tree is perfect for arum, as they resent wet in summer.

4 *Hosta* 'Halcyon'
Hostas are tolerant of far drier soils than is commonly believed, and here in the dry root zone of the oak is proof of that tolerance. One of the bluest of all hostas, *Hosta* 'Halcyon' has leaves that are similar in shape to the adjacent arum, but different enough – particularly in colour – to make a contrast. And one of the great advantages of blue-leaved hostas is that they are the least appealing to slugs and snails and tend not to be eaten.

5 *Digitalis purpurea*
Drifting throughout the Streamside planting are smatterings of common foxglove, *Digitalis purpurea*. These are all self-sown seedlings and are allowed to spread into available gaps as part of a welcome, shifting pattern within the planting. The value of self-seeding plants such as foxgloves in difficult conditions such as dry shade is that they will seed into places where it would be difficult or impossible to plant due to shallow soil or extremely dry soil.

6 *Tellima grandiflora*
Another self-seeding plant that fills in awkward gaps, *Tellima grandiflora* is tolerant of dry soil once established. Its small, bell-shaped flowers are borne in great profusion from late spring to mid-summer, creating a light, frothy effect and illuminating the shade. Here it is important as one of the first plants to flower.

7 *Gunnera manicata*
A beast of a plant and one requiring moist to wet soil to thrive, *Gunnera manicata* has the distinction of being the largest leaved hardy plant that can be grown in the British Isles. Definitely not suitable for small gardens it will, however, make a dramatic statement where space can be given, and is always a talking point.

8 *Cardamine pentaphylla*
This low-growing, free-flowering perennial has spread by rhizomes along the Streamside planting, and there is some concern that it may be becoming invasive further downstream. Attractive as it is, if the evidence is that it is 'escaping' then steps may need to be taken to eradicate it.

9 *Astilbe* 'Deutschland'
A low-key *Astilbe* with pure white flowers, *Astilbe* 'Deutschland' is also a very attractive foliage plant with bright green, finely toothed leaves. Such pale-coloured foliage helps to create highlights in a shaded planting, as do the white-coloured flowers. *Astilbe* prefer damp soil, as is the case here in a damp dip at the edge of the stream.

10 *Rodgersia aesculifolia* (bronze form)
Dominating the foreground of the planting and marking the edge of another path along Streamside, this is a form of *Rodgersia aesculifolia* with especially bronze leaves – they usually turn green before the flowers begin to form. Lush foliage is one of the bonuses that you get with many moisture-loving plants, and is a consequence of their adaptation to shade.

This is a caption for the pic on the left

CHAPTER TEN

The Potted Garden
Container gardening

Gardening in containers is a wonderful way of creating changing displays throughout the season, and is consequently a highly popular aspect of gardening. Moreover, for many people it is the only form of gardening available – if the outdoor space you have isn't at ground level or doesn't have any soil, then a container is likely to be the only option. Whether you have a small apartment balcony in London, a terraced house with a small backyard in Yorkshire or a rooftop terrace in New York, container gardening can provide the means to bring not only ornamental plants, but also fruit and vegetables to your door. In doing so, not only do we improve our own lives but we also enhance the environment around us. A cityscape full of planted balconies and rooftops must surely be something to aspire to, and in areas where the collective mentality has created exactly that, the effects can be as inspiring as any ground-level garden – perhaps even more so due to the particular challenges faced by container gardeners.

Planting in containers (left) enables gardeners with balconies, roof terraces and non-traditional gardens to grow a few choice plants, and if drought-tolerant species are used, the containers don't need much watering.

Why use containers?
For and against

Container gardening is arguably not a sustainable use of our precious resources. Water use and climate change impinge on container gardening possibly even more than terrestrial gardening because pots need regular – often daily – watering. This is especially true in hot, dry weather and in particular if little or no rain can reach them. For example, a container garden could receive no natural rainfall if it was on a balcony on the leeward side of the prevailing wind or rain or there were other balconies above yours.

There is also the problem of keeping pots watered when you are away for any length of time. People today live increasingly insular lives and may not have a neighbour or friend they can call on to fulfil this duty – and there are no guarantees that they will be as diligent in watering your pots as you are. Added to which, container gardening usually relies on changing plants on a regular basis, and refreshing soil annually.

With increasing concern over sustainability and the use of resources in general, container gardening sounds inherently unjustifiable. I believe, though,

that with a little common sense, a dash of BLOOM logic (see p.56) and some carbon trading, the benefits far outweigh the difficulties.

Carbon trading

Cities and towns need plants to alleviate what would otherwise be an entirely artificial environment, to improve the lives and spiritual and mental well-being of humans and to provide food and habitats for wildlife. Studies that have been carried out on how humans interact with green space – and what happens when it is taken away – have confirmed that without green space, our quality of life goes down.

The role of the container garden in enhancing the lives of individuals and the locale may seem rather modest, but when a whole block of individuals embraces the concept not only does it benefit individuals, the neighbourhood and the local

An eclectic mix of pots (below) filled with a selection of plants including vegetables and succulents makes an unusual display.

environment, it can also trigger a whole series of beneficial events. The neighbours you never really knew become gardening buddies, swapping tips and plants, and wildlife begins to appear: a woodpecker here, a bumblebee there. Fresh food can be grown in containers, cutting carbon miles and reducing the amount of packaging we use. Containers can help to bring the city and the country closer, and bring people together too. Not a bad achievement for a few pots. So given this context, the regular use of water and

changing of soil and plants is a minimal trade-off. And there are ways in which water use can be reduced, as well as the plants used in containers reused, or grown cheaply (in financial and environmental terms). Even the containers themselves can be obtained from scrap materials, everyday objects that someone else has discarded as waste. And there is no need to replace all of the compost in your containers when you repot. For example, the compost in a pot of tulips can be used for annuals or succulents once the tulips have gone over.

Using scrap objects as containers

There's no doubt that there are some lovely containers, troughs and window boxes available to buy, but with a little ingenuity and a dash of flair it is possible to create a container garden using found objects and recycled scrap. Depending on the type and size of plant you want to grow, scrap pots can be anything from clay drainage pipes to car tyres (very good for growing strawberries), old boots to complete WCs. A container is, after all, just a vessel to hold growing media, so why not experiment and use your imagination, rather than buying off the shelf?

Wooden boxes (above) can be turned into rustic-style containers for a range of plants, such as fuchsias.

Old chimney cowls (left) have been transformed into attractive planters using a selection of drought-tolerant alpine plants.

Even the smallest outdoor space (above) can become a haven for people and plants – all that is required is imagination.

Good container management
How to reduce watering

Containers have several shared characteristics, no matter what size or shape they are. Being above ground, the growing medium in containers warms more readily and maintains that warmth for a longer time than terrestrial soil. This leads to plants in pots growing and flowering earlier than in the ground, and consequently 'going over' earlier too. The upside of this is that early displays of plants such as spring bulbs can be enjoyed. The downside is that in prolonged hot weather the roots of plants can 'cook', causing stress to the plant, which then requires much more water than it would if it were in the ground.

Getting down to the roots

Because there is generally a much lower volume of soil or growing medium available to a plant in a container than one grown in the ground - even if the container is really big - the plant is unable to tap into moisture that might exist deeper down in the soil. The result is that the roots of plants in containers can quickly occupy every bit of space, reducing the area available for water and exhausting nutrients in the growing medium more rapidly, leading to the need to 'pot on' regularly.

In both instances there are solutions. Firstly, during prolonged hot spells a good way of keeping containers - and therefore plant roots - cool is to wrap the outside of the pot with hessian or muslin soaked in water. To increase the availability of water, you can use water-retaining crystals which, when mixed with the growing media when the container is planted up, can help to maintain the pore space available for water (see p.37) as well as physically absorbing water for gradual release to the plant. These crystals come as tiny, hard granules that swell to up to 100 times their original size when watered, which can then be released to the plant roots. They have an added advantage of keeping the soil a little cooler in hot weather.

Water-retaining crystals (above) swell to up to 100 times their original size when they are hydrated and gradually release moisture to the plant roots.

Using hessian to reduce water loss

During the heat of summer, the outside of a pot can become hot very quickly, making conditions tough for the roots of plants, which can then dry out. Terracotta pots are breathable, being porous, so wrapping a damp covering around the container can help to keep the heat down. You can use a length of hessian, muslin, old sacking or old clothes, as long as they are absorbent.

1. Damp down the covering before wrapping it around the pot, by submerging in a bucket of water. Wrap around the container.

2. Secure the damp covering by tying with string. Thereafter, damp down with water when watering the pot.

Drip feeding

Watering systems that 'drip feed' plants are effective ways of irrigating a garden with many containers, as the water is applied slowly and continuously at a measured rate, ensuring the growing media doesn't dry out – far better than a regime of deluge and drought. A drip-feed system can also be used to apply liquid feed to plants, something that is essential for long-term plantings such as trees and shrubs, which will rely on this application of feed as the growing media become progressively exhausted of nutrients.

To reduce the need for constant potting on and prevent the exhaustion of the growing media, thrifty plants – such as drought-tolerant plants, herbs, alpines and succulents – can be used, or even direct-sown annuals, all of which require less water and nutrients than many traditional container plants (see p.162). Choosing the right growing media will help too. Peat-based composts can dry out and be hard to re-wet, whereas loam-based media tend to be more stable.

The versatility of containers (above left) enables them to be used for growing plants that might not otherwise thrive outdoors, such as the banana, *Ensete ventricosum*.

A plastic-lined tray (above right), which has been filled with leaf litter, can act as a reservoir, holding excess water.

Rescuing dried up container plants

If your pots do dry out, and it seems impossible to get water back into the growing medium, here is a cheap, easy and foolproof trick. Fill a watering can with water and add a few drops of washing-up liquid to the can. The molecules comprising the washing-up liquid bind themselves with water – it's what makes them effective at cleaning crockery – which in turn helps the water to bind to the growing medium. If this is combined with standing the container in a bath or large bowl of water it is doubly effective. But don't put the washing-up liquid in the watering can and then add the water, unless you want bubble-filled pots!

Plants for containers
Sustainable planting

There is an extensive range of plants that not only look good in containers but also meet the criteria for sustainable planting, including herbs, alpines, shrubs, annuals and vegetables.

Low- to no-water containers
Just as in the terrestrial garden, there are many plants that will cope perfectly well in containers with a low- to no-water regime. These include the specialist plants listed in 'Don't Add Water' (see p.146), but also some of the alternative lawn plants such as succulents, alpines and herbs. A container planted with *Sempervivum*, *Echeveria* or *Aeonium* will look beautiful all year round without the need for excessive watering.

Herb pots
Herb containers have the advantage of providing flavouring for the kitchen, ensuring you have a year-round supply of fresh, tasty, 'zero carbon' herbs. By

placing them near the kitchen – or in a window box beneath the kitchen window – you need only reach out a hand to gather a flavoursome crop. Coriander, flat-leaved parsley, basil and oregano are all suitable – in fact just about every herb you could want to grow can be cropped from a pot.

Alpine pots
Alpines have a reputation for being extremely difficult to cultivate and therefore only really suitable for the cognoscenti, but there are actually many that are accommodating, tough and beautiful and ideal for gardeners with limited space, especially when grown in troughs and containers.

Alpine plants can often be so small as to be suitable for the tiniest of containers, or even soil-free growing environments such as tufa, an inert, lightweight volcanic rock that can provide everything that thrifty alpines require, with almost no need for watering at all. Alpines – and succulents – are often highly architectural plants that lend themselves to being used creatively as 'living sculptures', the tightness of their

Grouping pots together (below) with the same or similar plants maximises visual impact and keeps the pots cooler.

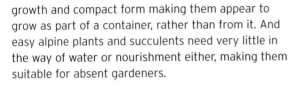

Shrubs and perennials (above) can survive perfectly well in pots. When they become too big, they can be planted out or divided.

Some alpines are compact (above), drought-tolerant and able to cope with full sun making them ideal for containers.

growth and compact form making them appear to grow as part of a container, rather than from it. And easy alpine plants and succulents need very little in the way of water or nourishment either, making them suitable for absent gardeners.

Perennials and shrubs in pots

If you have the space for larger containers, there is no reason why you cannot have the equivalent of a terrestrial garden entirely in pots. Flowering perennials, shrubs, ornamental grasses and even trees can all survive and thrive in a containerized garden, given the appropriate care. But eventually, with most containerized plants, the time will come when they become too big or run out of steam and start to become sickly. Rather than throwing away perennial

divisions or shrubs that have become too big, why not offer them to a local school, charity or community association for planting out in the ground?

Annuals

Direct-sown annuals make a great show in containers, cost very little and require minimal aftercare or water. The process is exactly the same as in a garden with soil borders, as described in New Planting Styles (see page 125). And, as annuals tend to be quite thrifty plants, you will find at the end of the season that the growing media in the compost still has a reasonable amount of life left in it. If you remove around half of the compost and then top up with fresh material, the pot will be ready just in time for a planting of spring bulbs such as narcissus or tulips.

Succulent plants (below) with fleshy leaves can be grown successfully with little soil or water.

The adaptations of lavender (below) to hot conditions and thin soil are just as applicable when growing in containers.

Container veg
Fresh from the pot

If you have ever been to a gardening or allotment show and marvelled at the oversized leeks, parsnips and carrots, each one a perfect specimen, then here's the secret – pots. Almost all 'competition' veg is grown in containers as the grower can manipulate the conditions more readily, growth starts earlier (usually by growing under glass), and pests and diseases can be managed more easily.

But you don't have to be a competition grower to use containers for veg. I use containers for lots of crops because the growing medium in pots warms up quickly, so it's possible to crop food like salad leaves much earlier in the season than with 'ground-grown' veg. Tomatoes and chillies grown in pots are also a real success, and have a better taste than those grown under glass as the ripening process takes a bit longer, increasing the sweetness – or hotness – of the fruit.

Microveg

Microveg is a new and exciting way to grow vegetables, even if all you have is the smallest of outdoor spaces or just a windowsill. Microveg growing simply means harvesting vegetables – principally leaf and herb crops – at seedling stage rather than allowing them to mature. All salad leaf and leafy herb crops can be grown and eaten as microveg, including lettuce, coriander, basil and celery. The flavour is often more

Herbs and veg suitable for pots (below, top left clockwise) are salad and herb leaves such as lettuce, rocket and sorrel; beetroot; flat-leaved parsley (grow in root trainers then harvest young); shop-bought garlic (you can rehydrate this in a small pot); potatoes (replace a single tuber when harvesting to get a second crop); chilli and bell peppers, and tomatoes (grow in a sunny spot).

intense than in the mature plant, making microveg popular with renowned chefs such as Raymond Blanc, and by sowing a succession of trays at fortnightly intervals it's possible to have fresh, tasty food for the whole summer, even if the only available space you have is a windowsill. If you have room for larger pots, why not sow seed trays with salads, use two-thirds as microveg and grow the rest on into mature plants by pricking out and potting on the seedlings?

Mini garlic

Garlic is one of our most popular food flavourings, but shop-bought bulbs can often be quite dry, even when put through a crusher. This wonderful way of growing garlic, shown to me by veg-growing legend Joe Maiden, ensures you have a regular supply of juicy mini garlic that can be harvested and used whole, like a spring onion. Simply take a small pot and fill it with potting compost. Push up to a dozen garlic cloves (you can use garlic bought from a shop) into the compost, with the top of each clove left proud. Place the pot outside or on a fairly cool windowsill, and in a few days these will sprout and grow grass-like, fleshy leaves. Although the cloves themselves won't grow much, they will rehydrate – rather than becoming more desiccated in the kitchen – and will taste fresher and juicier than dry, shop-bought garlic. They can be chopped or crushed whole, leaves and all, or used to add a flavoursome kick to a salad.

The never-ending potato pot

Potatoes are so good in containers that it is almost not worth growing them in the ground – I now grow all my salad potatoes in containers on my patio. But if space is at a premium and you only have room for one pot, you can still enjoy a succession of spuds throughout the season. In early spring, use a bucket-sized plastic pot and half fill it with compost. Place a chitted seed potato – the salad varieties such as 'Anja', 'Charlotte' and 'Pink Fir Apple' are most suitable – into the compost and top up the container with further compost to within 6cm (2in) of the rim. Keep the compost in the container moist and don't allow it to dry out. After six to ten weeks the potatoes will be ready to harvest, which can be done simply by upending the pot, providing enough potatoes from one container for between five and ten single servings. Then repeat the process by replacing one of the mature potato tubers back in the pot – in six to ten weeks you'll have a second crop and can start again.

Recipe pots (above) can be created to grow all the veg and herbs for a particular cuisine, such as Thai. Try lemon grass, coriander, Thai basil, chilli pepper and oriental salad.

Checklist: Growing crops in containers

1. Firstly, and most importantly, grow what you know you'll eat.
2. Use a loam-based peat-free compost with some water-retaining crystals and some grit for drainage.
3. Early sowings will need the protection of a greenhouse or conservatory, but if you don't have either then simply wait until outdoor sowings can commence, or buy pre-grown plug plants. Salad and herb crops that have been started from seed will need thinning out regularly from five to six weeks after sowing. Add them to mature leaves and herbs for a fresh salad.
4. Feeding is best done with a low-nitrogen liquid feed. Tomato fertilizer is suitable.
5. Regular watering is essential, especially for tomatoes.

CHAPTER ELEVEN

Garden Design
Bringing it all together

The idea of the garden as an 'extra room' was championed by designers such as John Brookes in the 1960s. Brookes worked on the principle that any outdoor space, no matter how small, can be designed in such a way that it will become a useful and beautiful extension to the building it adjoins. One of the techniques Brookes uses is to divide the garden into spaces that relate to the façade of the house - in effect transposing the width of the building, distance between windows and doors and height between floors onto the ground, so that these dimensions dictate the positioning of paths, borders and paving. In reality, few gardens can be planned in this way from the outset. But there is enormous value in having a clear idea of what elements you want to include in your garden and where to place them, and what kind of texture and structure you want the garden to have. This kind of planning also ensures that you select appropriate plants for your soil and microclimate, and that you allow them the space they will need to thrive.

The garden at Glen Chantry, Essex, UK, (left) has been designed with large, colour-themed mixed borders which contain a wide range of perennials, shrubs, roses and woody plants. Though the garden has been planned with great care, the effect is one of informality.

How to plan
At the drawing board

The starting point for any garden plan is to list the elements you want to include in it in order of importance, based on how you want to use the space. This list is likely to vary considerably, depending on your circumstances and who will be using the garden. It's important to think carefully and honestly about what you want, rather than opt for what you think you should have. For example, do you want to include an outdoor dining area, and if so should this be covered or partially sheltered so that it can be used throughout the year? Do you need a shed or similar structure to house garden tools? Would you like a patio or some other kind of seating area? Have you always wanted a water feature?

Once you have drawn up your wish list you can establish how much space each feature would require, based on your needs, the available space and the environmental considerations explored in this book, including soil type, aspect and microclimate, sustainability and wildlife enhancement. Armed with this information you can begin to plan on paper how your garden might look.

Make a plan on paper
It is impossible to dictate taste, as beauty is forever in the eye of the beholder, but there are tried-and-tested design rules and principles that can be applied to make even the smallest space attractive and usable. If you can get an overview of your garden, from an upstairs window or even the top of a ladder, take advantage of this by photographing the garden at various times of the day. You can then enlarge the photographs, ideally to A4 or A3 size, using a photocopier if necessary, and overlay them with clear acetate on which you can draw your ideas for the garden and how you would like it to be used. Alternatively, measure your garden – using fixed features such as walls to measure from – and draw it to scale onto graph paper. You can then use acetate as you would with a photograph to experiment in your planning.

Even if you are taking on an existing garden with established plants and features that cannot be changed, it can be re-planned to your own requirements, following the same principles as you would when planning a new garden. The most important (and expensive) decisions to make will be on the positions of the permanent features such as paths and paving.

Plot each area in detail
You need to be disciplined when planning the planting in your garden. Draw up a list of plants that meet the cultural requirements of your garden – the microclimate and soil – and then create a shortlist of favourites, noting their height and spread on the list. Use graph paper or an acetate overlay to plot exactly how large the planting areas in your garden are. Take note of their eventual size but bear in mind that herbaceous perennials can be manipulated more than most woody plants.

Mowing in shapes

If your garden is mostly lawn, a useful design tip is to mow in the shape of new borders and features. Allow the grass to grow a little longer than you would usually, then use a lawnmower on a low setting to follow the lines of your plan and mow the shapes into the grass. Once the features are mown in, spend some time – a few days – living with the shapes, looking at how borders and paths interact. Observe them from different parts of the garden and your home. If they don't look right you can simply let the grass grow, revise your design and try again.

I. Plant ideas for pond area

Plan borders in each area and sketch out the planting
Once you know what elements you want in your garden, and
some shapes and sizes, you can begin to sketch out how the
plantings might look. In my own garden I made a few simple
sketches to help me plan the look I wanted for each area:

(1) Around the pond and at its margins I opted for a mixture of
lush foliage plants including *Rodgersia* and *Ligularia*, with
Astilbe and grassy foliage plants; *Iris*, *Carex* and *Miscanthus*.

(2) This sunny border gets dry and hot in summer, so the
plants had to be drought-tolerant. *Sedum*, *Salvia*, *Allium* thrive
in these conditions, along with bearded iris and *Eremurus*.

(3) This border is partly in shade for half the day and as a
result has slightly more moist soil, so here I selected plants
such as *Monarda*, *Rudbeckia*, *Echinacea* and *Gillenia*.

2. Plant ideas for south-east facing border

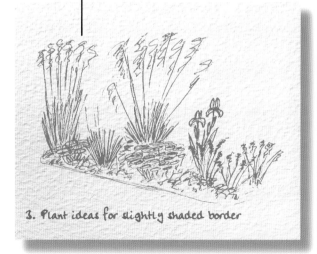

3. Plant ideas for slightly shaded border

Months of careful planning and planting (right) bear fruit in the
summer when the borders can be seen to their best effect.

Making the most of space
Working with what you have

Whatever your taste in plants and materials there are design principles that should be observed when setting out a garden that will help to accommodate all the elements you want to include, while making the most of the space you have. When designing a small garden it's tempting to make the central space – usually a lawn or paved area – as big as possible, pushing planting spaces out to the sides, usually into mean, narrow beds. In fact, the best way to make a small space appear larger is to divide it, so that you can't view the whole garden in one go but are encouraged to explore.

This can be achieved by drawing the eye in different directions. Examples of this are a path that turns a corner and heads out of sight, a dense planting that screens part of the garden, or a feature that leads the eye away. Or you can use a combination of these: a path that turns a corner, which is in turn hidden by planting or a structure, for example. Repeating certain features, a particular plant or a hard landscaping feature can lend a sense of rhythm and unity to a space but also draw the eye, making the garden seem larger. Water can also help to enlarge a garden, simply by reflecting light and the sky, so it is worth including purely from a design perspective, even if you don't consider the benefits to wildlife.

Although you should aim to maximize your outside space, do remember that to make the most of your garden it is essential to allow sufficient room for each of the elements it contains.

A space for plants

Among the most common mistakes made by gardeners are over-planting and under-planting. The former is usually a consequence of a love of plants and a desire to acquire: even when the plant label reads 'height and spread 3m x 3m (10ft x 10ft) and we know we only have half a metre (5ft) square available, we just have to have that beautiful specimen. And so plants end up shoe-horned into ever-decreasing spaces and the garden soon looks congested and lacking in structure. Under-planters allow too much space around plants or are mean with numbers of plants, and tend to enjoy bare soil as much as flowers and foliage – to the detriment of soil health and moisture levels.

A borrowed view (above) can be anything from a broad countryside vista to a tower block in a cityscape. By leading the eye out of the garden, the illusion of space is created.

Planned planting

Over-planting perennials isn't the end of the world as they can be lifted, divided and thinned out – in fact, it's a good way of bulking up numbers of plants for future borders. But getting it wrong with trees and shrubs can quickly lead to serious problems and result in plants becoming lopsided, misshapen and lacking in vigour due to excessive competition with their neighbouring plants.

When planning your planting, think about which plants complement or contrast with one another, which flower colours or foliage combinations are most

Setting border dimensions

One way to ensure the dimensions of a border look and feel right is to follow this simple rule: for every linear metre (3ft), make the border between 25cm (10in) and 50cm (20 in) wide. Therefore a border that is 3m (10ft) long should be between 1m (3ft) and 1.5m (5ft) wide, and certainly no narrower than 75cm (30in). Using this rule will ensure you have enough depth to create a tiered planting, including tall, medium and low-growing plants, or to include the odd tall plant at the front of a border. Mark out a border on the ground following these rules and you will find it looks naturally right.

The principle of repetition **(left)** can be applied regardless of the space available. Here, clipped box balls and hooped plant supports lead the eye to and past the central focal point.

A curving path **(middle)** that winds out of view will immediately rouse our natural curiosity.

Light-reflective materials **(below left)** instantly make a garden feel bigger, no matter how small.

effective or have particular value to wildlife, which plants can survive with little watering, and so on. Thorough plant research is immensely rewarding and will enable you to make the best selection for your garden, turning you into a better gardener before you have even committed a plant to soil.

Once you have your final list, take it with you every time you visit a nursery or garden centre and don't be tempted to deviate from the list. For compulsive plant purchasers this is tough but necessary if the right plants for your plot are the ones you take home with you from shopping forays.

The borrowed view

It is worth considering what aesthetically interesting feature in our surroundings can be used to draw the eye. A gap in a hedge, or a group of plants with a central dip can frame the feature. A path that lines up with it, or vertical plants or features will also draw the eye to the borrowed view.

Checklist: Planning your garden to make the most of space

1. Draw up a list of the elements you need in your garden, from the must-haves to the desirables.
2. Think about the space each of these elements will need and how much time you want to spend looking after your garden.
3. Get an overview photograph of your garden from a first-floor window or ladder and print it out on paper. Alternatively, measure the garden and plot it onto graph paper.
4. Use an acetate overlay to plot your designs over the photo or drawing.
5. Divide borders using a 1-m (3-ft) grid to enable you to calculate the number of plants you can use.
6. Draw up a list of plants appropriate for the conditions in your garden, their benefit to wildlife and ability to thrive without excessive intervention.

Special effects with plants
Plant design tricks

When you last visited a really well-planted garden, the chances are you came away with the impression that the planting looked effortlessly 'right', not contrived or out-of-place but beautiful, perhaps even perfect. In fact the planting was probably anything but effortless, but the result of careful planning and a deep understanding of the conditions in the garden and the plants themselves. It's true that some gardeners have an inherent knack for putting plants together, but even those lucky enough to be blessed with natural ability will have honed their skills through research and close observation.

When you have a small garden it can be all too easy to end up with plantings that appear 'dotty' – disjointed, and lacking structure and presence. This can be the result of using small numbers of many different plants, or sometimes a reluctance to use larger plants in a small space for fear of making the garden seem smaller. The most effective plantings are bold in their use of numbers and colour, use trickery such as repetition, and explore the one spatial plane in a garden that is, in almost all cases, limitless – the vertical.

Grouping plants

Trees and shrubs are more usually employed as single specimens to obtain the best effect, and a small garden is unlikely to be able to accommodate many. The way to create impact with smaller plants – herbaceous perennials, bulbs and grasses – is to use single species or cultivars in quantity. Depending on the style of planting, these may be grouped in drifts, or in the case of a matrix, 'scattered' through the border. Groups of plants in threes, fours, fives, and so on, create far more impact and unity than single plants and appear less contrived, as if the plants are living naturally in a community rather than as a result of obvious planting. Arranging single species in a tripod, diamond, or 'five on a dice' enables drifts to be interlocked with one another, ensuring that the space in the border is used to best effect. And because there are no straight lines in nature, these interlocking groups will appear more natural.

Giving your planting a vertical dimension (below) by using tall plants such as these *Verbascum* that utilize 'air space', creates a sense of expansiveness.

Using the vertical plane

No matter how narrow or short a garden might be, the space above it, the air, is free to explore with plants. Contrary to what we might think, using the vertical plane can actually make a garden seem bigger by drawing the eye upwards, away from the linear limitations and up into the big blue, or grey, depending on the weather. And as many tall plants occupy little linear space, preferring to show off their height rather than breadth, this exploration of the sky needn't come at the price of fewer plants. Some tall plants – *Eremurus* and foxgloves for example – have a fairly short flowering period and can be grown through other plants. Others, such as *Thalictrum* 'Elin' or *Verbena bonariensis* have a translucent quality that enables other plants to be viewed through them. And there are columnar or fastigiate trees and shrubs – *Prunus* 'Spire' and *Juniperus scopulorum* 'Blue Arrow' – that cast little shade and are unlikely to upset neighbours by spreading into their patch, making them perfect for inclusion where space is limited. Plants with vertical ambitions are among the best for creating a sense of rhythm through a planting, too.

Using repetition

The repetition of one particular plant or plants with the same form or colour can help to create unity and lead the eye through the garden, taking the viewer on a journey towards something we want them to see, or away from something we don't. It's an effective way of making a garden hang together and is a useful means of including a wide range of different plants in a small space without giving a disjointed effect. For example, the magenta flowers of *Echinacea purpurea* 'Rubinstern' can be repeated through *Lythrum salicaria* 'Lady Sackville', a plant with similar flower colour but a completely different shape.

Creating rhythm

Tall, airy ornamental grasses such as *Molinia caerulea* subsp. *arundinacea* 'Skyracer' can be used repeatedly through a scheme to create rhythm, and are especially effective once their foliage and flower colour fade to straw yellow, contrasting with surrounding colour. Another trick is to use topiary – clipped evergreens – to create the same effect, with the added advantage of winter presence. Cones of box, *Buxus sempervirens*, or columns of yew, *Taxus baccata*, work well, the former being small enough to accommodate where space is tight.

Grouping plants (below left) creates unity in even a small garden, and prevents plantings appearing disjointed.

Paired topiary evergreens (below) define the path through this planting, showing how repetition can create cohesion.

Colour, structure & texture
Mixing and matching

Of all the considerations involved in plant choice and garden design, colour has the potential to be the most divisive. Screaming cerise alongside ruby red may not be to everyone's taste, but then soft pastels can, for others, be far too boring and safe. But as important as colour is, the structural and textural qualities of different plants – not only foliage texture but flower shape and form, too – are there to be exploited when planning plantings.

We all know that colours can be either contrasting or complementary, and that some combinations look right, while others jar or fight with one another for attention. There are undoubtedly some colour combinations that bring out the best in each other, such as orange and purple, and others that combine to create a subtle shift from one colour to another, like pink and violet. There are also special effects that can be achieved using colour. For example, hot colours, including fiery reds and oranges, can be used to foreshorten a view. If your garden is long and narrow, planting a generous quantity of hot-coloured plants will make the garden appear shorter and wider. In contrast, the cooler, recessive colours such as silver, blue and white can extend a view, making a short garden appear longer.

In areas where light levels are high and the sunlight strong, pastel shades can seem flat and lifeless, burned out by the strong light, whereas hotter, darker colours show well and seem more at home. Against the dark foliage of an evergreen hedge or the backdrop of trees

Intensely contrasting colours (below) of *Sedum telephium* 'Purple Emperor' and pale blue *Elymus magellanicus.*

A mass of hot colours (below) can overwhelm. A dash of blue (here provided by *Agapanthus* 'Blue Giant') cools the effect.

The purple-blue of *Aconitum napellus* 'Bergfürst' (bottom) appears hot and spicy when planted with *Lythrum virgatum.*

Hot-coloured plants (bottom) such as the red *Crocosmia* x *crocosmiiflora* 'Emberglow' can help to foreshorten vistas.

and shrubs, lighter colours tend to show better and seem to lift the light levels, whereas dark, hot colours can seem turgid and dull. Colour contrast isn't limited to flower, of course, and coloured foliage can be utilized in exactly the same manner. The reddish purple leaves of *Cotinus* 'Grace' create a dusky, slightly sombre mood, whereas the silver blue *Elymus magellanicus* produces the opposite, being light-reflective and fine in leaf.

There are some combinations that are best avoided. Gold and silver is a brave but not always wise combination, and plants with differing types or colours of variegation nearly always bring out the worst in each other.

Structure and texture

The structural and textural qualities of plants are as important in a planting as flower colour, not just in creating rhythm and repetition but also in providing contrasting shapes, and surfaces with differing light-reflective qualities. The 'form' of plants – the shape they grow – can be used to create the rises and falls within a planting, either from the front to back of a border or when viewed head-on. Foliage offers limitless opportunities to contrast and complement, but also to change the scale within a planting. For example, the large, pinnate leaves of *Angelica archangelica* can be contrasted with the narrow, ribbed, grass-like leaves of *Crocosmia* 'Lucifer'. The small silver leaves of *Elaeagnus* 'Quicksilver' provide a light-reflective backdrop for flowering plants, especially those with blue, magenta, purple or violet flowers, while the golden inflorescences of *Stipa gigantea* create a hazy, shifting backdrop to a planting.

Flower shape is almost as variable as foliage, with single blooms or inflorescences ranging from flat umbels to tall spikes, globe-like heads to cheery, daisy-like flowers. Combining different flower colours with flower shapes creates even greater dynamism.

Mixed flower shapes (below) of *Echinops bannaticus* 'Taplow Blue' and *Achillea millefolium* 'Terracotta' create structure.

A dark backdrop of *Cotinus* 'Grace' (bottom) is softened by the grassy foliage of *Panicum virgatum* 'Strictum'.

***Aconitum napellus* 'Bergfürst'** (below) ceases to be hot when planted with the cool-coloured *Elymus magellanicus*.

Stipa gigantea and ***Verbena bonariensis*** (bottom) create an airy, translucent screen when mixed together.

The private garden
Screening eyesores, blocking out noise

In the modern world there are certain inevitabilities, and most of us put up with the sight of something we would rather not see, either inside or outside our gardens. Unless you live in a remote rural location, the ever-present background hum of traffic is another unwanted distraction. Screening an eyesore should be easy, but sometimes our efforts only serve to draw further attention to it. The easiest mistake to make is to try to cover up a solid, linear eyesore - a gas or oil tank, or dustbin area - with another solid, linear structure such as a fence or trellis.

Camouflage

The military may seem an unlikely source of gardening tips, but the design and implementation of camouflage can provide useful guidance on how to hide the things we would rather not see. During World War I a form of camouflage was developed for naval vessels that became known as 'dazzle ships'. The camouflage consisted of asymmetric, linear slashes of colour applied seemingly randomly in bands of different thicknesses and at different angles. The paint broke up the slab-like outline of big warships, making them much harder to spot; the painted faces of commandos on night patrol is an example of the same technique.

Rather than using a solid, straight-edged screen to hide a rectilinear object, it is better to break up the outline of the eyesore with plants of different heights. A solid fence only emphasizes what lies beneath, whereas a mixture of evergreen and deciduous shrubs, or perennials and grasses with different forms, will create a 'dazzle ship' effect, so that even if the eyesore is partially visible it will recede and apparently disappear. If the eyesore is harder to hide or outside the boundary of the garden, create a distracting feature or use hard landscaping to draw attention away from it. A path that leads towards something hidden will create a sense of anticipation and mystery, while at the same time encourage the eye away from an ugly structure. Alternatively, create a feature that is so distracting you simply cannot stop looking at it. The most diverting features in my garden are the bird feeders, which are often so full of feasting birds it is impossible to take your eyes off them.

Be careful that your garden path (below left) doesn't lead the eye to an unattractive garden structure such as a shed.

Screens made from natural or synthetic materials (below) are a great way of hiding dustbins, compost bins or water butts.

nature's **gardener**

Noise pollution

Background noise, specifically traffic noise, can be a harder proposition to tackle, as no amount of planting can dull the roar of vehicles. Standard practice on motorway verges is to erect tall fences that bounce the sound waves back, but this can be impractical to emulate in a garden, and you probably don't want to be hemmed in by 4m- (13ft-) high fences. However, noise is usually less intrusive if you cannot see what is making it, so if at all possible try to create a screen between your garden and the cause of the noise. Years ago I lived above a pub and I could only get to sleep by imagining that the hubbub of chattering customers was a babbling brook. It sounds implausible, but because I couldn't see the customers I was able to drift into sleep. Distraction is probably the better option when it comes to screening noise, and water is usually the most successful diversion. A small fountain in a self-contained feature - a pebble pond or container of some sort - often works well, or a wall-mounted feature that drips water into a bowl. By fitting a water feature that has a pump with an adjustable flow rate it is possible to achieve just the right volume of water and sound; too much can be worse than the noise you are trying to block out, not enough will be ineffective.

A natural hazel trellis (above) and tall plants such as sunflowers can create a sense of privacy in the garden.

The sound of falling water (below) created by a water feature can help to block out intrusive noises.

Materials & local vernacular
Inspiration on your doorstep

Is there a dominant style of architecture and building in the area where you live? Modern towns and cities typically include a mixture of old and new buildings, but individual streets or suburbs often have architectural characteristics in common. In older country towns and rural communities the pressures of change and development are usually slower to make their mark, and the regional influences tend to be as much to do with the availability of materials as architectural style. This local vernacular can be found in anything from municipal buildings to farm structures, and is worth observing in the garden, too.

Using local materials

In much of North Yorkshire, in the north of England, the dominant building material is locally quarried sandstone, which gives villages and towns a distinctive, cohesive feel. It's easy to spot the homes that were built in the 1950s and 60s made of brick or concrete blocks, when 'manmade' was considered preferable to natural, local materials, and planning regulations weren't as stringent as they are now. This is not to say that there aren't some very good modern buildings in the county, which respect the local vernacular while

being architecturally forward-looking, and, most importantly, fit for purpose. Of course, gardens don't have to relate to the local vernacular, but it is helpful to have an understanding of the materials in use in your area, and those that make up the fabric of your home. The latter will most certainly have a bearing on what will work in your garden.

The dry-stone wall is one of the quintessential features of the north of England and North Yorkshire in particular. Comprising chunks of local stone, its construction involves significant skill, from selecting the correct pieces of rock to fit, to tying the structure with 'through stones' that ensure the wall is solid. Many have stood for hundreds of years, some perhaps for more than a thousand. Incorporating dry-stone walling features into the local gardens makes perfect sense aesthetically and environmentally – the material is readily available (and doesn't necessarily need to be quarried as pre-used stone can be purchased) and the skills required to build the walls still exist, thanks to a

Building materials (below) used for this house in upstate New York are reflected in the stone and wood used in the garden. Both represent the local area's architectural traditions.

recent resurgence in traditional crafts. The aesthetic of the dry-stone wall can be brought into the garden not only in the pure sense – as a boundary – but can be modified as a feature, such as a living wall planted with alpine and succulent plants, perhaps given a twist by realigning sections of the stonework at an angle, or using different pieces of stone to create changes in direction. If stone is not a feature of your local vernacular there will almost certainly be a dominant material, either historically or currently, that can provide you with inspiration, from thatch to clapboard, oak to clay tile.

Know your garden's place

The advantage of respecting the local vernacular in a garden is that it will root your garden in the broader environment. It may well be that in using a local material you are also supporting a regional craft skill that is in danger of vanishing. Local materials are also more likely to be sustainable materials, attracting low carbon miles in their production and supply.

The local vernacular (right) is often expressed through the use of readily available materials, such as roofing thatch.

Dry-stone walls (below and right) are a feature of many parts of the UK, including North Yorkshire. Here, walling craftsman Dan Wright builds a dry-stone wall at Harlow Carr. As you can see, plants will often find homes in these walls, seeding into what little soil is washed into cracks and crevices.

Greening garden structures
Transforming the ordinary

Perhaps the two most common structures in or adjacent to gardens in developed countries are garages and the humble garden shed. Both are undoubtedly useful, but invariably utilitarian in design and construction and often painted unnatural colours that have no precedent in the landscape. With a little imagination there is no reason why a shed or garage can't be turned into a divertingly engaging addition to the garden, even a feature in its own right, and an environmentally friendly wildlife habitat, too.

Green roofs

Rather than repainting or hiding a shed or garage, why not make a green roof (see p.182-183) and clad the outside? Making a green roof is worthwhile for a variety of reasons. Firstly, it is visually less intrusive than roofing felt or bitumen paint. In addition there are fewer damaging processes involved in creating a green roof than a conventional one. Once completed and established a green roof can provide habitats and food sources for a variety of vertebrates and invertebrates, help in the drive to cut carbon emissions and reduce water run-off dramatically.

Using living and natural materials

And why stop at your shed and garage? There are a host of garden features that can be made more attractive by greening with living material, and new features that can be made from scratch. Conventional timber panel fencing – in short supply worldwide at the time of writing, due to the vast amounts of timber being used in the developing world – can be replaced with living willow screens. These not only absorb carbon as a crop prior to harvesting, but continue to

Ferns and logs (below) are perfect for cladding and planting a shaded shed. At Harlow Carr a brown painted shiplap shed has been turned into a haven for biodiversity.

do so as a living screen in the garden. And a living willow screen needs no preservative treatments that can damage the environment through their manufacture and disposal. Living willow can also be used to create pergolas, arches, plant supports – almost anything you can buy as a manufactured product can be made with it. As the willow grows it can be tied back in to the main framework or trimmed back in spring.

Dead willow screens are ephemeral, with a lifespan of three or four years at most. They can make an effective temporary screen while waiting for a hedge to establish, for example. They can, however, also be used as climbing supports for plants, where they quickly become assimilated into, in effect, a living fence. If you want to know more about willow weaving there are workshops run by numerous organizations.

Green sofas

Turf can also be used to create features in the garden, such as green sofas and even boundary dividers. Green sofas can be easily made by forming soil into the shape of a seat, consolidating it as you go by firming with your hands or the back of a shovel, and then simply laying turf over top as if laying it on a lawn. A turf seat needn't be as elaborate as the one we have at Harlow Carr (pictured), and can simply be a backless bench. As well as being extremely comfortable to sit on – in dry conditions only if a damp posterior is to be avoided – a turf bench will also provide a habitat for soil-dwelling animals.

And if you want to make something really pretty, planting a few wild flower plugs in the back and arms will create splashes of colour against the turf. Maintenance of a turf sofa or bench consists solely of a quick cut with hedge shears every two to three weeks, depending on growth rates.

A semi-shaded shed (top) has been transformed with a roof of shade-tolerant woodland plants such as bugle (*Ajuga reptans*), while the sides have been clad with dry-stone walling and timber.

Turf sofas (middle) are not only fun but also carbon-neutral garden accessories that are extremely comfortable to sit on – in dry weather. And when not available for sitting they act as a piece of garden sculpture.

Living willow (left) makes a superb alternative to a fence, or for use in garden features such as shelters and arbours.

How to make a green roof
A step-by-step guide

Commonly used roof coverings such as roof felting and bitumen expend energy and generate pollution in their preparation, and once in place do nothing to offset their carbon footprint. By carefully selecting sustainable materials or by recycling existing ones it's possible to create a green roof that is at least carbon neutral. Up to 90 per cent of the volume of a green roof can comprise water at any one time, and this is taken up gradually by the plants, slowly leached out or transpired. This will help to reduce water run-off which, during summer storms, can escalate into damaging flash floods. Green roofs can be planted with alpines, ferns, succulents, ornamental grasses, bulbs, herbs or wild flowers, or covered in turf. In general, any plant or plants that are drought-tolerant can be utilized on a green roof.

Cladding

The sides of a garden structure can also be beautified, with cladding. Sheds usually require regular painting with wood preserver which, depending on the manufacturing process, can be damaging to the environment, and also look unattractive. Cladding is an opportunity to let your imagination run riot as it can consist of just about any found or recycled material. At Harlow Carr we have three clad summerhouses: one clad with turf on a dwarf dry-stone wall, reminiscent of a Neolithic roundhouse, a second clad with logs and a third with stone and timber. Within the cladding we have included invertebrate nesting spaces under the eaves, in the form of cut lengths of bamboo, and in some of the gaps between the stonework and logs we have incorporated planting pockets to enable ferns and alpines to grow.

Depending on the structural integrity of the building you are roofing and cladding, you may need to strengthen it with buttress posts to support the roof weight. And if you are cladding with an organic material like turf, the walls will need to be made waterproof, either with a pond liner or by stapling recycled plastic compost sacks to them.

Chiastophyllum oppositifolium (right) is suitable for green roofs, growing to a height of about 15-20cm (6-8in).

Roof plants

Below is just a small selection of the many plants that are suitable for planting in green roofs.

Alpines and succulents
Anemone nemorosa
Aquilegia bertolonii
Chiastophyllum oppositifolium
Haberlea rhodopensis
Saxifraga 'Freckles'
Saxifraga x urbium 'Variegata'
Sempervivum 'Blood Tip'
Sedum acre
Anchusa cespitosa
Phuopsis stylosa
Erodium spp. and cultivars
Verbascum 'Letitia'
Lewisia spp. and cultivars

Grasses and sedges
Molinia caerula var. arundinacea 'Moorhexe'
Festuca glauca
Stipa tenuissima
Poa labillardierei
Carex testacea

Ferns
Dryopteris erythrosora
Asplenium scolopendrium
Athyrium niponicum var. *pictum*
Polystichum setiferum
Blechnum penna-marina
Blechnum spicant

Building a green roof

To create a green roof using plants (other than shallow-rooted sedum) you will need to construct a timber frame that sits on top of the roof. This needs to be filled with growing media, ready for planting into. For most small sheds a frame made from 15cm x 3cm (6in x 1in) softwood, which can be recycled from old pallets, is ideal. On larger sheds you may want to make something more substantial from 20cm x 5cm (8in x 2in) softwood. In this case the whole structure will require strengthening with heavier timber supports to hold the roof, such as the railway sleepers used here.

1. Build a timber frame from 15cm x 3cm (6in x 1in) softwood to fit on top of your chosen roof. Then divide the frames internally to create eight individual cells of equal size. Apply a light-gauge pond liner to the roof and secure it with staples. Drag the frame into position on the roof and screw it firmly in place.

2. The additional weight of the timber roof frame needs supporting with six 10cm x 10cm (4in x 4in) posts. They should be dug into the ground and lean into the shed at an angle of about 30 degrees, so that the tops are in contact with the wooden frame. The posts act like buttresses, absorbing the weight from the roof and transferring it down to the ground.

3 Fill each cell of the frame with a 5-cm (2-in) layer of free-draining, lightweight material such as vermiculite. Top up the remaining space with loam-based compost with a little added grit to further enhance drainage. The roof is then ready to plant. Use small (9-cm/4-in) potted plants as these will establish without the need for irrigation. A completed roof (right) will provide food sources and habitats for wildlife and benefit the environment by absorbing carbon dioxide.

CHAPTER TWELVE

Perfect Partners
Create the look

It's a cliché, but true, that gardening is a lifetime of learning. In the course of my gardening career I have been fortunate enough to work in many different gardens, each with its own particular microclimate and soil type. Perhaps the most important thing I have learned is that plants invariably have the answer to our needs, providing we respect their needs. The frustrated gardener blames the plant for failing to thrive, the wise one accepts that the wrong choice was made in the first place and resolves to try something more suitable. These Perfect Partner selections draw from my own knowledge of growing plants in different places for different effects. Each selection contains six plants that require the same type of growing conditions, are of a similar size and, should you wish, form an instant shopping list for your garden for you to take away when hunting for plants. For each plant I have added my own observations, taken from my notebook, to help you grow them successfully and enjoy them more.

Christopher Lloyd's garden at Great Dixter (left) shows how it's possible to create plantings that not only look good but that also thrive with the minimum of trouble, by using plants that form perfect partners.

Hot & dry conditions

Six low-growing plants (below 75cm/30in)

Stipa tenuissima

This tough, easy-to-grow grass, native to Mexico and Argentina, makes a great foil for hard surfaces such as paving or rockwork. The common name of hair grass is particularly apt as this is among the most tactile of all plants, just asking to have fingers run through its fine, soft leaves.

- **Height and spread:** 60cm x 30cm (24in x 12in)
- **Flowering time/colour:** Summer, greenish-white fading to buff
- **Notes:** Produces abundant seed that can be collected and sown, or allowed to self-set. Seedlings grow away quickly and seem to establish better than divisions.
- **Pests and diseases:** None.

Sternbergia lutea

There are many lovely, drought-tolerant autumn bulbs, such as sternbergia. Known as the autumn daffodil, this free-flowering, tough plant found from Spain to Afghanistan adds splashes of golden-yellow to the autumn garden.

- **Height and spread:** 15cm x 8cm (6in x 3½in)
- **Flowering time/colour:** Autumn, deep yellow
- **Notes:** Sternbergia seem to enjoy a tough, sun-drenched life but only divide them if flowering becomes less profuse.
- **Pests and diseases:** May be affected by narcissus flies and eelworms, although shingle mulch seems to reduce this.

Elymus magellanicus

Perhaps the best and most intense of all of the blue foliaged grasses, hailing from southern Chile and Argentina. It is a tidier and longer lived plant than some of the blue festuca, and it's an ideal foil for the hot flowers of *Zauschneria* and the dark foliage of *Sedum telephium* 'Purple Emperor'. In hot, dry conditions, the stems turn more silvery but in less severe conditions, they become a blue-grey colour.

- **Height and spread:** 20cm x 30cm (8in x 12in)
- **Flowering time/colour:** Summer, buff
- **Notes:** Rather than cutting this grass back to the ground, which seems to weaken it, it is best to just comb out any dead leaves with your hands.
- **Pests and diseases:** None

Zauschneria californica 'Dublin'

When in flower, this shrub is a truly spectacular sight, smothered in funnel-shaped scarlet flowers, which in the wild in north-western America are pollinated by hummingbirds. The tiny leaves are blue-green and covered in fine hairs.

- **Height and spread:** 25cm x 30cm (10in x 12in)
- **Flowering time/colour:** Late summer through autumn, scarlet
- **Notes:** Wait until the risk of frost has passed before trimming back the old foliage – it will help to protect the plant. Use a sharp gravel mulch to ward off slugs.
- **Pests and diseases:** Slugs can be a problem on young foliage.

Sedum telephium 'Purple Emperor'

The deep, glossy purple foliage of this handsome garden hybrid is one of its strong selling points, topped with dusky pink to red blooms that are loved by bees and butterflies. It makes a striking combination with silver and blue foliage plants.

- **Height and spread:** 40cm x 30cm (16in x 12in)
- **Flowering time/colour:** Late summer into autumn, varies from dark pink to red
- **Notes:** As with all of the 'border' sedums, this plant responds well to the 'Chelsea Chop' (see p.122).
- **Pests and diseases:** Slugs and snails may attack young foliage.

Allium cristophii

The huge blooms of this ornamental onion, which can reach 20cm (8in) in diameter seem almost too big for its diminutive size, but the metallic light purple colour of the star flowers is quite lovely and unlike anything else in the garden. This is an excellent plant for growing 'through' later-flowering plants or under deciduous shrubs. Native to Turkey and Central Asia.

- **Height and spread:** 30-60cm x 5cm (12-24in x 2in)
- **Flowering time/colour:** Early summer, pinkish purple
- **Notes:** Don't be tempted to remove the seedheads after flowering; as with most ornamental onions they provide form and interest right into late summer.
- **Pests and diseases:** May be affected by white rot and onion fly.

Hot & dry conditions
Six medium-sized plants (between 75cm/30in and 1.2m/4ft)

Eryngium x oliverianum
Steel blue isn't a common colour in the garden, making this sea holly all the more desirable. The strong shape of the foliage and flowers associates superbly with ornamental grasses and the steely tones help to cool plants with very strong flower colours, like *Zauschneria* and *Eschscholzia*. This plant is a garden hybrid between *E. x alpinum* and *E. x giganteum*.

- **Height and spread:** 90cm x 45cm (35in x 18in)
- **Flowering time/colour:** Summer into autumn, steel-blue
- **Notes:** Excellent plants for cutting. Flower stems that are cut and hung for a few days will retain their colour for months.
- **Pests and diseases:** Slugs and snails may damage young foliage; inadequate drainage can lead to root rot.

Echinops bannaticus 'Taplow Blue'
A handsome garden hybrid that has both architectural presence and strikingly beautiful flowers, *E. bannaticus* 'Taplow Blue' is a magnet for nectar and pollen-feeding insects. Its globe-shaped flower heads associate well with plants that have flowers borne in flat umbels.

- **Height and spread:** 1.2m x 65cm (4ft x 26in)
- **Flowering time/colour:** Mid to late summer, bright blue
- **Notes:** I love using this plant to cool the bright colours of bright red *Achillea* or purple-red *Knautia macedonica*, both of which have contrasting flower shapes.
- **Pests and diseases:** May be affected by aphids.

Eremurus stenophyllus
Native to central Asia, *Eremurus* have the common name of 'desert candle' which is very apt. These plants illuminate the garden for the brief time that they are in flower and create a sense of anticipation every year as the flowering time beckons.

- **Height and spread:** 1m x 60cm (3ft x 24in)
- **Flowering time/colour:** Early to midsummer, dark yellow
- **Notes:** *Eremurus* are always best planted in autumn, bare root on a bed of grit about 10cm (4in) deep, with the fleshy roots just below the soil and the central crown just visible above the soil.
- **Pests and diseases:** Slugs may be a problem.

Euphorbia characias 'Portuguese Velvet'
This is a fine architectural plant with wonderful, blue-green foliage and zingy, acid-yellow bracts that light up the garden from early spring. It's especially lovely after rain or heavy dew, when water droplets caught in the fine hairs covering the leaves appear as glass beads, spangling the whole plant. The sub-species is from south-east Europe.

- **Height and spread:** 1.2m x 1.2m (4ft x 4ft)
- **Flowering time/colour:** Spring to summer, acid-yellow
- **Notes:** If allowed to set seed, it will often hybridise with *Euphorbia wulfenii* cultivars, sometimes with interesting results. Weed out inferior forms or they may take over the garden.
- **Pests and diseases:** Generally trouble-free.

Kniphofia rooperi
Red hot pokers are among the most dramatic of all garden plants and are especially good at creating rhythm through a planting, or as 'punctuation marks'. *K. rooperi*, which comes from South Africa is noteworthy as it is one of the latest to flower with large, almost egg-shaped racemes.

- **Height and spread:** 1.2m x 60cm (4ft x 24in)
- **Flowering time/colour:** Early autumn to early winter, orange-red
- **Notes:** Don't be afraid of using this plant at or near the front of a border, where it will appear innocuous for most of the season before bursting into life in autumn.
- **Pests and diseases:** None.

Caryopteris x clandonensis 'Dark Night'
This tough shrub, a garden hybrid, can often be found adorning public landscapes and mixed shrub borders, but it deserves a place in a drought-tolerant planting because of its attractive grey foliage and lovely deep blue flowers.

- **Height and spread:** 1m x 1.5m (3ft x 5ft)
- **Flowering time/colour:** Late summer to autumn, dark blue
- **Notes:** *Caryopteris* should be pruned back to a framework in spring to ensure good flowering, but in a zero irrigation garden it is best to wait till the risk of frost has passed.
- **Pests and diseases:** None.

Hot & dry conditions

Six taller plants (above 1.2m/4ft)

Ozothamnus rosmarinifolius

A tough and fast-growing shrub from south-eastern Australia with aromatic silvery foliage, *O. rosmarinifolius* is also covered in fragrant flower heads in early summer. It can be short-lived in extremely hot and dry situations.

- **Height and spread:** 2.5m x 1.5m (8ft x 5ft)
- **Flowering time/colour:** Early summer, white
- **Notes:** Don't get too attached to this plant; it lives fast and tends to die young. However, it is well worth growing for its ability to fill space quickly, and if you plan ahead you can take cuttings to replace it, or grow something different.
- **Pests and diseases:** None.

Callistemon pallidus

The common name for these plants is the bottlebrush and they add a genuine taste of the exotic to temperate gardens, as they come originally from Australia. They are hardier than their appearance suggests, but in very cold areas, they benefit from the protection of a wall.

- **Height and spread:** 1.5m x 2.5m (5ft x 8ft)
- **Flowering time/colour:** Spring to mid-summer, creamy yellow
- **Notes:** *Callistemon* benefit from a light trim after flowering to remove the old flowering growth, which can become unsightly. They will also tolerate hard pruning.
- **Pests and diseases:** None.

Elaeagnus 'Quicksilver'

One of the finest deciduous silver foliage shrubs and often used as a foil for other plants, *E.* 'Quicksilver' also has small but highly fragrant flowers. It tolerates pruning well so it can be manipulated to fit into smaller spaces. This is a garden hybrid but the species ranges from southern Europe to China.

- **Height and spread:** 4m x 4m (13ft x 13ft)
- **Flowering time/colour:** Summer, creamy yellow
- **Notes:** Although this plant is known for producing suckers they are easy to remove by tearing from the ground.
- **Pests and diseases:** Damaged, dying wood can become infected with coral spot fungus.

Stipa gigantea

Native to Spain and Portugal, this grass has become extremely popular in recent years and rightly so. With shimmering, oat-like panicles comprising spikelets that ripen to the colour of old gold and remain beautiful well into winter, it is one of the most graceful of all ornamental grasses.

- **Height and spread:** 2.5m x 1.2m (8ft x 4ft)
- **Flowering time/colour:** Summer, purplish-green ripening to gold
- **Notes:** Although a tall plant, *S. gigantea* has a wonderful, see-through quality that enables it to be used nearer the front of a border than a plant of this size otherwise would.
- **Pests and diseases:** None.

Echium pininana

This plant, which hails from the Canary Islands, is so wonderfully monstrous that you cannot help but be impressed. *E. pininana* grows like a foxglove on steroids up to a massive 4m (13ft), forming a tottering column smothered in blue flowers. The ultimate talking point in the dry garden.

- **Height and spread:** 4m x 90cm (13ft x 35in)
- **Flowering time/colour:** Mid to late summer, blue
- **Notes:** A really cold wet winter will probably finish off *E. pininana*, so have a stock of plants grown from seed as back-up, and keep them under cover in winter.
- **Pests and diseases:** Young growth may be damaged by slugs.

Genista aetnensis

Found growing in the wild on the islands of Sardinia and Sicily (hence its common name of Mount Etna broom), this is a most graceful tree with weeping branches. Its linear leaves are only produced on young foliage and soon fall, so the whole effect of the plant is light and airy with little shade cast. When in full, fragrant flower, it is a beautiful sight to behold.

- **Height and spread:** 8m x 8m (25ft x 25ft)
- **Flowering time/colour:** Mid to late summer, yellow
- **Notes:** The fast way to kill *Genista* is to cut back into the old wood because they really don't like it.
- **Pests and diseases:** Aphids.

Semi to full shade
Six low-growing plants (below 75cm/30in)

Epimedium x versicolor 'Sulphureum'
One of a group of understated but invaluable garden hybrids with handsome foliage and attractive spring flowers, *E. x versicolor* 'Sulphureum' is a spreading, evergreen form that is especially useful for its tolerance of dry soils and conditions ranging from shade to full sun.

- **Height and spread:** 30cm x 1m (12in x 3ft)
- **Flowering time/colour:** Mid to late spring, yellow
- **Notes:** With the exception of *E. perralderianum* all *Epimedium* show their best if the old foliage is removed in late winter, allowing the flowers and attractive young foliage to show.
- **Pests and diseases:** May be affected by vine weevil.

Tiarella cordifolia
The common name of 'foam flower' gives the perfect description of this plant when it is covered in its frothy, creamy white flower racemes. Found in the wild in North America, this is a tough plant, capable of tolerating a range of conditions from full sun to deep shade and, once established, fairly dry soils. It will gradually spread to form a sheet of attractive foliage.

- **Height and spread:** 30cm x 30cm (12in x 12in) plus
- **Flowering time/colour:** Summer, creamy white
- **Notes:** Although tough and accommodating, *T. cordifolia* won't like standing in wet soil during winter.
- **Pests and diseases:** May be affected by slugs.

Trillium sessile
Trillium are among the most unusual of woodland plants, with foliage and flowers that are distinctive enough to make them instantly recognizable. *T. sessile* may not be the most glamorous of the trilliums, but is arguably the easiest to grow and tolerant of drier soil than others. *Trillium* are native to north-east USA.

- **Height and spread:** 30cm x 20cm (12in x 8in)
- **Flowering time/colour:** Late spring, red-maroon
- **Notes:** *Trillium* require moist acid to neutral soil and benefit from mulching with leaf mould in autumn.
- **Pests and diseases:** Slugs may affect young leaves.

Pachyphra macrophyllum
This is a charming little woodland plant, originating from north-east Turkey, which illuminates shaded corners with its pure white flowers. Although fairly slow growing, once established it will form a carpet of glossy, semi-evergreen foliage that is ideal for under-planting with spring bulbs.

- **Height and spread:** 30cm x 80cm (12in x 2½ft)
- **Flowering time/colour:** Early spring, white
- **Notes:** In the wild this plant favours deciduous woodland, where it gets plenty of leaf litter in autumn and reasonable light levels until the canopy closes in early summer.
- **Pests and diseases:** Slugs may be a problem.

Hosta 'Halcyon'
Hosta are surprisingly accommodating plants, found in the wild in conditions as varied as volcanic mountainsides and damp meadows and from full sun to deep shade. They are foliage plants par excellence but many forms are also blessed with lovely flowers. The garden hybrid *H.* 'Halcyon' has bright blue foliage, making it one of the best blue hostas.

- **Height and spread:** 40cm x 65cm (16in x 26in)
- **Flowering time/colour:** Summer, lavender-grey
- **Notes:** *Hosta* have a reputation of being the favourite food of slugs and snails. 'new gardening' principles and a biodiverse garden are the best way to control molluscs (see p.68).
- **Pests and diseases:** Slugs and snails.

Dryopteris erythrosora
One of the most strikingly beautiful ferns, hailing from Japan and China, *D. erythrosora* is especially lovely in spring when its new fronds are forming. These are coloured copper-red to dusky pink, eventually turning shiny dark green. Although preferring moist soils, it seems tolerant of drier conditions once established.

- **Height and spread:** 60cm x 40cm (24in x 16in)
- **Flowering time/colour:** Fertile fronds appear in spring
- **Notes:** Ferns need the best soil preparation you can give when planting and benefit from a generous mulch of leaf litter each year.
- **Pests and diseases:** None.

Semi to full shade

Six medium-sized plants (between 75cm/30in and 1.2m/4ft)

Polystichum setiferum

The cultivars of polystichum (see Notes) are among the most bizarrely named in the plant world. Fortunately, the parent plant is easier to pronounce and simpler to grow, preferring fertile soil but also tolerating deep shade and dry conditions once it is fully established. Originates from Europe.

- **Height and spread:** 1.2m x 90cm (4ft x 35in)
- **Flowering time/colour:** Fertile fronds in Spring
- **Notes:** Of the many oddly named varieties – 'Plumosomultilobum' for one – the compact form 'Herrenhausen' is one of the loveliest, and at 50cm (20in) high is ideal for smaller spaces.
- **Pests and diseases:** None of note.

Digitalis purpurea

A common woodland plant throughout much of Europe, the foxglove is to my mind uncommonly beautiful, capable of colonizing large areas by setting and shedding prodigious amounts of seed each year. This leads to great variability in flower colour, further adding to its charm.

- **Height and spread:** Varies from 1m-2m x 60cm (3ft-6½ft x 24in)
- **Flowering time/colour:** Early summer, from white to purple
- **Notes:** *D. purpurea* can be either biennial or a short-lived perennial. To ensure continued stock, allow it to self-seed, but also collect some seed for sowing into pots or into the ground.
- **Pests and diseases:** Leaf spot and powdery mildew.

Polygonatum x hybridum

This graceful woodland hybrid has small, snowdrop-like flowers that hang like bells beneath arching stems, making it both distinctive and instantly recognizable. In really good, moist soil it can reach 1.5m (5ft), but in my experience – and in less rich soil – 1.2m (4ft) is more usual. *Polygonatum* originates from Yunnan and Sichuan in China.

- **Height and spread:** 1.2m x 1.2m (4ft x 4ft)
- **Flowering time/colour:** Late spring to summer, white
- **Notes:** The one big drawback with *Polygonatum* is sawfly larvae damage, which can be so extreme as to lead to defoliation. Squash the larvae between thumb and forefinger as soon as you spot them.
- **Pests and diseases:** Sawfly larvae.

Anemone hupehensis 'Hadspen Abundance'

The 'wind flowers', which are native to China, are some of the prettiest and most useful of late summer flowers, tough enough to spread via suckering shoots to form natural colonies. *A. hupehensis* 'Hadspen Abundance' has dark pink blooms held on wiry stems above attractive, dark green foliage.

- **Height and spread:** 90cm x 40cm (35in x 16in)
- **Flowering time/colour:** Mid to late summer, dark reddish-pink
- **Notes:** Because of their rambunctious nature, I plant wind flowers with other robust plants that can tolerate their spreading tendencies.
- **Pests and diseases:** Powdery mildew and slugs

Lysimachia clethroides

One of the most attractive features of this plant from China and Korea is its flower racemes, which are pendant and curved in bud but gradually straighten to almost vertical with a slight curve to each tip, making it one of the most graceful plants for sun or semi-shade.

- **Height and spread:** 90cm x 60cm (35in x 24in)
- **Flowering time/colour:** Mid to late summer, white
- **Notes:** *L. clethroides* will benefit from protection from the heat of the midday sun, disliking soil that dries out, so is best sited in the lee of trees or in a border that catches the early morning sun.
- **Pests and diseases:** Slugs and snails may damage foliage.

Deschampsia cespitosa 'Goldschleier'

The parent plant of this attractive grass can often be found growing at the edges of woodland clearings, where its silvery flower spikelets illuminate the shade. The hybrid *D. cespitosa* 'Goldschleier' has bright silvery yellow spikelets with a graceful, airy form. The flowerheads turn golden in the autumn giving it a long season of interest.

- **Height and spread:** 1.2m x 1.2m (4ft x 4ft)
- **Flowering time/colour:** Early to late summer, purple, turning silvery yellow with age
- **Notes:** The majority of deciduous grasses are best divided in spring or early summer rather than autumn.
- **Pests and diseases:** None.

Semi to full shade
Six taller plants (above 1.2m/4ft)

Viburnum tinus 'Gwenllian'

This compact evergreen shrub has been a mainstay of 'landscape' plantings for some time, and so could be viewed as being too municipal for gardens. But that is to ignore its strengths; good foliage all year round, a profusion of pink-flushed white flowers that open from pink buds, followed by dark blue-black fruit.

- **Height and spread:** 3m x 3m (10ft x 10ft)
- **Flowering time/colour:** Spring, white flushed with pink
- **Notes:** *Viburnum tinus* cultivars are tolerant of very hard pruning, including cutting back hard to the ground (stooling).
- **Pests and diseases:** Trouble free.

Miscanthus sinensis 'Silberfeder'

In northerly gardens, *Miscanthus* can sometimes be shy to flower. However, this cultivar is one of the most reliable and free flowering. Although often thought of as a plant for a sunny border, in the wild *Miscanthus* can be found growing at woodland edges, where it looks perfectly at home.

- **Height and spread:** 2m plus x 1.5m (6½ft plus x 5ft)
- **Flowering time/colour:** Late summer to mid autumn, silver to pale brown
- **Notes:** *Miscanthus* look good right through winter and so should be left standing until early spring, then cut back to within a few centimetres of the ground.
- **Pests and diseases:** None.

Osmunda regalis

Rightly known as the royal fern, this is one of the largest of the hardy ferns, and a plant of great presence and beauty. It is tolerant of full sun but only if planted in permanently wet soil or at the margins of a pond - otherwise a shaded spot and moist soil will do. It is widespread in temperate regions.

- **Height and spread:** 2m x 4m (6½ft x 13ft)
- **Flowering time/colour:** Fertile fronds in summer, rust-coloured
- **Notes:** The Victorian craze for ferns almost put paid to the royal fern in the wild in some European countries, but in an interesting reversal it is now escaping back to the wild - from gardens.
- **Pests and diseases:** None.

Ligularia przewalskii

This handsome perennial is as impressive in leaf as it is in flower. Large, deeply cut leaves are topped with towering, dark purple stems bearing racemes of clear yellow flowers. It is best planted where there is plenty of space to appreciate its aristocratic elegance. A native of northern China.

- **Height and spread:** 2m x 1m (6½ft x 3ft)
- **Flowering time/colour:** Mid to late summer, yellow
- **Notes:** *L. przewalskii* is prone to wilting in soils that dry out or if given too much sun. Provide a thick mulch and shelter from the midday sun to keep it happy - dappled shade is ideal.
- **Pests and diseases:** Slugs and snails can damage young foliage.

Rodgersia podophylla

Thriving at the margins of a pond or a woodland edge, *Rodgersia* are impressive foliage plants, hailing from Korea and Japan. This form has crinkled, dark purple-bronze leaves when young that become smoother and green as they mature. The flowers are greenish-white, and in autumn the foliage turns bronze red.

- **Height and spread:** 1.4m x 1.8m (4½ft x 6ft)
- **Flowering time/colour:** Mid- to late summer, greenish-white
- **Notes:** *Rodgersia* grow best where there is some protection from cold winds, as their large leaves are quite easily damaged. They prefer moist soil but will tolerate drier conditions in a sheltered spot.
- **Pests and diseases:** Slugs may damage emerging foliage.

Aruncus dioicus

A tough, robust plant that seems capable of putting up with anything from deep shade to full sun and moist to dry soil, *A. dioicus* has attractive, fern-like foliage and big panicles of creamy white flowers. Found in the wild from Europe to Siberia and eastern North America.

- **Height and spread:** 2m x 1.2m (6½ft x 4ft)
- **Flowering time/colour:** Early to midsummer, creamy white
- **Notes:** *A. dioicus* is a dioecious perennial - plants are either male or female. The flower panicles vary accordingly, the male being whiter and more upright, the female greener and pendant.
- **Pests and diseases:** Sawfly larvae can damage foliage.

Bulbs
For naturalizing in grass

Galanthus nivalis
The common snowdrop, a European native, is one of the most evocative of all wild plants and has, consequently, become a plant around which an entire subculture of enthusiasts has built up. Huge sheets of snowdrops make for a truly awesome sight in winter and they have a lovely honey fragrance.

- **Height and spread:** 10cm x 10cm (4in x 4in)
- **Flowering time/colour:** Winter, white with green
- **Notes:** Snowdrops are best increased through division, and although this is usually carried out after flowering they will tolerate being split before, during and after flowering.
- **Pests and diseases:** Narcissus bulb fly.

Ornithogalum nutans
This vigorous, tough bulbous perennial can, along with Camassia, provide the last major display from a spring bulb planting in grass. It is taller than earlier bulbs as well, thus ensuring it will be visible above the grass, which by late spring will be in active growth. Native to Europe and south-west Asia.

- **Height and spread:** 50cm x 10cm (20in x 4in)
- **Flowering time/colour:** Spring, white
- **Notes:** O. nutans can become something of a pest in borders due to prolific seeding, but in grass this tendency can be a positive advantage, creating gradually spreading colonies over time.
- **Pests and diseases:** None.

Crocus tommasinianus
Flowering from late winter into spring, C. tommasinianus can vary greatly in colour, and there are a number of cultivars available in which this colour variation is stable. Spreading by offset bulbils and seed, it will quickly form colonies where naturalized. Grows wild in central Europe.

- **Height and spread:** 8cm x 2.5cm (3½in x ¾in)
- **Flowering time/colour:** Late winter to spring, variable, pale silvery lilac to purple and deep red
- **Notes:** Some cultivars are sterile – such as C. tommasinianus 'Ruby Giant' – which means they cannot spread by seed.
- **Pests and diseases:** Crocus are a food source for mice, voles, squirrels and some birds.

Erythronium dens-canis
A pretty spring flower that appears delicate yet is remarkably robust. E. dens-canis is variable in flower from white through pink to lilac and the petals of each bloom are recurved – that is they bend back on themselves. The foliage is mid-green with brown marbling. Tolerant of dappled shade.

- **Height and spread:** 10cm x 10cm (4in x 4in)
- **Flowering time/colour:** Spring, variable, white to lilac
- **Notes:** Unlike the more exotic Japanese and North American Erythronium, this European/Asian E. dens-canis revels in the tougher conditions posed by grass. It can often die out if the soil is too rich.
- **Pests and diseases:** Slugs can damage young foliage.

Narcissus obvallaris
The best daffodils for naturalizing are those with uncomplicated flowers and compact growth, and N. obvallaris has both. Found wild in south Wales and western Europe, it is vigorous enough to build up into large colonies over time, making it one of the best daffodils for grass. Tolerant of dappled shade.

- **Height and spread:** 30cm x 10cm (12in x 4in)
- **Flowering time/colour:** Early spring, golden-yellow
- **Notes:** As with all naturalized bulbs it is essential not to cut the grass until the foliage of the bulbs has fully died back, usually by midsummer depending on the plants used.
- **Pests and diseases:** Narcissus bulb fly.

Camassia cusickii
Hailing from north-east Oregon, USA, C. cusickii is the tallest of the bulbous plants here and one that creates a beautiful haze of blue above the grass when planted in quantity. The cultivar 'Zwanenburg' has even deeper blue flowers and is also suitable for naturalizing. The slight variation between parent and cultivar can make for a subtle colour shift when used together.

- **Height and spread:** 70cm x 10cm (28in x 4in)
- **Flowering time/colour:** Late spring, steel-blue
- **Notes:** Camassia enjoys fertile, moisture retentive soil, making it suitable for naturalizing in gardens with clay or loam soils.
- **Pests and diseases:** None.

Full sun or partial shade
Six low-growing naturalistic perennials (at or below 75cm/30in)

Nepeta racemosa
A tough, drought-tolerant and long-flowering plant with aromatic foliage that is much loved by cats (felines are likely to devastate the foliage if they get the taste for it). *N. racemosa* makes the perfect border edge plant. Native to Caucasus.

- **Height and spread:** 30cm x 40cm (12in x 16in)
- **Flowering time/colour:** Summer, violet to lilac-blue
- **Notes:** *N. racemosa* will produce flowers sporadically over a long period during summer. Cutting back hard after the first flush of flowers means strong new foliage will be followed by a full second flowering.
- **Pests and diseases:** Mildew on the foliage in dry weather.

Crocosmia x crocosmiiflora 'Solfatare'
There are many crocosmia available in a range of sizes and colours but 'Solfatare' marries beautiful, grassy, bronze-tinged foliage with apricot-yellow flowers. Considered borderline hardy a few years ago, it is now reliably hardy in all but the coldest, wettest temperate gardens. It comes originally from Caucasus.

- **Height and spread:** 60cm x 10cm (24in x 4in)
- **Flowering time/colour:** Summer, apricot-yellow
- **Notes:** Crocosmia are good plants to grow 'through' others, such as low-growing geranium. The apricot-yellow flowers can be set off beautifully against the intense blue of *Geranium* 'Rozanne'.
- **Pests and diseases:** Can be affected by red spider mite.

Geranium 'Rozanne'
In my experience this is about the longest in flower of all hardy geraniums, starting in early summer and still producing flowers when the first frosts arrive. It has deeply cut foliage marked with dark blotching and intensely blue blooms.

- **Height and spread:** 50cm x 60cm (20in x 24in)
- **Flowering time/colour:** Summer to autumn, blue
- **Notes:** Unlike other geranium there is no need to cut *G.* 'Rozanne' back hard to encourage a second flush of flower, as it never seems to stop flowering!
- **Pests and diseases:** Vine weevil larvae, slugs, snails and powdery mildew in hot, dry conditions.

Echinacea 'Art's Pride'
One of a number of new *Echinacea* on the market, 'Art's Pride' isn't the easiest to grow as it requires faster draining soil than its brethren. But if you have that, and plenty of sun, it will reward you with its deeply cut flowers of the loveliest burnt orange colour. A drought-tolerant garden hybrid.

- **Height and spread:** 50cm x 30cm (20in x 12in)
- **Flowering time/colour:** Summer, burnt-orange
- **Notes:** Adding plenty of grit into the soil before planting. Dress around the neck of the plant with more grit to reduce the risk of rot and attack by slugs.
- **Pests and diseases:** Prone to damage from slugs and snails.

Achillea millefolium 'Fanal'
Achillea are useful front to mid-border garden hybrids. Their flat umbels of flowers are perfect for contrasting with vertical plants such as *Lythrum* or those with globe-shaped flowers, including *Echinops*. *A. millefolium* 'Fanal' has bright red flowers that can be hard to place in a planting, but associate well with blue, violet and magenta.

- **Height and spread:** 75cm x 60cm (30in x 24in)
- **Flowering time/colour:** Summer, red
- **Notes:** Divide every three or four years. If cut back after the first flush of flower they will produce a full second flush.
- **Pests and diseases:** Powdery mildew can affect the foliage in dry weather.

Hemerocallis 'Burning Daylight'
There are a bewildering number of day lily hybrids on the market, and although this one has been around for some time, it is still one of the best. Intense orange flowers show beautifully against purple, violet and magenta, and 'Burning Daylight' produces them in spades.

- **Height and spread:** 50cm x 60m (20in x 24in)
- **Flowering time/colour:** Summer, orange
- **Notes:** Try jazzing up a salad with a few day lily flowers, which are perfectly edible (although tasteless). Wash thoroughly before use to remove any lurking pollen beetles!
- **Pests and diseases:** None of note.

Full sun or partial shade
Six medium-sized naturalistic perennials (between 75cm/30in and 1.5m/5ft)

Echinacea purpurea 'Magnus'

The name *Echinacea* derives from the same root as echidna: meaning a spiny, hedgehog-like mammal. Looking at the central, bristly, cone-shaped flower disc from which its horizontal ray florets are held it is easy to see why. A tough yet beautiful plant that deserves a place in any planting, naturalistic or not.

- **Height and spread:** 1.3m x 50cm (4½ft x 20in)
- **Flowering time/colour:** Summer to autumn, deep purple
- **Notes:** *Echinacea* are among the most 'choppable' of 'Chelsea Chop' plants (see p.122).
- **Pests and diseases:** Slugs and snails can damage young foliage.

Perovskia 'Blue Spire'

Perovskia provides the perfect foil for the intense flower colour of *Echinacea purpurea* 'Magnus' and *Knautia macedonica*. The cool mixture of silver foliage and violet-blue flowers, allied to its airy, see-through form, make this plant a must-have. In addition, it is tolerant of coastal sea spray and is drought-proof.

- **Height and spread:** 1.2m x 1m (4ft x 3ft)
- **Flowering time/colour:** Late summer into autumn, violet-blue
- **Notes:** During winter the naked, grey stems of *P.* 'Blue Spire' create a similar effect to those of *Rubus*, but on a scale more suitable for a very small garden.
- **Pests and diseases:** None.

Calamagrostis brachytricha

One of the later warm-season grasses, *C. brachytricha* is compact enough to be accommodated in most gardens. In late summer this handsome grass produces bronzy pink, foxtail-like inflorescences that gradually fade to light grey, and in autumn light have a ghostly, ethereal effect.

- **Height and spread:** 1.2m x 80cm, variable (4ft x 2½ft)
- **Flowering time/colour:** Late summer, green fading to bronzy-pink
- **Notes:** I have found this grass to be completely drought-proof, tolerating high temperatures and low rainfall with apparent ease.
- **Pests and diseases:** None.

Helenium 'Rubinzwerg'

There can be a touch of snobbery when it comes to *Helenium*, as some gardeners find them rather coarse plants. But their long-flowering, trouble-free nature makes them perfect for the naturalistic approach. *H.* 'Rubinzwerg' has flowers of reddish-brown from summer into autumn.

- **Height and spread:** 1.2m x 70cm (4ft x 28in)
- **Flowering time/colour:** Summer to autumn, reddish-brown
- **Notes:** *Helenium* benefit from support by twigs or other plants, such as *Miscanthus*. Or use the 'Chelsea Chop' (see p.122).
- **Pests and diseases:** None.

Monarda 'Gardenview Scarlet'

Despite having a reputation for developing mildew, the long-flowering period during summer, followed by straw-coloured stems topped with blackened seedheads in winter make *Monarda* well worth growing. This cultivar has proven to be the least prone to mildew, and has beautiful bright red blooms.

- **Height and spread:** 1.2m x 80cm (4ft x 2½ft)
- **Flowering time/colour:** Summer, bright red
- **Notes:** The aromatic foliage of *Monarda* can be used to make a tea and, if steeped in hot water overnight, the fresh leaves make an infusion for the bath. Check with a herbalist before trying this out.
- **Pests and diseases:** Young foliage can be damaged by slugs; some cultivars are prone to mildew in hot weather.

Gaura lindheimeri

For some reason this plant isn't grown as widely as it should be. Its butterfly-like flowers are borne on thin, wiry stems, so that the flowers appear to dance in a breeze. It is lovely when allowed to cascade through other plants and is drought-proof. It needs well-drained soil.

- **Height and spread:** 1.5m x 90cm (5ft x 35in)
- **Flowering time/colour:** Summer, pink buds, opening white then fading to pink
- **Notes:** At 1.5m (5ft), *G. lindheimeri* has an arching habit, making it suitable for planting close to the front of a border.
- **Pests and diseases:** None.

Full sun or partial shade
Six taller naturalistic perennials (above 1.5m/5ft)

Veronicastrum virginicum 'Fascination'
One of those plants for exploring the vertical axis! Although tall at 1.8m (6ft), *V. virginicum* 'Fascination' is quite narrow, making it suitable for a smaller garden where height is sought. Its slender racemes of mauve-pink flowers add to the upright, sky-searching look. A fairly drought-tolerant garden hybrid.

- **Height and spread:** 1.8m x 50cm (6ft x 20in)
- **Flowering time/colour:** Summer to autumn, mauve-pink
- **Notes:** The stems and flowers can become strangely flattened and curving - a phenomenon called fasciation, where cells mutate and create strange growing habits - something to show to friends!
- **Pests and diseases:** Mildew.

Miscanthus sinensis 'Kaskade'
An especially graceful form of *Miscanthus*, which I grow at home near the edge of a path as a 'punctuation mark', and where its fine, arching, feathery flowers cascade, positioned to catch the late afternoon sun. In winter it lends structural interest to the garden, and the crown and stems make an ideal habitat for overwintering insects.

- **Height and spread:** 1.8m x 70cm (6ft x 28in)
- **Flowering time/colour:** Late summer, reddish-pink
- **Notes:** I prefer to provide a little space between individual plants of *Miscanthus* to allow light around them, rather than clumping them into a group, where they can appear a little heavy.
- **Pests and diseases:** None.

Sanguisorba officinalis 'Red Thunder'
Sanguisorba are wild looking plants, usually found growing either in meadows, prairies or at woodland edges. Many are early- or mid-summer-flowering, but the garden hybrid 'Red Thunder' is one of the latest, gracing the garden with its thimble-like ruby flowers held on upright stems from late summer into autumn.

- **Height and spread:** 2.7m x 1m (9ft x 3ft)
- **Flowering time/colour:** Late summer and autumn, ruby-red
- **Notes:** The small but lovely flowers of *Sanguisorba* look attractive cascading through the flower heads of *Miscanthus*.
- **Pests and diseases:** Slugs may attack the young foliage.

Thalictrum 'Elin'
A big, purposeful garden hybrid that is worth growing for its foliage and stems alone; the leaves are red in spring, becoming glaucous blue before dark flower stems surge up to 2.3m (7ft), topped by airy flowers. It prefers shade in the hottest part of the day or a deep mulch to keep the roots cool.

- **Height and spread:** 2.3m x 60cm (7ft x 24in)
- **Flowering time/colour:** Summer, mauve and cream
- **Notes:** *Thalictrum* can take a season or two to settle in, especially if planted late in the season or moved - which it seems to dislike.
- **Pests and diseases:** None.

Eupatorium purpureum
A statuesque plant found in damp pasture and woodland edges in North America, *E. purpureum* has attractive, purple-tinged foliage and stems that are topped with large, domed flower clusters that are usually pinkish-purple but can range from pink to white. Rich in pollen and nectar, the flowers are loved by butterflies, bees and moths.

- **Height and spread:** 2.2m x 1m (7ft x 3ft)
- **Flowering time/colour:** Mid-summer, pinkish-purple
- **Notes:** A great transitional plant, *E. purpureum* can be used to create a wild look in a garden, or connect a gardened space with surrounding countryside.
- **Pests and diseases:** Slugs and snails can damage young foliage.

Rudbeckia laciniata 'Herbstonne'
A big, bold and free-flowering garden hybrid *R. laciniata* 'Herbstonne' has great character and presence. It has attractive, glossy foliage that from mid-summer is topped with distinctive daisy flowers with deeply cut ray florets and conspicuous, conical disc florets.

- **Height and spread:** 2m x 90cm (6½ft x 35in)
- **Flowering time/colour:** Mid-summer to autumn, yellow
- **Notes:** I grow this plant with a similarly big and colourful companion, *Kniphofia* 'Prince Igor' - the combination of orange and strong yellow is certainly bold.
- **Pests and diseases:** Slugs can damage young foliage.

Winter interest

Six low- to medium-sized plants for full sun or partial shade

Cornus alba 'Sibirica'

There is a range of new *C. alba* cultivars available, but 'Sibirica', a garden hybrid which has been around for years, has stood the test of time as a beautiful, easy-to-grow plant. The glossy red stems are a real treat in winter, preceded by good autumn colour.

- **Height and spread:** 3m x 3m (10ft x 10ft) but with annual pruning usually attains 1.5m x 1.2m (5ft x 4ft)
- **Flowering time/colour:** Late spring to early summer, white
- **Notes:** Rather than hard pruning to the ground to ensure good stem colour, I find it more effective to cut the plant back to 20cm (8in) from the ground, or to cut just half the stems back hard.
- **Pests and diseases:** Generally trouble-free.

Sarcococca confusa

A highly fragrant winter-flowering shrub from China, *S. confusa* also has attractive glossy foliage resembling that of box (the common name is sweet box). The flowers are inconspicuous, making the power of their scent all the more surprising, and on clear winter days, it is a seasonal garden highlight.

- **Height and spread:** 2m x 1m (6½ft x 3ft)
- **Flowering time/colour:** Winter, creamy white
- **Notes:** With its tight, dense growth and good foliage, *Sarcococca* makes an interesting alternative to clipped topiary, and can be lightly pruned after flowering to enhance the shape.
- **Pests and diseases:** None.

Erica carnea cultivars

Heathers have suffered from the stigma of being fashionable plants 30 years ago – making them deeply unfashionable in the intervening years. But there are few better winter-flowering plants. *E. carnea* cultivars have flowers in a range of colours and many have attractively coloured foliage.

- **Height and spread:** 40cm x 40cm (16in x 16in)
- **Flowering time/colour:** Winter, white through light purple to deep wine-red
- **Notes:** Try planting heathers with ornamental grasses and stem colour plants rather than conifers.
- **Pests and diseases:** Can be affected by fungal infections.

Carex oshimensis 'Evergold'

Although not a winter plant as such, this garden hybrid sedge is one of the best golden variegated foliage ground cover plants. It also retains its smart appearance through winter, making it a great foil for dark- or red-stemmed shrubs including *Cornus alba* 'Kesselringii' and *Salix daphnoides* 'Meikle', as well as purple-flowered forms of hellebore.

- **Height and spread:** 30cm x 40cm (12in x 16in)
- **Flowering time/colour:** N/A
- **Notes:** Unlike many other golden-leaved plants, *C. oshimensis* 'Evergold' seems less prone to scorch, making it suitable for sunny locations.
- **Pests and diseases:** None.

Helleborus x hybridus cultivars

An ever increasing group as breeders exploit the tendency of hybrid hellebores to, well, hybridize. Colours range from primrose yellow 'Citron' to dark purple 'Pluto', with many shades in between. Keep an eye out for seedlings in your own garden – something interesting might crop up!

- **Height and spread:** 45cm x 45cm (18in x 18in)
- **Flowering time/colour:** Winter, from purple to greenish-yellow
- **Notes:** Removing the old leaves prior to flowering will reduce the risk of fungal diseases such as black rot and leaf spot and help to set off the flowers to best effect.
- **Pests and diseases:** Slugs and snails, black rot, leaf spot.

Euphorbia amygdaloides 'Purpurea'

An evergreen garden hybrid that has dark purple foliage – the perfect counterpoint to golden *Carex* and *Erica*, as well as light-stemmed *Cornus* such as *C. sanguinea* 'Midwinter Fire'. In early spring the stems are topped by acid yellow flowers, making a dramatic contrast with the foliage.

- **Height and spread:** 40cm x 40cm (16in x 16in)
- **Flowering time/colour:** Spring, acid-yellow
- **Notes:** Euphorbia have milky sap that can cause dermatitis in some people, so you should always wear gloves and eye protection when pruning.
- **Pests and diseases:** Grey mould may affect the foliage.

Winter interest
Six medium-sized to taller plants (full sun or partial shade)

Chimonanthus praecox

The wintersweet, native to China, is among the most fragrant of all winter plants, its scent wafting a long way on clear, sunny winter days. During the rest of the year it has little to offer – reasonably attractive if unremarkable foliage, but it is worth growing for those wonderfully fragrant flowers.

- **Height and spread:** 4m x 3m (13ft x 10ft)
- **Flowering time/colour:** Winter, sulphur-yellow
- **Notes:** Perhaps the best way to grow wintersweet is as a wall trained shrub, where its fragrant blooms can be enjoyed in winter and its foliage can provide a backdrop for other plants.
- **Pests and diseases:** None.

Helleborus argutifolius

Although less glamorous in flower than other hellebores, *H. argutifolius* is a plant with great architectural presence and the ability to cope with hot, dry and sunny locations as well as dry, semi-shaded sites. Its pale green flowers and serrated foliage look good in either setting. Native to Corsica.

- **Height and spread:** 1.2m x 1m (4ft x 3ft)
- **Flowering time/colour:** Late winter, early spring, pale green
- **Notes:** Although appearing evergreen, *H. argutifolius* actually produces biennial foliage. Remove any old, diseased leaves each winter to keep the plant healthy.
- **Pests and diseases:** Slugs and snails, black rot, leaf spot.

Rubus thibetanus

Another plant that owes its winter interest to the presence of a thick white bloom on its stems, *R. thibetanus* is better behaved than its larger cousins *R. biflorus* and *R. cockburnianus*, both of which tend to 'run'. It has the added benefit of attractive, fern-like foliage, and purplish red summer flowers followed by black fruit. A native of western China.

- **Height and spread:** 2.5m x 2.5m (8ft x 8ft)
- **Flowering time/colour:** Summer, purplish-red
- **Notes:** Rubus can be hard pruned back to the ground, keeping the overall size down and ensuring a succession of fresh, white bloomed stems.
- **Pests and diseases:** Grey mould can affect the foliage.

Salix acutifolia 'Blue Streak'

As with a number of winter-interest plants, the garden hybrid *S. acutifolia* 'Blue Streak' has a bloom that coats the stems; in this case the stems are blue-black and the bloom bluish white.

- **Height and spread:** 10m x 12m (33ft x 40ft), but with annual pruning usually attaining around 2.5m x 1.5m (8ft x 5ft)
- **Flowering time/colour:** Early spring, silver
- **Notes:** Interesting effects can be created by allowing a single 'leader' stem to form, to which the branches are pruned each year. This allows space underneath for bulbs or ground cover plants.
- **Pests and diseases:** Aphids, caterpillars, willow scale and anthracnose may affect willows.

Viburnum x bodnantense 'Charles Lamont'

Winter-flowering *Viburnum* are 'must have' plants if space allows, their beautiful, frost-resistant blooms filling the garden with fragrance on still, sunny winter days. These hybrids are easy to grow.

- **Height and spread:** 3m x 2m (10ft x 6½ft)
- **Flowering time/colour:** Winter, bright pink
- **Notes:** Although requiring little pruning to thrive, I prefer to remove up to a third of the oldest stems each year after flowering to prevent the plant becoming too congested.
- **Pests and diseases:** Honey fungus and viburnum beetle may be a problem.

Prunus maackii

Although the birches are usually considered the finest of winter-interest trees, along with *Acer griseum*, two cherries are of note; *P. maackii* and *P. serrula*. Originally from north-east Asia, *P. maackii* has peeling, orangey brown bark that is conspicuous in winter, and also bears fragrant white blossom followed by black fruit.

- **Height and spread:** 10m x 8m (33ft x 25ft)
- **Flowering time/colour:** Spring, white
- **Notes:** To bring out the best in trees with good stem colour, a little intervention is required with a sponge and warm water, to wash away algae that can spoil the effect.
- **Pests and diseases:** A number, including attacking bullfinches.

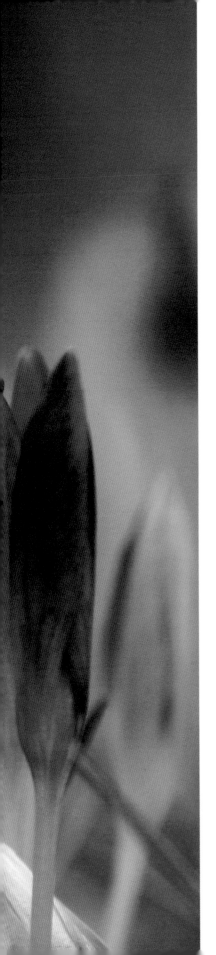

REFERENCE

Reference
Further information

Learning about the process of creating a garden has taught me much more than just gardening, and I have been fortunate indeed to have contact with so many enlightened people who have helped guide and inform me. In this section I have listed some – by no means all – of the books that have made a significant impact on my way of thinking, along with useful websites that relate to each chapter of the book. These should help you if you wish to carry out further research and deepen your knowledge not only of gardening, but the environment, wildlife, recycling, permaculture and so on. There is also a chart for quick reference prompts. For me it is the variety of other subjects and issues that gardening touches which makes gardening so important today; not as an insular hobby, but as a significant factor that helps contribute to our understanding of the planet, and a means by which we can put something back of value, rather than just take.

Crocus tommasinianus **(left)** is a beautiful crocus that is easy-to-grow and long-lived. It has goblet-shaped flowers that appear in late winter/early spring. It thrives under trees such as beeches and red maples, though it can also be planted in lawns, where it tends to naturalize, forming large colonies.

The gardening year
Spring & summer

SPRING

Can you dig it?
✳ Carry out the final cultivation of new borders that have been made using the 'layer cake' method (see p.41).
✳ As soon as the foliage of perennials and bulbs begins to show and providing the soil is neither waterlogged nor frozen, mulch borders using an appropriate soil improver.
✳ Try to vary the material each year depending on your soil type, any deficiencies it has and the plants you are growing. Use lightweight materials to improve drainage and heavier organic material to improve the nutrient levels and moisture retention in thin soils.
✳ Take care not to mulch over the crowns of perennials. It is a good idea to use an inverted pot to protect them if need be.
✳ Plants that are prone to slug and snail damage or neck rot can be given a dressing of grit immediately around the base. Although, it won't stop molluscs entirely, it can help.

The wildlife hotel
✳ In early spring cut back the grasses and perennials that have been left standing in your garden through winter. Put the material near the back of a border or under a hedge to provide a habitat for insects.
✳ Cut short lengths of hollow perennial stems to make homes for invertebrates. Secure them with string into bundles and then place these bundles of stems in the cracks in walls or between the rocks in a rock garden.
✳ Put up nest boxes for insectivorous birds close to where you have problems with aphids.
✳ Keep bird feeders well stocked. This will attract a range of birds – including those that eat seeds and insects – to your garden.
✳ Keep an eye out for animals that have emerged from hibernation unseasonably early – in the UK the hedgehog is the most commonly seen mammal that hibernates – and put out appropriate food for them. Your local wildlife organization can advise you.
✳ Avoid disturbing the nests of birds and mammals that may be in hedges, trees or evergreen plants in your garden.

Planting
✳ Lift and divide perennials that have become too big, died out in the centre or are no longer flowering well. Late spring is also the optimum time for dividing grasses from warm climates, such as *Miscanthus*.
✳ Don't forget that when re-planting divisions they will require the same careful soil preparation, mulching and watering-in as pot-bought plants.
✳ Prepare the soil for direct-sown annuals and carry out a first sowing during late spring.
✳ Plant autumn-flowering bulbs now, either naturalized in grass or as border plants.
✳ When buying new plants check that they are suitable for the soil and microclimate.
✳ In late spring, plant drought-tolerant containers for the season ahead, using water-storing granules to ensure watering is minimal.
✳ Prune winter-flowering plants and cut back winter stem-interest plants, leaving at least 30cm (12in) of stem above ground level to ensure early leafing. This will provide the plant with the food it needs and will also minimize feeding and watering. Don't forget to mulch with organic matter after pruning.

Reuse, recycle, sustain
✳ Install a water butt or rainwater harvesting system for the year ahead.

SUMMER

Can you dig it?

✳ Your well-mulched borders should be fairly free of weeds, but once they do start to appear try hand pulling rather than hoeing, as this will reduce soil moisture loss.

✳ Use the clippings from your lawn to provide additional mulch around trees or shrubs or beneath a hedge that hasn't been mulched.

The wildlife hotel

✳ In hot, dry weather put a bird bath out for visiting animals. This can be a very important source of water for birds, and is definitely not wasteful.

✳ Hold off from cutting your hedges – they will still be providing nest sites for birds.

✳ Make or buy invertebrate habitat boxes to provide over-wintering habitats for beneficial insects. Putting them up in late summer means they are more likely to be 'found' and used.

Reuse, recycle, sustain

✳ Once the temperature starts to rise and rainfall decreases, remove the grass box from your mower to allow the clippings to mulch back into the lawn. This will return some of the moisture and nutrients back into the sward.

✳ Don't over feed lawns with spring/summer fertilizer – this will promote lush growth but will also require a lot of watering to maintain.

✳ If your lawn is small, why not offer your powered lawnmower as a swap for a push mower? And if you only have a few metres of hedge, do you really need powered hedge trimmers?

✳ If you are planning to replace garden furniture or features, why not see what is available from local suppliers first, or log on to a recycling website – or even visit a scrap yard for inspiration. You might be able to find a new home for the items you are replacing as well as finding replacements.

Planting

✳ Avoid planting at this time of year. Only plant if the weather is damp enough to allow it, or you can be absolutely sure that you can keep newly planted plants supplied with only harvested water, or that the plants concerned are drought-proof and will only need watering-in and no subsequent irrigation.

✳ Carry out a second sowing of direct-sown annuals in early summer to ensure a good succession of flowering. This is best done when the soil is moist after rain or heavy dew.

✳ In late summer, cut down the grass and foliage where naturalized spring bulbs have flowered. The later you can leave this the better – assuming there are no autumn bulbs to come, in which case an early summer cut will be required. The long grass provides a habitat for animals. It will look unsightly and scorched after cutting if done when the weather is hot.

The gardening year
Autumn & winter

South by southwest?
✳ Crown lift evergreen shrubs to improve light levels beneath. This can be carried out from late autumn through to winter.

Can you dig it?
✳ This is the best time of year to start soil preparation for a new border. Mark out the shape of the border following the suggestions in *Garden Design* (see Chapter 11) and prepare the soil, having first checked pH and soil type, with the advice given in *Can You Dig It?* (see Chapter 2). There is no reason you cannot apply a second mulch at this time, providing the soil conditions are suitable.

The wildlife hotel
✳ Cut hedges, having first checked to ensure there are no nesting birds remaining - some species can have second or third broods quite late in the year. Don't forget to provide a good layer of mulch beneath the hedge when conditions allow.
✳ Make a simple log pile, or, if you feel more adventurous, why not consider making a log pile bench as described in this book (see pp.72-73)?

✳ Cold, crisp autumn days are perfect for the one bit of serious digging that I would advocate: making a pond. If you have the space and the time to do so, it will repay all your efforts and become the hub of all the wildlife activity in your garden.

Planting
✳ Now is the time to cut mini meadows. First check that any amphibians or small mammals (they may not be immediately visible) have vacated the area.
✳ If you don't have a mini meadow but want one, now is the perfect time to start the process.
✳ Plant potted perennials, trees, shrubs and dry spring-flowering bulbs (which can be planted up until Christmas).
✳ Plant a mini garlic pot on a cool windowsill or outdoors.
✳ Autumn provides a second opportunity to lift and divide perennials, or simply move plants around, including smaller woody plants that have yet to establish extensive roots systems. However, ornamental grasses are better left untouched until spring.

Garden design
✳ If you haven't already started one, begin a photographic record of your garden through the seasons to help you to make adjustments to areas that need improvement or change. Attempting to do this in spring without some kind of visual record can be difficult - our memories can often fail!
✳ Using your photographic record as reference, reorganize borders to improve structure, texture and colour.
✳ Planning a new border? Try using the 'cutting corners' method, mowing out the shape of your proposed new planting on the ground and then living with it for a while before deciding whether to commit, or try something new.
✳ Increase your skills by enrolling on a course to learn willow weaving, hedge laying or dry stone walling. It doesn't matter if you only learn the basics; you can employ a craftsperson to do work for you and help out as they do it. Organizations such as the RHS run courses.

WINTER

South by southwest?
✳ In late winter, after cutting back perennials, pruning and tying in climbing plants, repaint walls and structures (using light-reflective paint in shaded gardens). Use environmentally friendly paints – suppliers can advise you on which these are.
✳ If you want a native deciduous hedge, now is the time for it to be laid. If you don't want to tackle it yourself then contact the National Hedgelaying Society, which can help put you in touch with a local practitioner. If you don't have a native hedge, why not remove the fence and plant a beautiful, biodiversity-rich native-species hedge instead?

Can you dig it?
✳ In a dry, warm winter there is nothing to prevent you from continuing to cultivate new beds and improve the soil in existing borders.

Reuse, recycle, sustain
✳ Make a compost heap in readiness for the new season, and/or buy a wormery. In some areas local authorities give these away for free or for a nominal charge.
✳ If you haven't already done so, install a water butt. Again, these can sometimes be obtained for free or next to nothing from your local water company.

The wildlife hotel
✳ Clean out bird nesting boxes in readiness for the season ahead. Wear gloves and long sleeves to prevent bites from fleas and ticks.
✳ Put up new habitat boxes, especially bird-nesting boxes, in preparation for the new nesting season. If you really want to make the most out of the experience, why not install a box with a built-in video camera?

Planting
✳ In late winter, prune winter-flowering plants and cut back winter-stem interest plants, leaving at least 30cm (12in) of stem above ground level to ensure early

leafing that will provide the plant with the food it needs to grow and minimize feeding and watering. Alternatively remove a third of the stems down to ground level, keeping the rest intact.
✳ Now is the time to carry out formative pruning of young trees and shrubs.
✳ Plant bare root trees, shrubs and roses. Roses always establish best – and are more economical to buy – as bare root specimens.
✳ From late winter cut back the spent stems of flowering perennials and ornamental grasses, leaving the grasses until last. Add the spent material to the compost heap.
✳ Winter is the best time to start the ground preparation for mini meadows and direct-sown annual beds, providing the soil is dry enough to dig.

Garden design
✳ Let your imagination run riot and green up your garden structures (sheds and so on) – or make new ones such as a turf seat.

Glossary

Biodiversity The word is a contraction of 'biological' and 'diversity'. It is used to encompass all living things on earth and the complex inter-relationship between them; in effect the web of life.

Carbon footprint Our individual and collective contribution to carbon dioxide overall emissions that we produce as a consequence of our daily lives.

Carbon neutral Refers to a process, product or activity that generates no carbon emissions, or that absorbs as much or more carbon during its life than it emits thereafter; for example a tree being utilized as timber in a building.

Carbon trading Balancing carbon-emitting activities (such as driving a car or flying) with those that absorb carbon, such as tree planting, or by signing up to a trading scheme that balances the carbon your lifestyle generates.

Cultivation A generic term referring to the cultivation of plants (i.e. growing) and the cultivation of soil (i.e. digging over, adding organic matter etc).

Cultivated As in 'cultivated plants'. These are plants that do not occur naturally in the wild but have been selected through breeding. Cultivar is the name given to these plants (a contraction of cultivated and variety). Cultivar names are expressed in inverted commas (see Ornamental plants).

Cultural clearance Using methods other than chemicals – such as hand weeding, hoeing, mechanical clearance or the cover up method – to remove weeds, turf etc., prior to cultivation for planting.

Double digging A method of soil cultivation particularly suitable for plants requiring a rich, deep root run (such as some vegetable crops) or as a first time cultivation on thin, fast-draining soil. Topsoil is removed in a trench, the subsoil dug over and organic matter added and the topsoil then replaced. Also referred to as trenching.

Friable structure Refers to soil that has been broken down through cultivation to the point where it crumbles in the hand, while still retaining enough moisture for it not to turn to dust. Soil is unable to stay in this state for more than a few hours; it is more prone to soil structure problems (and the vagaries of the weather) when finely cultivated than at any other time.

Glyphosate The chemical name for a popular garden herbicide (weed killer), glyphosate is systemic – i.e. it acts on the whole plant killing both roots and foliage. Its increased use, as a consequence of the banning of many other weed killers, is leading to fears that some weeds are forming resistance to it.

Invasive plants A plant, often alien but not exclusively, that spreads (through seed or vegetatively) in a way that is damaging to the environment. In the UK examples include Himalayan balsam, giant hogweed, Japanese knotweed, and *Rhododendron ponticum*.

Layer cake method A non-technical term for the surface application of soil improvers such as organic matter and grit, which are then either allowed to naturally break down into the soil or are lightly forked in.

Macroclimate The prevalent climate in an area, district or country.

Microclimate The discreet climatic conditions that can be highly variable in a comparatively small space, such as a garden.

Natural cycles The encouragement, through reduced intervention, of self-sustaining levels of predators, pests, soil fauna and so on. Also encompasses the natural improvement of soil fertility and structure through the absorption of fallen leaves etc.

Natural pest controls These are naturally occurring or introduced pest predators, or preventative organic treatments (such as barrier sprays) used to deter or control plant pests.

Nitrogen fixing Plants, such as legumes, that have developed root nodes that 'fix' nitrogen in the soil.

No-dig regimes A method of soil management where soil improvement is carried out without digging, by applying soil improvers to the soil surface (see layer cake method) in order to preserve soil flora and fauna.

Offsets Typically referring to bulbs that produce small offsets to the side of the main bulb in order to increase/reproduce.

Organic matter In a garden sense this refers to material that can be used as a soil improver or mulch, such as farmyard manure, processed straw etc.

Ornamental plants A loose definition for plants that are either cultivated hybrids – plants selected by growers for a particular characteristic such as flower colour, fragrance or disease resistance. It is also used to describe species plants that are not native to the country in which they are being grown, but are native somewhere in the world. The former category often includes hybrids of genuinely native plants – for example, the cultivar of the European spindle tree, *Euonymus europaeus* 'Red Cascade'.

Permaculture The creation of sustainable human habitats that take heed of the natural world. Permaculture uses the diversity, stability and resilience of natural ecosystems to provide a framework for people on a local, national or global scale to develop their own sustainable solutions to the problems facing their world.

Permeable barriers A vertical barrier through which wind can pass, slowing as it does so, rather than a solid barrier that wind passes over, causing eddying.

Plug plants Small, young plants grown in cells or root trainers ready for planting or potting.

Rain shadow An area in the lee of a solid or permeable structure that is sheltered from, and therefore doesn't receive, rain. Rain shadows are usually also free from frost.

Root ball The roots and soil around a plant, but more specifically one that has been grown in a field and then dug out and the root-ball covered in a hessian sack; as in root balled.

Scarifying The method used to remove a build-up of dead grass, moss and weeds from turf. This involves vigorous raking or the use of a machine to the same effect. The term is also used in reference to scarifying seeds to remove the naturally occurring outer layer that delays germination.

Single digging A method of cultivation similar to double digging but at half the depth.

Soil improver Material added to the soil to improve structure, drainage, nutrients.

Sub soil The soil below the topsoil.

Sustainable A process, activity or product that can be carried out/produced without adversely affecting the environment, throughout the lifetime of the process, activity or product.

Tilth Cultivated soil. For example a 'fine tilth' is soil that has been dug over and raked ready for sowing seed, whereas a 'coarse tilth' is roughly culitvated.

Top soil The top layer of soil that has the greatest effect on plant growth, as it is where the bulk of plant roots are to be found. The topsoil is the layer of soil that gardeners seek to 'improve'.

Vernacular Principally referring to the language of a country or place, it also relates to a local style of architecture, building etc and the materials used.

Virtuous circles The establishment of a natural balance between the use of resources and their preservation. Also the establishment of a self-sustaining balance in the garden where minimal intervention is required due to the use of appropriate plants, cultivation and maintenance techniques and the presence (in balance) of pests and predators.

Water table The natural level of water beneath the soil when the soil is at field capacity; i.e. the soil cannot absorb any further water.

Understanding plant names

Plant names comprise the following elements:
* The family (rarely used)
* The genus (e.g. *Digitalis*)
* The species (e.g. *purpurea*)
* The cultivar, variety or subspecies, (e.g. 'Alba')

The use of italics for genus and species is deliberate, while cultivars are always shown in quotes and not italicized. Cultivar means, simply, 'cultivated variety' – that is a plant that has been selected and bred rather than one that occurs in the wild. Varieties are naturally occurring variations of a species that have been identified in the wild and then propagated and made available to buy.

Further reading & RHS Gardens

These few books have shaped my thinking during my career and provided inspiring references whilst writing this book. Below these are the addresses of RHS gardens.

Beth Chatto's Damp Garden
by Beth Chatto and Steven Wooster
Published by Cassell Illustrated, 2005.

Beth Chatto's Gravel Garden
by Beth Chatto and Steven Wooster
Published by Frances Lincoln, 2000.

Beth Chatto's Woodland Garden
by Beth Chatto and Steven Wooster
Published by Cassell Illustrated, 2006.

Colour by Design
by Nori & Sandra Pope
Published by Conran Octopus, 1998.

Designing with Plants
by Piet Oudolf with Noel Kingsbury
Published by Timber Press, 1999

Flora Britannica
by Richard Mabey
Published by Sinclair-Stevenson, 1996

How to Make a Wildlife Garden
by Chris Baines
Published by Frances Lincoln, 2000.

Meadows
by Christopher Lloyd
Published by Cassell Illustrated, 2006.

Pocket Guide to Ornamental Grasses
by Rick Darke
Published by Timber Press, 2004.

RHS Plant Finder 2006-2007
Published by Dorling Kindersley, 2006.

Saving The Planet Without Costing The Earth
by Donnachadh McCarthy
Published by Fusion Press, 2004.

Sharp Gardening
by Christopher Holliday
Published by Frances Lincoln, 2006.

Silent Spring
by Rachel Carson
Published by Houghton Mifflin, 2002

The Well-Tempered Garden
by Christopher Lloyd
Published by Weidenfeld & Nicolson, 2003.

The Well-Tended Perennial Garden
by Tracy DiSabato-Aust
Published by Timber Press, 2006.

What Perennial Where?
by Roy Lancaster
Published by Dorling Kindersley, 1997.

The Wild Garden
by William Robinson
Published by Sagapress (a reprint of the fifth edition first published in 1895), 1994.

Wildlife Gardening for Everyone (RHS)
by Malcolm Tait
Published by Think Publishing, 2006.

RHS Garden Harlow Carr
Crag Lane, Beckwithshaw, Harrogate, North Yorkshire HG3 1QB Tel 01423 565418

RHS Garden Hyde Hall
Buckhatch Lane, Rettendon, Chelmsford, Essex CM3 8ET Tel 01245 400256

RHS Garden Rosemoor
Great Torrington, Devon, EX38 8PH Tel 01805 624067

RHS Garden Wisley
Woking, Surrey, GU23 6QB Tel 01483 224234

Websites

The following websites are a useful source of information on gardening and related topics covered in this book.

General

THE ROYAL HORTICULTURAL SOCIETY
www.rhs.org.uk

Traditional crafts

NATIONAL HEDGELAYING SOCIETY
www.hedgelaying.org.uk

Soil

THE SOIL ASSOCIATION
www.soilassociation.org.uk

PERMACULTURE.NET
www.permaculture.net

Recycling and sustainability

THE CARBON TRUST
www.carbontrust.co.uk

RAINWATER HARVESTING ASSOCIATION
www.rainharvesting.co.uk

RECYCLEMORE.CO.UK
www.recycle-more.co.uk

THE SOURCE FOR RENEWABLE ENERGY
www.energy.sourceguides.com

THE GREEN ENERGY WEBSITE
www.greenenergy.org.uk

WORLD RAINFOREST INFORMATION PORTAL
www.rainforestweb.org

GREENPEACE
www.greenpeace.org/international_en

ENVIRONMENT INVESTIGATION AGENCY
www.eia-international.org

FOREST STEWARDSHIP COUNCIL
www.fsc.org.uk

FREECYCLE
www.freecycle.org

THE WATER GROUP
www.watergrouppromotions.co.uk

Wildlife

THE WILDLIFE TRUSTS
www.wildlifetrusts.org

ROYAL SOCIETY FOR PROTECTION OF BIRDS
www.rspb.org.uk

THE INVERTEBRATE CONSERVATION TRUST
www.buglife.org.uk

LANDLIFE (WILDFLOWER CONSERVATION)
www.landlife.org.uk

NATIONAL WILDFLOWER CENTRE
www.nwc.org.uk

FLORA LOCALE
www.floralocale.org

THE AMERICAN SOCIETY OF MAMMALOGISTS
www.mammalsociety.org

PLANTLIFE INTERNATIONAL
www.plantlife.org.uk

Planting

THE SOCIETY OF GARDEN DESIGNERS
www.sgd.org.uk

THE ARBORICULTURAL ASSOCIATION
www.trees.org.uk

THE WOODLAND TRUST
www.woodland-trust.org.uk

PICTORIAL MEADOWS
www.pictorialmeadows.co.uk

Index

Acknowledgments

Picture Credits

All photographs taken by Lee Beel for Octopus Publishing Group Ltd unless otherwise stated as below:

Christian Barnett/Gardens Illustrated: 182, 183(1, 2, 3, 4); W.G Baxter/Corbis: 36; Richard Bloom/GPL: 193br; Stuart Blyth/GPL: 187tl; Mark Bolton/GPL: 62 (Design: Alan Capper, RHS Chelsea 06), 107b, 120, 121, 203tl, 209tr; Phillipe Bonduel/GPL: 88l; Botanica/GPL: 107t, 191cr; Nicole Brown/Bridgewater Books (Design: John Brookes) 167r; Jonathan Buckley/The Garden Collection: 2tcl & 64-65 & 129 & 138 & 139 (Design: Sue & Wol Staines), 2bcr & 148-149 (Design: Judy Pearce), 17r (East Ruston Old Vicarage), 23t & 186r (Design: Christopher Lloyd), 30cr & br (Beth Chatto), 34t (Helen Yemm, Ketley's), 46r (Design: James Fraser, London), 69tl, 69bl, 76 & 132r (Design: David & Mavis Seeney), 79r (Coton Manor, Northamptonshire), 92c (Design: Simon Hokinson), 99tl, 116l (Lady Farm, Somerset), 147(4), 193cl, 195tl, 199bl, 199br, 201cl, 205tl, cr, 209tl; Burke Triolo Productions/GPL: 46l; Nigel Cattlin/FLPA: 35(2); Torie Chugg/The Garden Collection: 24c, 69br, 92t (Design: Fran Forster), 100, 147(1), 153(5), 158 (Design: Sheila Fishwick, RHS Hampton Court 05), 193tl, 203tr; Hugh Clark/FLPA: 71bl; Eric Crichton/GPL: 80br, 199cr; Geoff Dann/GPL: 78, 99tr; Francois De Heel/GPL: 205bl, 209br; Joan Dear/GPL: 191bl; David Dixon/GPL: 2tr & 44-45 (Design: Kate Frey); Philip Downer/Oxford Scientific 37l; Ecoscene/Corbis: 60r; Liz Eddison/The Garden Collection: 50 (Design: Cleve West, RHS Chelsea 06), 128b (Design: Marney Hall), 150l (Design: Kevin Cooper & Linda Fairman), 159cr (Design: Geoffrey & Josh Whiten), 176r (Design: Melanie Thornhill & Martin Seacombe), 179br (Design: Mary Reynolds), 181b, 189tr, 201cr, 213 (Whichford Pottery); David England/GPL: 81r; Sklar Evan/GPL: 80bl; Raymond Gehman/Corbis: 60l; Suzie Gibbons/GPL: 96t, 102t; John Glover/GPL: 97t, 189tl; Derek Gould/Garden World Images: 189bl; Anne Green-Armytage/GPL: 187cl; Tony Hamblin/FLPA: 82; Marcus Harpur/Harpur Garden Library 144-145; Derek Harris/The Garden Collection: 2tcr, 2br & 172 & 184-185 (Design: Christopher Lloyd), 68, 104-105, 147(3), 163bl, 201tl, tr, 207tl; Paul Hart/GPL: 37r; Sunniva Harte/GPL: 193bl, 207bl; Charles Hawes: 63tl, tr, bl, br (Design: Dennis Hennesey); Jacky Hobbs 114r: (Design: Piet Oudolf); Neil Holmes/GPL: 2bcl, 118, 119, 191br, 197tl; Anne Hyde/GPL: 96b, 151t; Michele Lamontagne/GPL: 81l; Andrew Lawson/The Garden Collection: 2bcl, 112-113, 140-141 (Sticky Wicket, Dorset), 20, 21, 24b, 31cl (Beth Chatto), 38l, 88r, 115 (Design: Oehme & Van Sweden), 132l, 133, 147 (2,5,6,7,8,9), 150r, 153 (1,2,4), 171c, 187bl, br, 193tr, 193cr, 195cr, 197tr, bl, br, 199tl, tl, tr, cl, 203cl, br, 205tr, 207tr, cr, br, 209bl; Marianne Majerus 131; George McCarthy/Corbis: 80tr; Marie O'Hara/The Garden Collection: 2bl & 156-157 (Design: Paul Williams), 23b, 92b, 163br, 205br; Jerry Pavia/GPL: 189br; Doug Pearson/JA1/Corbis: 19; Martin Pope/Camera Press: 26bl, br, 27bl, bc, br, 165; Howard Rice/GPL: 187tr; Royal Horticultural Society 35; Brad Simmons/Corbis: 178; JS Sira/GPL: 191cl; Paul Spracklin 131 (Design: Paul Spracklin); Derek St Romaine/The Garden Collection: 2bc, 23c & 171b (Design: Phil Nash), 34b (Design: Carol Klein), 105r & 166-167 (Glen Chantry), 117 (RHS Wisley), 122 (RHS Rosemoor), 151b, 153(3), 164bc, 195tr, 207cl, 209cl, cr; Nicola Stocken Tomkins/The Garden Collection: 2tl & 16-17 (East Ruston Old Vicarage), 38r, 47, 51, 69tr, 95, 110, 114l, 171t, 173r, 176l, 177t, b, 189cr, 195cl, br, 197cl, 203cr; Fredrich Strauss/GPL: 159l, 164bl; John Swithinbank/GPL: 191tl; John Swithinbank/Garden World Images: 18; Roger Tamblyn/Garden World Images: 31cb, 87; Steve Terrill/Corbis: 57b; Matthew Wilson: 57t, 59t, 73, 83(1,2,3,4), 98t, 102b, 130tl, bl, bl, br, 134-135, 141r, 154, 155, 164br, 169, 173l; 250cl; Nik Wheeler/Corbis: 179t; Jo Whitworth/GPL: 39; Steven Wooster/GPL: 97b; 191tr; Steven Wooster/The Garden Collection: 170 (Eion Edgar); Kit Young/GPL: 79l.

Author's Acknowledgments

Without the following people this book wouldn't have happened, and I owe them a great debt of thanks.

Susie Behar, Michael Whitehead and their colleagues from Bridgewater Books who have shown grace under pressure and helped guide me through the nuances of making a book. Helen Griffin and colleagues from Mitchell Beazley and Susannah Charlton and her colleagues at RHS Publishing have given support and made helpful and tactful suggestions throughout. Lee Beel for his excellent photography and companionship. My colleague Liz Turner for her organizational skills and ability to remain calm, even when I have not. To Steven Edney and Jane Smith and their colleagues from Octopus Publishing Group for their enthusiasm and willingness to take on board and sell *Nature's Gardener*.

To the horticultural practitioners, conservationists, designers and writers who have had a profound influence on the thinking behind this book. They include Sir David Attenborough, Professor Chris Baines, John Brookes, Beth Chatto, Geoff Hamilton, Roy Lancaster, Christopher Lloyd, Richard Mabey, Piet Oudolf, Dan Pearson, Tom Stuart Smith, Cleve West and Robin Williams.

To Richard Taylor (bench maker), Dan Wright (dry stone waller), and Phil Bradley (willow weaver), for agreeing to have their work, and/or themselves, featured in the book; Stephanie Harrod from Harrod Horticultural Sneeboer Tools Holland; Just Green; Geoff Whiteley at Strulch; and Damien Handslip at Pictorial Meadows. Also thanks to Dennis Hennesey, Paul Spracklin, Judy Pearce, Wol and Sue Staines, Kim and Stephen Rogers, Alan Gray and Graham Robson and many others for the inspiring gardens that feature in these pages. And of course my colleagues at RHS Gardens Hyde Hall and Harlow Carr who have embraced the principles of 'new gardening'.

Lastly, my thanks to Michelle Pearson for reminding me that nature and wildlife should never be subservient to the needs of gardening; to Mike Snowden, one of the most sensible, practical and inspirational gardeners ever to wield a hoe, for showing me how I could garden and yet still embrace nature; Kylie O'Brien from *The Daily Telegraph* for getting me back into writing; and David Lamb from Mitchell Beazley, with whom, more than five years ago, I started a conversation about a new type of gardening book that might meet the needs of gardeners in a changing world.

This book is dedicated to the memory of my father, Peter Wilson, who started me on this journey many years ago, but departed before its course was determined, and with love to my mother, Connie Wilson, who has never stopped believing in me. Thank you.